Trust Again

Trust Again

Overcoming Betrayal and Regaining Health, Confidence, and Happiness

Debi Silber

ROWMAN & LITTLEFIELD
Lanham • Boulder • New York • London

Published by Rowman & Littlefield
An imprint of The Rowman & Littlefield Publishing Group, Inc.
4501 Forbes Boulevard, Suite 200, Lanham, Maryland 20706
www.rowman.com

6 Tinworth Street, London SE11 5AL, United Kingdom

British Library Cataloguing in Publication Information Available

Library of Congress Cataloging-in-Publication Data

Names: Silber, Debi, author.
Title: Trust again : overcoming betrayal and regaining health, confidence, and happiness / Debi Silber.
Description: Lanham : Rowman & Littlefield, [2020] | Includes bibliographical references and index. | Summary: "At a time when we need support the most yet we're the least likely to seek it, this book will provide comfort, support and community for those struggling to heal from a painful experience with betrayal. Readers will learn about, and move through the proven five stages from betrayal to breakthrough which were one of the three discoveries made during Dr. Debi's study, and will be lovingly guided with tools and strategies along the way. They'll also learn how predictable healing can be as they read not only Debi's journey through betrayal, but the stories of "The Fab 14"; the brave study participants who shared their experiences so that these discoveries could be used to help others ready to heal"—Provided by publisher.
Identifiers: LCCN 2020007292 (print) | LCCN 2020007293 (ebook) | ISBN 9781538140635 (cloth ; alk. paper) | ISBN 9781538140642 (ebook)
Subjects: LCSH: Trust. | Betrayal—Psychological aspects.
Classification: LCC BF575.T7 S55 2020 (print) | LCC BF575.T7 (ebook) | DDC 158.2—dc23
LC record available at https://lccn.loc.gov/2020007292
LC ebook record available at https://lccn.loc.gov/2020007293

∞™ The paper used in this publication meets the minimum requirements of American National Standard for Information Sciences—Permanence of Paper for Printed Library Materials, ANSI/NISO Z39.48-1992.

To you. Yes you, the reader. This book was written for you so that you can have the tools, support, and strategies you need to heal right at your fingertips. I know how much betrayal hurts, and I also know what's waiting for you when you move through the Five Stages of Betrayal. You deserve a life that's filled with love, laughter, meaning, and fulfillment. Although that may seem like a far fetch from where you may be right now, my wish is that you use this experience as an opportunity to become the highest and best version of you—one that you never imagined existed yet one that's patiently waiting to be revealed.

Contents

Part 3. Moving Forward as a Brand New You

Foreword

Wm Paul Young

I've known Wm Paul Young for a few years and have enjoyed many deep and meaningful conversations about life, love, betrayal, remorse, regret, growth, trust, grief, forgiveness, God, and spirituality. During our last conversation, we spoke in depth about trust—the precious nature of this sacred and earned gift, the devastation created when it's been shattered through betrayal, as well as the unique opportunity it provides for growth and transformation. I'm so grateful for his insight and perspective, and it's an honor to share his beautiful words with you.

To take the risk to love is to expose yourself to possible betrayal. To choose to trust will also create the space for potential betrayal. When one is allowed the honor of entering the "story" of another human being, often it will be framed around the themes of love, trust, loss, and betrayal. These light and dark threads are woven into the fabric of our shared human condition and illuminate the angel and the beast who coexist in the human heart and experience.

I would love to write that I have never betrayed anyone. I have. And while there are moments that the regret for destructive choices, regardless of motivation, seems almost consuming, I have learned to live with regret as part of grieving and not part of shame's whisper of accusation. But that took years of work, therapy, community, truth telling, exposure, and grace.

It would also be wonderful to tell you that I have never been betrayed, that I don't understand the cataclysmic dismantling of experiencing trust violated and destroyed. I have been. The closer the proximity of betrayal's bomb, the deeper and wider the devastation. To be betrayed by someone to whom you have given your deepest trust and around whose love you have built your sense of belonging, is to experience a death and the shattering of the heart. It is a death in which it seems impossible there ever could be resurrection.

Perhaps it is the circles I wander, but I know almost no one, except for some children, who has not been betrayed. That is incredibly sad and sobering. Even the God whom I have come to know and love has experienced betrayal at the hands of human beings. I see Jesus as the ultimate expression and incarnation of complete Love and the crucifixion and cross as our corporate response of betrayal.

Is it possible that betrayal can be justified? Can infidelity and disloyalty ever be redemptive? Can such a loss be reconciled?

The prophet Jeremiah, in the Hebrew Scriptures, announces in no uncertain terms that God has divorced Israel. Why? Betrayal. Specifically, adultery: relational betrayal. The answer to the first question is no. Betrayal is never justifiable! There is never justification for adultery, for infidelity, for lying and gossip, and for all the other forms of betrayal.

The second and third questions, can these losses ever be redemptive and reconciled? If they could not be, there would be no hope for any of us. At the beginning of 1994, my wife caught me in a three-month affair with one of her best friends. I blew up our world. Absolutely not a shred of that could possibly justify such a betrayal. That began an 11-year dismantling journey of redemption and reconciliation. It was a journey through hell, one that I would never, ever want to experience again but for which I am grateful every second of every day. As someone once said, "Religious people believe in hell, but spiritual people have been there." What was shattered in a moment took years to rebuild: trust. And it required staying present, not running. It meant being exposed, and, as painful as that is, it is essentially necessary. The unexposed is the unhealed. One has to face the wind of fury and consequence and do the arduous, incremental hard work of taking down all façades and masks and in the rubble finding the good, the true, the right, the beautiful, and the worthy. It is inviting others into the spaces where no one has been allowed to enter and offering again the gift of trust. This is no simple task. My friend Debi has experienced this, has studied this, has done this, and has created a road map so you can do it too.

I have a dear friend who played semiprofessional rugby for 25 years. There is a phrase in rugby: "First to the breakdown." It has layers of meaning. I will be there when things start to fall apart. I have your back.

I am all in. In the journey of knowing God, the divine, love, you must often travel through the wilderness of atheism, where you begin to no longer believe in who you thought God was in order to open your heart to something truer. So too, the journey toward wholeness of the soul will go through the wilderness of breakdown, where the true has an opportunity to usurp the power of the false. With the resurrection of the true will also arise your capacity to trust again. To that end, I offer you (with permission) this poem, written by my poet friend David Tensen.

> Dear Breakdown,
>
> When I saw you coming
> over the horizon
> I braced myself.
>
> With your strong gaze
> and constant gait
> I began to suspect
> you were on assignment
> or I had summoned you
> unknowingly.
>
> I'd seen what you
> had done to others.
> Their lives resembled wrecks.
> Many lost hope and
> all sense of pride.
> And you were coming
> for me now.
> And I was unprepared.
>
> Sure, these people recovered
> and discovered
> they couldn't arrange galaxies
> with their false personas.
> But who wants to go through hell for that lesson?
>
> And yes, some claimed
> they loved deeper
> laughed louder

and found their true selves.
But who wants to submit to your
painful ways?

So much in me
told me
you were not welcome.
Too many memories
of failing and falling
had me questioning your nearness
once more.

But then
you had your way.

I expected you to hit and run
but you were more
committed than that.
I had you all wrong.
Sure, it hurt.
And sure, I died many deaths.
But you allowed me to see
that I was never in charge
never that strong
never going to wake up
to the Presence of all things
unless you came
to my rescue.
So, thank you,
Breakdown.

davidtensen.com

Trust Again will bring rivers of healing to many. You are in good hands. —Wm Paul Young, *The Shack*

Acknowledgments

*W*riting this book would never have been possible without the help of many incredible people I'm blessed to know. To Suzanne Staszak-Silva and Rowman & Littlefield for inviting me to be part of their publishing family. To Mike Olah and Dreamscape Media for the opportunity to reach even more people through the audio recording of this book. To Celeste Fine and Jaidree Braddix for their efforts in ensuring this book finds the right home for publishing. To Sofia University for the opportunity to study betrayal, forgiveness, trust, and healing—my experiences there were life changing. To my PhD dissertation committee Dr. Alyssa Rockenbach, Dr. Joan Rosenberg, and Dr. Marilyn Schlitz, my program chair—for your guidance and support so that these discoveries regarding betrayal could be made. To the Fab 14—it's because of your bravery that we know about Post Betrayal Transformation, Post Betrayal Syndrome, and the Five Stages from Betrayal to Breakthrough. Thank you for your willingness to share your stories so that others could benefit from your experiences. You've helped more people than you'll ever know. To my mastermind family, who always inspires me to play bigger, and to my coaches J. J. Virgin and Karl Krummenacher, who continually demonstrate what's possible with vision, inspiration, strategy, and support.

To the PBT Institute community of warriors who are healing from their betrayals along with the Certified PBT Coaches and Practitioners who've healed from their own betrayals and are now paying it forward by serving others. To my friends who each show their love and support in their own unique ways. To Thom Neil for your technical brilliance and continual support behind the scenes. To Tania Johnson—your support and belief in my mission has made the PBT Institute possible.

xiv *Acknowledgments*

Thank you for always being there, for your dedication and contribution—I could never have done any of this without you. I'm so grateful
to be on this journey with you since this dream began. To William P.
Young for your life-changing wisdom. To Guy, Anna Miranda, and
Paul Saladino—your spiritual guidance has given me the faith I needed
to make this journey possible. I'm grateful for your friendship and insight. To my extended family—Chris, Susan, Zach, Abby, Lydia, Jay,
Jamie, Hannah, Shayna, Talia, Cynthia, Molly, and Keely—I love having all of you in my life. To my in-laws Dr. Mike Silber and Lenore
Silber—thanks for all of your love and support since 1984. I love you
both. To my family, Adam, Dani, Dylan, Camryn, and Cole—I never
imagined the depth of faith, strength, resilience, forgiveness, friendship,
compassion, and love you've all helped me experience. You are my
world. To my mom—I miss you every day and feel your love and pride
from your bird's-eye view.

Introduction

My Story

I'd been through what I'd considered so much already. It started with 11 days in the ICU unit after contracting peritonitis, a deadly infection that was slowly shutting down my organs and spreading throughout my body back in 1997. My stomach slowly started becoming distended as if I were six months' pregnant. Soon after that, I passed out, was rushed to the hospital, and was told that I had a 104-degree temperature and my blood pressure was 88/44. Because the pain was in my midsection, the doctors thought it was appendicitis, so they quickly scrubbed up and gave me an emergency appendectomy. That's when they saw the infection. Knowing time was running out, they immediately opened me up from top to bottom and suctioned out between a pint and a quart of strep pneumonia.

I was so infected that I was quarantined in a portion of the ICU unit, and only those who were protected could come into the room to check on me. I was so out of it that I don't remember the first few days at all, but I do remember the sweet voice of the nurse teaching me how to use the morphine drip that lay by my bedside. For days, I alternated between passing out from the intense pain, waking up, and hitting the morphine drip until I eventually passed out from the pain again.

Pass out, wake up, hit the morphine drip, pass out, wake up, hit the drip. This routine went on for more than a week, over and over again. When I was conscious enough, my thoughts would drift to my 16-month-old and my newborn baby. I asked myself questions like "How can you possibly take care of them if you don't get out of this ICU unit?" The pain was so unbearable that after about a week of my pass-out/wake-up/morphine drip routine, I remember saying to myself, "This is too hard, you don't have to do this. It's okay, just close your eyes and drift away."

What happened next was something that felt like a fierce decision, a command. It rose up from deep within me with an intense resolve I'll never forget. At that moment, I pictured my husband and two young babies who'd been holding vigil in the hospital waiting room while I spent those days in ICU. In a shockingly clear moment, I pictured my children, and it hit me that they came into this world with the understanding that I was their mom. That was our agreement and understanding. That was what we all decided on and agreed to as our new family was created. It was as if we signed a contract; we each knew our roles, and my drifting away because the pain was too intense would have meant breaking my end of our deal. The struggle was intense because it would have been so easy at that moment to let go and to stop using my energy to outlast the unbearable pain. It was so tempting because I couldn't see any sign of light at the end of the dark tunnel I was in. Then, with whatever energy I had left, I put those thoughts aside and got furious.

The next thing I knew, I heard myself scream. I'll never know if it was only in my head or out loud, but I remember the words so clearly: "God, Universe, divine energy, anyone . . . *help me get out of here!*" That was the turning point. That was the moment I started healing, and that decision, command, mind-set shift, or whatever you want to call it saved my life.

A few days later when I eventually left the hospital, I remember the doctors saying that being young and healthy saved my life. I knew they had to attribute my healing to something because they'd never heard of anyone who'd survived that type and degree of infection. Intuitively, while I knew that my health and age definitely helped, I knew that it was the fierce determination to stay alive for my kids that got me out of there.

A few years later, I lost my mom, had a miscarriage (before eventually having my two other children), and finally cut the toxic ties to my original family after years of mental, verbal, and emotional abuse. Those years of torment had me question my value, worth, and sanity, and while I didn't understand it, I knew that on some level, these lessons would somehow serve in the future, even if I couldn't see how.

While it was all painful, each trauma in its own way helped me create a level of strength and resilience I never had. Many lessons were learned during that time, but even with all of those lessons, I wasn't prepared for what was next.

From that point until 2015, I had been raising four kids and six dogs and had a successful and thriving online and offline business. I'd healed from a second health crash in 2011 and learned the hard way that an overstressed and chaotic lifestyle was a recipe for stress-related disease. After endless doctor appointments to get to the bottom of a laundry list of symptoms I'd been struggling with, I learned that all were stress related.

Why was this a good thing? Knowing that the way I interpreted and managed my stress could lead to illness and disease also led me to realize that a new way to think and feel may be able to turn these symptoms and conditions around. I remembered how that decision back in 1997 saved my life and felt assured that if my mind-set could help me heal from that, my mind-set could also help turn around some of the thoughts, beliefs, and behaviors that were creating these stress-related disorders.

With some new mind-set strategies and lifestyle habits in place, that's exactly what happened, and I was excited to share what I'd learned with others so they could prevent the same things from happening to them. The work was meaningful, and I was blessed to be able to see clients around my kids' schedules. It looked great from the outside, but from the inside, it was a very different story. Yes, I was doing it all, but there was emptiness, loneliness, and a hollowness I couldn't seem to get rid of. Keeping busy was my distraction of choice, and as long as I kept myself busy, the feeling would be kept at bay.

My husband Adam and I were barely communicating during this time. His real estate business was taking off, and he was becoming someone I no longer had much in common with. It seemed like the more money he made, the more extreme and reckless he became. With his flashy cars, excessive spending, and attention-seeking behavior, I barely recognized who he was anymore, and, having no time to find out, I simply hoped he'd snap out of it. Here's a picture of what our life looked like during that time.

I was exhausted running my business, taking the kids to their clubs and events, maintaining the house, and caring for the six dogs. For me, fun meant a walk in nature or just laughing with the kids. Adam had no patience or interest in being involved in any of that. Instead, whenever he had the chance, he'd have the top down on his lime green Lamborghini, music blasting, driving 100 miles per hour on the highway in order to get to Times Square in New York City. Once in the heart of one of the most densely populated areas in New York, he'd cruise through just slowly enough to be able to take in all of the comments, stares, thumbs-up, and women who expressed their interest in a ride and more.

It made me cringe. That scene couldn't be further from who I was, what I found entertaining, or what I wanted any part of at this stage of life. Each time Adam drove away, my heart would sink, and I'd be left shaking my head, embarrassed and saddened by how different he was from the sweet guy I met back in college. I was searching for more to fill the emptiness and thankfully stumbled on spirituality. Here I found the connection that allowed me to feel a deeper sense of connection with something bigger than me. I felt like I wasn't alone. I dove in, reading anything I could get my hands on. I started going to events, listened to recordings, and soaked up spiritual wisdom from some of the greatest thought leaders of our time. It was the first time I'd ever felt that kind of connection with something greater than my small world. I was learning that there was a reason for everything and how the Universe has my best interests in mind. I felt like I just discovered the best-kept secret and wanted to share what I was learning with Adam because by 2015, it had become a daily part of life, giving me the perspective, patience, and vision I needed to manage my busy life. He had no interest in hearing about my new discovery, and looking back it's easy to see why. While I found spirituality, he found another woman.

In July 2015, I received and read the e-mail that changed my life. It was from the husband of the woman Adam had been having an affair with back in 2008 along with all of the painful details that went with it. I was at an event in New York City, and he was with my kids when I called to confront him. After a long and painful pause, he confirmed it. I ended the call and walked back into the event, trying to act as if my world hadn't totally collapsed a minute earlier.

Since it would be a few hours until I'd be home, he immediately sat the kids down and confessed it all. I was taking the train home from New York City, and in anger, sadness, and disgust, the kids, now teenagers ranging in age from 13 to 19, left him to meet me at the train station. They knew I'd be in no condition to drive and lovingly guided my numb, lifeless self to the car, drove me home, and walked me to my bed.

Shock. That's all I could feel over the next few days after I had him pack his bags and leave. The shock soon turned into gut-wrenching, soul-crushing pain. I was barely functioning, and not wanting to burden the kids, I tried as hard as I could to be there for them, crying the minute I was alone. I didn't tell my friends; I was humiliated. They knew Adam for years and loved him, and although they would have lovingly supported me, I was afraid of their judgment, anger, and pity. My clients were counting on me for strength, direction, and support, so I did whatever I could to muster up the strength I needed before every coaching session, crashing with exhaustion the minute the session was over. I was barely functioning and was living a private hell.

While my world was rocked, so was his. Dark, lonely nights by himself and without his family must have brought lots of clarity because within three days, he'd already sold his fancy car, trading it in for something more modest. He stopped wearing the loud and flashy clothes and started spending quality time with the kids. It was as if his dark secret, now exposed, was the shock he needed to realize who he'd turned into. He was filled with shame and disgust, seeing through our eyes who he'd been as a husband, father, and friend.

The kids were hesitant to trust him but kept telling me how different he seemed. Even though the affair had ended years earlier, he was now experiencing the consequences of those decisions he'd made during that time. It must have been the ultimate wake-up call. Knowing how he'd broken my heart impacted him on one level, but knowing he'd lost the respect and trust of his four children must have been another. From an extremely raw and vulnerable place, he was starting over with each one of the kids, rebuilding their trust and faith in him in the specific way each needed to see it. They were slowly believing that his changes were real. My heart hurt too much to listen.

We started talking. His remorse was so deep and real, and so was my pain. He took full responsibility, saying that it was his emptiness, ego, and false persona he'd created that left a gaping void he was trying to fill through his behavior, the same void I was filling through spirituality. We started communicating, really communicating, and it felt like we spoke more in that first month we started speaking again than in the past 10 years. He was starting to remind me of the guy I met 30 years earlier. But my foundation was so rocked that I didn't trust what I was feeling. I felt so duped, so taken for granted, so taken advantage of, so disregarded by the massive lying, betrayal, and behavior that I couldn't see straight. With him out of the house, a new awareness slowly settled over me. I could survive this. I could be a single mom, raise my kids on my own, and heal. And I was slowly gaining the strength I needed to think clearly. What also became clear was what I needed from a husband, partner, and friend. I wasn't willing to compromise ever again; I'd never again put my needs on hold and not speak up in order to keep the peace. A new strength was emerging that was slowly becoming a powerful force. I was changing and never willing to settle again for less than I deserved.

At the same time, he was willing to do anything, whatever was needed, to repair the massive destruction he caused me and the kids. Seeing his remorse and desire to rebuild what he'd torn down allowed me to slowly believe that if I was willing to keep even the slightest bit of hope alive, he'd show me it wouldn't be in vain. It felt like a terrifying risk, but I knew that I was changing so much and wondered if it was possible for him to change too.

His changes were undeniable and becoming obvious to all of us. It was as if the crash led to a fog that lifted, allowing him to see us all so clearly. Losing it all showed him what mattered most, and while I'll never understand how we destroy what's most important only to realize how much it means, that's exactly what happened.

With new rules slowly emerging, I was also no longer willing to tolerate a partner I had nothing in common with. Since spirituality was something so important to me, it was something nonnegotiable if we were to continue to speak about things other than the kids. I'm not sure why this new common interest was so important to me, but intuitively, I sensed it would have us understand each other at a new and different level.

He started sending me pictures of paragraphs from books he was reading, and he'd text feelings I never knew he had. I texted back how much pain I was in from the loss of a marriage, friend, and partner that no longer existed. Just like the kids were saying, I was starting to see how he was becoming a different person right before my eyes, but being blindsided before, I didn't trust him and didn't trust myself. It seemed like it would have been so much easier to just move on. To try to put the past behind me and start to move forward with my new life seemed much easier than facing and moving through all that pain.

That's when all of the spirituality I'd been learning rushed on me with new ideas I struggled to consider. What if this was just what we both needed? What if this had to happen to shake us both up and put us on a path greater than the one we were certainly headed for? What if this was an act of divine intervention and our souls were somehow in cahoots to bring about the best in us both? A battle raged within me between my ego and my soul, and while that idea was plausible, I wasn't sold.

When I looked at it from a spiritual perspective, it all made sense. He needed a crash to "wake up" and be the husband, father, and friend he signed up to be. I needed the crash to realize that I had been settling, that my boundaries were constantly being overstepped and it was time to put my needs back on the list and be treated with the love, honesty, and respect I deserved. The marriage and partnership we both wanted would never happen based on the paths we were on.

My human perspective, however, was absolutely blinded by my ego where pride, protection, resistance, and fear tried to "protect me." I tortured myself thinking about what it would mean if I took him back. Was I doing it because I was afraid I couldn't make it on my own? Was it out of fear? No. I'd proven to myself that during that time alone, I could do it if I wanted to, so those questions no longer remained, and I could take on the next set of questions. What about the kids? What message would I be sending to my girls if I took him back and we started over? Would they learn a message of weakness, giving up or giving in? Or would they learn about forgiveness, second chances, and starting over? What would my boys learn about how to treat a wife? Would they learn it's acceptable to cheat, lie, deceive, and betray a sacred trust? Or would they learn that people can tragically lose their way but that if they take responsibility and do all they can to make it up to the person they hurt, a new and even stronger relationship could be possible?

Finally, did I love him, could I forgive, and could I ever trust him again? I had long conversations with myself and with all of the kids. They saw my strength and shared that they'd be okay and would support whatever decision I made. It was completely and totally up to me. Somehow, that cleared the path to think about what would serve us all best, and I could breathe a little bit easier.

My soul was urging me to try again, and my ego was saying hell no, don't even think about it. My body was caught in the middle, and I felt as if this darkness and heaviness would drown me if it continued.

The battle waged for weeks, and I thought that if I gave him, us, and our family a second chance, we could begin to rebuild a friendship first and see where it goes. I cautiously had him come home knowing in the back of my mind that our future was completely up to me. If I couldn't do it, at least I tried my best for the sake of our future, the kids, and myself. Having my plan B gave me the green light to try again.

Any loss is painful, and anyone who's been through a traumatic loss knows that pain. There's a mourning period, and for me, it was a mourning of the old relationship, partnership, friendship, and marriage I thought I had. That pain is so real that it can feel physical. I kept saying how my heart hurt as I just struggled with the reality of my new world. I was now in a club I never wanted to be in, and while I knew his actions really had nothing to do with me, the lesson he was learning about what mattered most in his life were learned at my expense. It felt so unfair, so unjust, and I struggled with it all. What did I do to deserve this? I was trying my best to raise a family, run a business, grow, and still find time for him. The sense of rejection, being so disregarded and cast aside, was too hard for my confidence and self-esteem to take. That was my ego speaking up. Then my soul would kick in with thoughts of a new beginning, a new chapter, a new opportunity that we never would have had access to had this not happened.

Before I knew it, my heart started to really physically hurt. I remember being on a coaching call and breaking into a sweat. My heart felt tight; my breathing was shallow; I felt nauseous, light-headed, and dizzy; and I felt like I was about to faint. I quickly ended the call and sat on my office floor until the nausea subsided. Words are powerful, and I was afraid I was manifesting a heart attack from this excruciating pain, anguish, suffering, and the very words I was using to describe it all. I didn't know it at the time, but it was my first panic attack, something I'd never had before and something not uncommon when we're reeling from the shock and heartbreak of a painful betrayal.

The feeling subsided, and I remember a week later feeling good enough to go to my Sunday yoga class, where I looked forward to my instructor Maria's weekly life lesson before each class. This week, it was about scars and how scars mean we've been through something, so instead of being ashamed of them, they're a reminder of strength and something to be proud of. So, because my heart was now physically hurting, I imagined that the physical pain was due to a scar that was forming on my heart, trying to mend what had been ferociously ripped apart. It didn't work. The pain kept getting worse. I'd heard how heart attacks were silent killers, especially for women, and, not wanting to create a panic within my family, I promised myself that if it didn't subside within a day, I'd go to the hospital.

It got worse, and now the pain was very real and very frightening. Now I was afraid to drive myself, fearing I'd have a heart attack on my way to the hospital. I'm not a hypochondriac, and I tend to minimize pain, so when things were only getting worse, I knew this was getting serious. Adam drove me to the emergency room, and within a short period of time, I was hooked up to an EKG machine with wires everywhere and doctors surrounding me. I was terrified, and then, as if a bucket of cold water had been thrown onto me, I realized, "I don't belong here; this place is for sick people!" If they didn't unhook me from all of this nonsense, I was about to do it myself, and thankfully, within a short time, I was unhooked from all of the wires, and when they confirmed that it was a panic attack just like the other ones I started having over the past few weeks, I was discharged and sent home.

This was all so hard, but I knew I had to get my mind under control because if I didn't, my thoughts, which were running rampant, would eventually kill me. That trip to the emergency room was a warning I needed to take seriously. I wasn't going to start drinking or take anything to distract myself from this pain. I needed to face it head-on in order to deal with it. I remember hearing, "What we resist, persists," so I surrendered to wherever these waves of pain would take me. Sure, I was willing to take this on, but I couldn't do it alone and suffer in silence anymore. I needed support, guidance, and direction. Was I doing the right thing, or was I making a mistake? I didn't know whom to trust. I questioned everyone's intentions. That's when I made an appointment to see Anna, a spiritual and intuitive coach who seemed to have the Universe on speed dial. If I couldn't yet trust myself, I reasoned that, at the very least, I could trust the Universe.

Anna confirmed it all. Without my saying a word, she told me exactly why it happened and how it was "divinely orchestrated" with such precision that we'd one day look at it as the greatest gift that could have happened to us both. I wasn't anywhere close to accepting that yet, but I kept listening. She told me about all it would lead to and how my pain was exactly what I needed to change the course of my life and put me on a path to share it with those who'd find hope and strength through my story. She told me we'd both use this experience to change so many lives for the better, as others would see how catastrophe, then growth and change, can radically alter the course of your life. I was hearing from the Universe itself how hitting rock bottom opens up your eyes, your heart, and your mind if you're willing to be open to the messages they're meant to teach.

At the same time, I wanted Adam to speak with someone he could confide in to work through whatever possessed him to make the decisions he made. Anna suggested Paul, another spiritual counselor with a no-nonsense approach. Adam had his first appointment, and the minute he walked in, without Paul knowing a thing about him, said, "You were such an asshole!" I knew Adam was in the right place and would get the "spiritual smackdown" he needed.

Could I believe the message Anna shared from the Universe? There was so much to gain if I did. I'd keep our family together and finally have the husband, partner, friend, and future I wanted. Everything I was seeing and hearing from Adam showed me he was transforming. He was seeing Paul every week, going to the ocean to watch the sunrise to marvel at its beauty. He was watching every Wayne Dyer video he could get his hands on, quoting spiritual leaders and being attentive, kind, and loving to the kids and me. His entire office kept saying he was becoming calm, so much different than he'd ever been, even lecturing everyone in his office about how to not screw up your entire life and the lives of those you love. He started going into New York City on Saturday mornings to feed the homeless, sitting with them to let them know they mattered. Paul would share with me how radically different he was becoming, how differently and clearly he saw me now, and how sorry he was for the pain he had caused. Knowing how extreme Adam could be, he was now embracing this new path with a passion and gusto that was unmistakable. It seemed as if there wasn't a cell left from the "other guy," and while his transformation was becoming obvious, I was still struggling with mine.

Everything was a trigger, and it seemed like I'd take one step forward and take two steps back. I'd try to be my highest self, then, within moments, images, thoughts, and the reality of what he did would consume me. The waves of pain lessened a bit, but the battle between my ego and my soul was something I had to take on once and for all. Am

I going to give this marriage another try, or am I going to call it quits? Enough of this torture already—I wanted relief. The battle came to a head one night, one that was so brutal that I can only describe it as the "dark night of the soul." I woke up from a restless sleep picturing my ego grabbing one of my arms and my soul gently embracing the other with my body caught right in the middle. Who would win? I couldn't keep this up; it was exhausting, debilitating, consuming, and frustrating and filled me with grief and despair. I had every reason to let my ego win. I'd been hurt, betrayed, cheated on, and lied to. I'd been duped by someone living a double life many years before that I never knew about. I could justify it all, and the kids would know I tried my best, and I just couldn't do it. No one could blame me.

My soul, however, was whispering a different message in my ear, letting me know that if I could move through this, there'd be a seed of greatness left in the wake of this nightmare. I was realizing that we learn our greatest lessons not from our successes but from our failures. I was seeing that our greatest teachers often aren't the ones who treat us the best but rather the ones who hurt us the most. I was learning that if we're able to take the messages meant to be learned from our pain, that's how we grow and transform. My soul was whispering to me that I had a huge lesson to learn from my childhood about boundaries getting crossed, being treated unfairly, and not standing my ground, and since I still must have been struggling to learn that lesson, the Universe provided me with an "opportunity" to learn that lesson once and for all. It started making sense. The lesson was learned and hit me hard because at that moment, I realized that if I could do this, I could do anything. It was about 3:00 a.m. when I made my decision—I let my soul win.

I felt like I'd entered into a dark, lonely tunnel. I was determined to come out the other side transformed but didn't yet know how I'd do it. With my decision made, I could at least focus on how I'd now heal myself, using this opportunity to become the highest and best version of me that would be birthed as a result of all this pain. It wasn't enough motivation just to know I had saved my family and my marriage. I know that may sound selfish, but the pain was so deep that that just wasn't enough to balance the injustice and unfairness I felt. I needed to know deep in my bones that this pain would serve a bigger purpose, and it motivated me to think that if I could somehow heal physically, mentally, emotionally, psychologically, and spiritually from this, I'd have a powerful message to share with others who were searching for a lifeline to heal from their own traumas.

In a desperate search for answers, this experience catapulted me into a PhD in transpersonal psychology. I needed to understand how the mind works, why we do the things we do, and how I could heal. While I was there, I did a study on how we experience betrayal—what holds us back, what helps us heal, and what happens to us physically, mentally, and emotionally when the people closest to us lie, cheat, and deceive. That study led to three very exciting discoveries.

The first is that while we can stay stuck for years, decades, or even a lifetime, if we're going to go from betrayal to transformation, we're going to go through five stages (which you'll soon learn all about). The second discovery was that healing from betrayal is very different from healing from other types of life crises (like the death of a loved one, disease, natural disaster, etc.). When we can make meaning out of our event and create a new life as a result; it's called Posttraumatic Growth, and I'll go into it in much more detail later in this book. But healing from betrayal involves many different aspects of healing in addition to that. Besides grieving, mourning the loss, and more, with betrayal, we also have to rebuild aspects of the self that were destroyed by the painful experience. Self-esteem, confidence, a sense of rejection, abandonment, belonging, worthiness, and trust all take a hard hit and need to be rebuilt as well. So, this specific type of healing needed a new name. That new name is Post Betrayal Transformation (PBT), and that's exactly where this book is taking you.

The third discovery is that there's a collections of physical, mental, and emotional symptoms so common to betrayal that it's become known as Post Betrayal Syndrome (PBS). We've had thousands of people take the PBS assessment/quiz on our website to see to what extent they may be struggling, and what we've learned from the data we're collecting, along with what I learned through the study as well as my own experience, is nothing short of life changing.

These discoveries led to an entirely new business, brand, and life where every day, we're helping people move through these Five Stages from Betrayal to Breakthrough. It led to the opening of the PBT Institute, the website https://ThePBTInstitute.com, a thriving membership community for support and healing, certification programs to train others to become Certified PBT Coaches or Certified PBT Practitioners, a three-phase supplement line to support whichever stage of betrayal you may be healing from, the *From Betrayal to Breakthrough* podcast, and so much more. What else did it lead to? Adam and I didn't renew our vows; instead, not long ago, we married each other again with new vows, intentions, rings, and all, with Anna and Paul officiating the ceremony and our four kids as our bridal party.

So many experiences, realizations, and healing have happened since my experience only a few years ago, and I'm going to share with you exactly how I did it. I'm also going to introduce you to the Fab 14, the 14 heroes who participated in my study allowing us to discover the Five Stages from Betrayal to Breakthrough as well as the concept of PBS and PBT. You'll see how the Fab 14 made meaning and peace and healed from their betrayals so that you can as well. The intention is that the "divine downloads," concepts, ideas, and wisdom that have been gained from all of this will help you too.

Are you ready? Now it's your turn.

I

UNDERSTANDING BETRAYAL

• 1 •

Why We Get Blindsided

The Nature of Trust

*Y*ou couldn't brace yourself because you never saw it coming. You thought you were safe, so you gave your heart, your time, your loyalty, your trust. Then, out of the blue and in one life-altering moment, it's as if that person closest to you just pulled off their mask and revealed who they've been all this time—lies you so easily believed and actions you dismissed because it *never crossed your mind* that the one you trusted the most would ever hurt you. You thought this person had your back. You believed the two of you were honoring the same rules, sharing the same moral code, and respecting the same beliefs. This was the one you loved, trusted, and believed in the most.

Your sense of safety and security is shattered in an instant, and the shock is forever imprinted on your body and mind. You can't comprehend what you just learned. Nothing makes sense. Your heart breaks, you feel like you got sucker punched, and the shock is so raw, consuming, and overwhelming that you can barely breathe. You feel totally alone, rejected, abandoned, and confused. You don't know how this could have happened, and you can't make sense out of what you just learned. You don't know what to do or what to think. The only thing you know for sure is that life will never be the same.

This is what it feels like to be blindsided by betrayal.

Many of us know the feeling of betrayal because we've experienced it on some level at some point in our lives. It may result from a partner's affair; discovering an important detail later in life that was withheld by a parent; a business partner stealing the company funds; physical, sexual, or emotional abuse in childhood; or a best friend revealing your secrets. Maybe it's a boss, coach, therapist, or counselor who took advantage of their position of power. Maybe it's a sibling who turns on you in a time of need. Maybe it's a series of "micro-betrayals" that accumulate to create a "death by a thousand cuts" from a coworker who repeatedly takes credit for your idea. And maybe it's a self-betrayal as you continue to dishonor yourself and your truth out of fear, shame, or a belief that doesn't support you.

Betrayal leaves many physical, mental, and emotional symptoms in its wake, and one of the most common is the effect that betrayal has on your sense of trust, which is foundational to any relationship. That trust can take a lifetime to build and only moments to be destroyed. But it's not just your betrayer that you no longer trust; it's also yourself because *how could you not see this coming*? As if that weren't bad enough, you start battling an array of physical, mental, and emotional symptoms that can make it nearly impossible to function. Even after you manage to get back on your feet (because people are counting on you, so what choice do you have?), the effects linger. If left unhealed, this massive experience looms in the background, keeping you sick, sad, and stuck for a lifetime. It can taint and plague every experience that's meant to be filled with joy. It can prevent you from ever trusting again and feeling safe, loved, honored, and treasured in future relationships. I've met so many people who believe that life will just never be as good as it used to be, that *they* will never be as good as they used to be. But it doesn't have to be this way. There is a way to move forward and heal from *all* of it.

THE NATURE OF TRUST

We're going to begin our journey by understanding what happens to us when we're betrayed, and that means understanding the nature of trust. Of course, I'll be giving you strategies to move forward, but it's important to start at the very beginning. So, here's how trust works. Relationships rest on a foundation of trust. It's what allows us to feel safe and secure. These relationships can be with family members, partners, friends, coworkers, or anyone else who is a part of our day. Every relationship you have has its own set of spoken or unspoken rules. Those rules govern us and give us a sense of order and an understanding of how that particular relationship "works." While we have different rules for different relationships—for example, you probably expect one thing from your partner and have a completely different set of expectations for your friend or your accountant—what matters most is that both parties abide by the rules. When that happens over time, we feel increasingly safe, secure, and comfortable in the relationship. We can rest easy because we have a sense of trust.

When we have trust in our relationships, we're more confident and feel freer to explore, learn, and grow. That's because while we may feel awkward or unfamiliar in certain arenas, we always have that safe circle of trust to return to. It acts as the perfect foundation on which to build a solid and sturdy self. Without it, the world can be a scary and unsettling place. Without it, we question everyone's intentions because we believe that our safety and security are at risk. Coming from a foundation of trust, however, we can more easily trust in ourselves, others, and the world around us. This is how trust works in our lives, and it isn't something we need to be taught. It's an understanding that's primal and common to all of us. Here's an example.

Years ago, when I first brought my kids to preschool, I remember that some of the other kids ran happily into the classroom while mine always stayed close by and hung on to my leg. If I were to pry them off of me and force them into the classroom, they wouldn't have felt safe. On some level, their trust that I'd be there for them when they needed me may have been questioned. To prevent that, the teacher sat me down on one of those tiny chairs and handed me a book to read. My job was to be there physically but to focus on reading the book and not play with my kids. It never failed. First, each child would hold on to my leg, sizing up the scene but staying right by my side. Eventually, they'd venture off and come running back. Soon enough, they realized it was much more fun playing with the other kids, and I was free to go, trust maintained.

When the rules that give us a sense of safety, security, and trust are violated, that's a betrayal. Trust is shattered, and there's no order. Instead, there's chaos because the rules that gave us structure, parameters, and an understanding of how to be within that relationship can no longer be relied on. There's no more foundation or sturdy ground on which to feel safe, and we are left with frightening questions, such as "If the people we trusted the most prove to be untrustworthy, whom can we trust?" and "If the ones we'd run to when *others* cause harm are the ones *causing* the harm, where do we turn?"

Betrayal is defined as "a violation of a person's trust or confidence." I define it as the deliberate breaking of a spoken or unspoken rule within a relationship. The more we trust and are dependent on the person who breaks the rules, the greater the harm, the deeper the hurt, and the bigger the betrayal. For example, let's take a child who completely trusts and depends on their parent. If that parent does something abusive or harmful, that's going to have a bigger impact then, let's say, a coworker who takes credit for your idea. They're both betrayals because trust has been violated, but they won't have the same impact. Betrayal can have many faces. Here are just a few.

THE MANY FACES OF BETRAYAL

Let's say you're religious and you were raised to believe that if you go to your place of worship and pray, you'll be kept safe. Then something tragic happens. This can leave you to feel that you've been betrayed by God. Maybe you have a relationship with someone in a position of authority like a parent, teacher, employer, therapist, doctor, mentor, or coach. Spoken or unspoken, the understanding is that if you follow their direction, they'll guide and support you appropriately. Then let's say they do something harmful or inappropriate. The rule or understanding that you'd be guided appropriately is broken, and that's a betrayal. Maybe you have a sibling, and the understanding is that you both will support your parents financially or otherwise when they need assistance as they age. The time comes when your parents need your support, and your sibling denies they ever agreed to anything. The rule is broken, and that's a betrayal. Maybe you and your best friend have an unspoken rule that you tell each other secrets that stay between the two of you. You later learn that your friend told your secret to someone else. That's a betrayal. Maybe you're working on a project with some coworkers. It was understood that you're working as a team and would share the project with your boss when you're all together. They finish the project early and present it to your boss without you so they can take full credit. That's a betrayal. Of course, there are other types of painful betrayals, but you get the idea. In all of these examples, the trust that the relationship was built on is shattered. Which betrayals hurt the most? The ones that involve the greatest amount of trust, sacrifice, commitment, depth of the relationship, and heart.

TRUST IS FOUNDATIONAL

Trust is the very foundation on which our relationships are built, and that's why that shattering of trust leaves us on shaky and unstable ground. Also, that shattering of trust doesn't just happen when others have betrayed us. It can happen when we betray ourselves. We can believe our bodies have betrayed us, as in the case of a diagnosis or disease. We can experience self-betrayal when we repeatedly stay quiet when we know we should speak up, when we break promises we've made to ourselves, when we negate or abandon our needs, or when we make decisions that cause self-harm. We're going to examine the full life cycle of trust—how trust is built, maintained, and shattered. This understanding is the first step to healing—once and for all.

Trust is sacred and fragile, and earning someone's trust is an honor and a sacred gift. To me, building trust is similar to building a nest. Each twig and branch being used to build that nest is an integral part of its foundation and structure, just as each exchange with someone is an opportunity to build trust. Each time we question something and expectations are met, trust continues to be built just as each twig being used to build the nest is another opportunity to build a safe and secure home for its inhabitants. Over time, with many twigs carefully placed, that nest is built, which represents a sense of safety and security. It's the same thing with trust. Over time, and with many opportunities for trust to be built, we can slowly feel safe, rest easy, and trust because we're supported within that nest of security. Over time, we slowly and confidently believe we're safe because of how the person we grew to trust showed up in countless situations, giving us many opportunities to feel secure. They demonstrated that they're trustworthy, and we have nothing to fear. If the rest of the world is confusing and chaotic, we can trust that all is well within our "nest" of safety.

That's why it's always a shock when we're met by something we didn't expect. We felt safe and secure. We were vulnerable; we let our guard down and truly believed that there was a mutual understanding around what was agreed on (spoken or unspoken) within the relationship. When we're betrayed, that trust, safety, and feeling of security that we grew to count on is shattered in one life-altering moment. That "nest" is completely and totally shattered. So, now picture what would happen if a nest were shattered. Any living being within that nest would lose any sense of safety and security they may have had. What are the only options? Scramble to find a way to somehow survive the experience or else perish. When we discover a betrayal, it takes only that brief moment to feel as if the rug has been completely pulled from under us, sending us into a scary and unfamiliar space and giving us those same options. Survive the experience or else allow it to destroy us.

THE BRICK WALL OF TRUST

Here's another visual that explains how trust works. Imagine a huge brick wall. That wall was built by adding one brick at a time, brick by brick and slowly over a certain period; those bricks accumulate to become a solid and strong structure. It can take years to build, and the only way to build it is by adding one brick at a time. There's no shortcut to building that wall any faster, and the only way to build it is by carefully adding one brick at a time.

Now, imagine that huge brick wall tumbling down because of something tragic and unexpected. You're looking at the rubble that used to be this enormous brick wall, and you can't imagine how that wall can ever be repaired.

Here's what I believe. I believe it can't be *repaired*, but it can be *rebuilt*. You're looking at a pile of bricks that took years of consistency, repetition, and attention to build. If the entire wall came tumbling down, patching it up simply won't work. With the brick wall down, you also have an opportunity to see if it can be rebuilt any better, bigger, stronger, or more beautiful.

You have another option too. That option is to decide if it's even *worth* the effort and energy it would take to rebuild or if you'd be better off walking away. If you choose to rebuild a new wall, however, what's the only way to put it back together again? Brick by brick by brick. Sure, you can stare at the rubble of bricks and decide that it's too big and too exhausting of a task to build again. You can question if it's worth the effort and energy that it will take to rebuild and how you'll approach this new project. But that's totally up to you. That's how trust works. It can take years to build trust with someone and only moments for it to be torn down. While it can most definitely be built again, however, there are unfortunately no shortcuts here. Building that trust couldn't be rushed when it was originally being built, and it certainly can't be rushed when it comes to building it again, especially if the intention is to rebuild that trust with the person who hurt you. Let's dive into this a bit more.

Rebuilding trust in yourself and your decisions and trusting in something bigger, in life, and in your healing is completely up to you. (In a later section, I'm going to teach you my four-step process to do just that.) Rebuilding trust in the person who hurt you involves a few other steps, so let's start there. First, it may or may not be an option. If the person who hurt you is unwilling to take responsibility for their actions, if they're denying what they did or said, or if they somehow blame you for the betrayal, you really don't have much to work with here when it comes to rebuilding trust with that person. Trying to rebuild trust when you're met with this response isn't the best use of your time and energy. Your experience may also leave you with the fact that the person who hurt you may no longer be alive or in any capacity to begin this new trust-rebuilding project. So, here it's best to focus on yourself and your healing so that you can move on. As promised, how to do this is coming up, so stay with me.

However, while some people are unwilling to rebuild trust with the person they hurt, some betrayers can be open, available, and eager to rebuild a new and better brick wall of trust if given the opportunity. These people have a very different response. These are the "bricklayers," the ones ready and willing to do what it takes to build a new wall. They're grateful for the opportunity, and it's as if the fog has been cleared for them to see you and what truly matters so clearly. These are the people who (if *you* are willing to try too) are going to do all they can to build something new and beautiful. Once realizing how deeply they hurt you (while being remorseful, taking full responsibility, and, if they're willing, doing what it takes to regain your trust), you can slowly see the potential here. If this is your betrayer's honest response to the pain they caused and you're willing to consider slowly and carefully rebuilding a new relationship with that person, you're both in a position to see that brick wall slowly become rebuilt. Here's what it can look like in the case of a romantic betrayal.

Maybe you're triggered by something that has you feeling unsafe and insecure. The person working on rebuilding that trust reassures you that now that they see things so clearly and differently, they understand exactly why that trigger would create your fearful response and show you through their behavior that they wouldn't behave that way again. You'd slowly see how your response was really to the painful *trigger*, not to what you're seeing in them now. That simple exchange between you and your betrayer is like one brick added to that brick wall. Maybe a few days later, your trauma has you questioning your partner's schedule. In a flash of insecurity, you call them only to find that they were exactly where they said they'd be. That's another brick added to that brick wall. Maybe you're about to have a conversation and you're thinking about how the "old them" would respond as you brace yourself for an uncomfortable exchange. You're met with their new loving perspective that sounds completely different than the old version of them that you grew to know. You exhale a sigh of relief and realize that that's another brick added to that brick wall.

Through opportunities to be pleasantly surprised because you'd grown to expect the old behavior and you're met with the new, it's as if each exchange is a brick being placed in that new brick wall. When you see over time that you simply can't "catch" the person lying and deceiving and instead you're catching them valuing and respecting what they now see so clearly, trust can slowly and carefully be rebuilt. This process can also show you that people can and do change if they're willing to "face it, feel it, heal it," which, whether you're the betrayer or the betrayed, is something I'm going to teach you how to do. Let's keep going.

THE TRUST WE PUT IN OTHERS

As I mentioned, betrayals involve a violation of a spoken or unspoken rule. While these rules may be initially established due to convenience, these same rules over time "take on the characteristics of a moral obligation," which is why friendships as well as partnerships experience pain, hurt, and shock when they discover that these rules have been broken.[1] The betrayal within a friendship, for example, can be especially upsetting in that a betrayal can be felt as an attack to a sense of self, leaving the betrayed feeling enraged and devastated at the realization of being treated so deceitfully and unpredictably.[2] Friendships are based on trust and openness where one friend confidently reveals aspects of himself or herself to the other.[3] This creates a vulnerability to being betrayed when that trust is violated. The relaxing of defenses, the opening of ourselves to others, and the freedom we feel to express ourselves openly leave us particularly vulnerable to betrayal. Does this mean it's wrong or a bad idea to relax our defenses or be vulnerable with others? Of course not; it's what creates close bonds, intimacy, and friendship. Betrayal, however, is a potential outcome and possibility that we risk when we trust and when we love another. But here's where I truly believe in that saying "Better to have loved and lost than never loved at all," even if we need to put ourselves back together again after a heartbreaking betrayal.

Betrayal by a partner or close friend can be so upsetting. Young adults often trust their friends with their secrets. Think back to when you told your best friend whom you had a crush on when you were in middle school and swore him or her to secrecy. In exchange for trusting your friend with your intimate secret, you expected loyalty in return.[4] That's why when these rules are violated, painful negative reactions occur. In fact, the violation of trust when a secret is shared was found to be the type of betrayal among friends that brings about the most anger because the act of breaking that trust is seen as mean and intentional.[5]

DEFINING BETRAYAL

So, let's dive in with a few more definitions of betrayal so you can get a true perspective on just how damaging it can be to our sense of safety and security. According to the *Macquarie Dictionary*, to betray is to seduce and desert, to disappoint the hopes or expectations of another, to deliver up to an enemy, to deceive or mislead, and to be disloyal or unfaithful.[6] Betrayal has also been defined as "to reveal something meant to be hidden."[7] Betrayal involves one partner in a relationship acting in a way that conveys how little the betrayer values or cares for the spoken or unspoken rules and values that serve as the foundation of the relationship. A betrayal can also show that the betrayer doesn't value the person they're betraying or the relationship and can be interpreted as complete rejection.[8]

The underlying feeling we experience through betrayal is that the betrayer's interests and needs are seen as a greater priority than the value of the relationship. This interpersonal rejection leaves us feeling devalued, unsafe, and alone as the person we trusted and/or were dependent on violates that trust.[9] This is why we take it so personally when we're betrayed and the shock is felt at a deep level, going much deeper than simply learning about the betrayal at the cognitive level.[10] Pain and hurt are felt at the very core.[11]

THE CHAOS BETRAYAL CREATES

There are lots of emotional responses to betrayal based on how deeply we depended and trusted the person. A sense of being out of control, fear, helplessness, agitation, the desire to numb, social anxiety, and panic are a few responses that are common.[12] At the highest levels, when, for example, a child experiences physical or sexual abuse by a caregiver, the child can struggle with depression, posttraumatic stress, anxiety, and hallucinations.[13] These traumas affect the body with a rush of stress-related hormones, body memory of the trauma, the loss of body integrity, and the inability to cope with what the betrayed person is experiencing and how it's being interpreted.[14] From this point, it's easy to see how the person who was betrayed would view the world as a dangerous place or how, on some level, they come to think that they possibly deserved the mistreatment.[15]

As if that's not enough reason to heal from betrayal, here are some other reasons. Let's start with the fact that while both women and men experience betrayal and the trauma it creates, women experience higher rates of betrayal trauma than men.[16] Women also experience higher rates of posttraumatic stress disorder (PTSD) than men and experience more than twice the level of abuse when compared with men.[17] The higher rates of PTSD in women also lead to higher "experiential avoidance."[18] What's experiential avoidance? Experiential avoidance is "when an individual is unwilling to experience private events, such as thoughts, memories, emotions, and bodily sensations, and takes action to change the experience or the frequency of these events and the contexts in which these events may arise."[19] That's a fancy way of saying that we're not facing our pain because, well, it's too painful. What does that mean when you play that out? It means that if more women experience the trauma of betrayal and those same women are more likely to experience PTSD symptoms than men and if those painful PTSD symptoms lead to a greater likelihood that they'll avoid moving through their experience instead of finding the tools and support to help them heal and reduce symptoms, then how women manage their work, families, and selves doesn't look hopeful. Here's where the tools and support you'll find here are needed more than ever.

When compared to men, women who've been betrayed also experience a greater loss in terms of a sense of belonging and abandonment.[20] Studies also found that women experience lies and deception more negatively than men.[21] This is why that violation and shattering of trust hurts as much as it does. As if a breaking of trust through betrayal weren't bad enough, for women with children, it's even worse. Not only do these betrayals affect a woman's physical, mental, and emotional wellness, but they directly impact the wellness of their children. This means that a mom's pain directly impacts her children on so many levels. So, strategies to heal help not only us but also future generations.

As children see their moms not only healing from betrayal but using it as a launchpad to greater growth, purpose, and meaning, their children can learn to work through their own experiences as well. These children, instead of choosing a more harmful or dangerous coping strategy when they're faced with challenges (for example, drugs or alcohol), may instead be able to make more empowering choices. They may crave the deeper meaning and more fulfilling relationships they see their mom able to experience as she learns and grows from her challenge. They may be able to move into their future with a steadier and more solid foundation because of the example they're seeing through their mom. When this happens, their mom has been able to become an inspiring role model who has taken her greatest challenge and turned it into her biggest gift. If you ask me, those are some pretty powerful incentives. Let's keep going.

Trust is shattered when we're deceived, and deception can be viewed in many ways, such as nondisclosure (or white lies), half-truths, and full-scale lies.[22] Studies have found that women and men view deception a bit differently, too, with women finding lies and deception as a more hurtful transgression than men.[23]

While romantic betrayal hits us right in the heart, betrayals of others we've trusted hurt as well. Another infuriating violation of trust is when we're betrayed by a company or product we've grown to feel safe with. Imagine an asthma medication that was found to cause constriction;[24] a water filtration system that, instead of purifying the water, contaminates water;[25] and a sunscreen that, instead of protecting against skin cancer, causes it.[26] It's been found that people are willing to take on a greater risk from a product in order to avoid the possibility of their trust being shattered by that product. That means that we want to avoid the shock and realization of being "duped" at all costs. Once a company or product has our trust, we're more angry and disappointed if we're deceived by them than if the product or company simply didn't meet our expectations. That means that if given a choice, we'd rather be disappointed in a product's results than experience a violation made by a company or product that made a promise to protect us and didn't.[27]

Although customers can be loyal to a particular company or product, betrayal is a primary motivator leading customers to restore fairness by whatever means they feel they need to.[28] This drive to restore fairness is experienced when a customer believes that a company intentionally violated the spoken or unspoken rule that was created in the relationship between the customer and the company.[29] This desire for retaliation is known as the "love becomes hate" effect, which happens when customers feel that a company has tried to exploit them, lied to them, taken advantage of them, violated their trust, cheated, broken promises, or disclosed confidential information.[30] So, even though betrayals of those we're closest to hurt most deeply, betrayals of anyone or anything we've grown to trust cause pain as well.

It's the promise to protect and the violation that's experienced that destroys trust. Whether it's a personal violation (for example, romantic betrayal) or a company that deceived us, when we're betrayed by our friends, coworkers, and more, these are all violations of trust that we experience as acts of betrayal.

So, now that you know what the shattering of trust looks and feels like, we're going to move on to what happens to us physically, mentally, and emotionally when that trust is broken. Meet me in the next chapter, where I'll be sharing some of the most common symptoms we experience after a betrayal. As you learn about these symptoms, you're going to be nodding your head in agreement as you realize a few things. First, you're going to realize that you're not crazy. Your symptoms are very real, and they're part of the "leftovers" left in the wake of your experience. Next, you're going to learn that you're not alone. Unfortunately, betrayal isn't uncommon. It happens to so many of us, sometimes more than once, at some point in our lives. These repeat betrayals especially happen when we haven't used the experience as an opportunity to learn and grow. When this happens, it becomes a pattern, and although it feels terrible, it feels familiar, so we keep finding ourselves in this dark and painful space. When this happens, we also feel as if we're in a club we never asked or wanted to be in, but, sure enough, here we are, and we don't know how to "cancel our membership" and get out. Finally, here's the good news. You're going to realize that as long as you're willing to do the work, you'll be able to heal from all of it.

· 2 ·

What Happens When Someone Betrays Our Trust

*D*iane and Sue were best friends who had talked for years about opening a wellness center together. When they finally decided to make it happen, they were so excited to join forces. They worked well together, both willing to put in the time and effort necessary to make their center successful. Diane was the more business-minded partner, focusing her attentions on investments and expenses. Sue seemed to be a natural at attracting and maintaining clients. Both felt confident that their individual strengths would work well together to help the business succeed.

About five years into their venture, Diane noticed the client flow had slowed and Sue wasn't coming in as often as she used to. The center was costly to maintain, and without a steady stream of clients, Diane was earning much less money each month. She became worried about whether she could afford to keep the business open.

One day, Diane bumped into an old client of Sue's. She asked her how things were going, and to Diane's shock and surprise, the woman said, "I'm still struggling, but it's been easier to come in since you opened up your second office two years ago. The discounted price really helps keep me on a regular schedule of appointments."

Where was this second office? As it turned out, the office was in the garage-turned-renovated-office-space in Sue's home. She had opened it without telling Diane and had been taking clients away from their shared business. It was a betrayal that impacted Diane in so many ways—her financial well-being, her relationship with her best friend, her confidence in her own business acumen, and so on. The fallout from a betrayal can be wide ranging—so much so that it shocks the body and mind.

You're about to learn why, when we're blindsided by someone close to us, it can tear our hearts out and turn our worlds upside down. As relationships grow and develop, it becomes easier to share our deepest feelings, reveal aspects of ourselves, and open ourselves up to another person. We become vulnerable because we trust that our feelings are safe in another person's hands. So, when that trust is violated, it's deeply painful. We're forced to realize that the other person didn't respect or hold the same beliefs or expectations we've been holding. Being blindsided with that realization shocks us on a physical, mental, and emotional level, especially when it comes to sexual and emotional infidelity, deception, and lying, which are the most common forms of betrayal.[1]

EMOTIONAL RESPONSES TO BETRAYAL

Fear, rejection, sadness, depression, anxiety, shock, anger, repression, numbing, and denial are just a few of the feelings that can emerge as a result of a betrayal. Depending on the severity of the betrayal and our own emotional reactions to it, we can also experience symptoms of posttraumatic stress disorder (PTSD) where we are triggered by a thought, memory, person, place, or event that brings us right back to our pain. When this occurs, we're not just thinking about the betrayal; we also respond and react as if we're reexperiencing it all over again.

We can also feel shame if we find ourselves obsessing over the event. Shame is common, especially if we become hypervigilant following a betrayal. We may find ourselves taking on behaviors to see if our betrayer or others are continuing to lie or withhold information. We may also feel shame when it comes to sharing our experience with others because we're afraid we'll be judged or pitied. Or it may be that your friend or partner is loved and highly regarded by others and we're ashamed to share the truth of what we've discovered because, as heartbreaking and crazy as it seems, people can look at us like somehow there was something lacking within us that drove their behavior.

This shame is an understandable and an exhausting reaction to broken trust. It's also a response that prevents our healing and contributes to even more pain. It was also one of the biggest motivators for me to write this book. After an experience with betrayal, we need support, tools, and strategies more than ever. Unfortunately, it's also a time when we're the least likely to seek that support. Why? Because it's common to feel ashamed that it happened in the first place, as if somehow we weren't enough and a betrayal is proof that we're "less than." Perhaps we feel embarrassed that we'd been taken advantage of or duped. It's also often because we're protecting the betrayer (at our own expense) or because we're trying to prevent ourselves from receiving judgment from others, pity, or whatever.

HOW SHAME HAS US SUFFERING IN SILENCE

After my betrayal, I was completely ashamed for just about every reason I mentioned here. I clearly remember how my friends rallied when I shared my story about my family betrayal. I felt like I had the support, I needed to know that I wasn't crazy, and I wasn't alone. Telling these same friends about the betrayal from my husband felt different. While my friends would have been supportive, I also knew they loved my husband and I didn't want to hear or feel their anger or disappointment toward him. I didn't want to be influenced or swayed in *any way* from anyone with their advice or suggestions during this fragile time. I didn't want to hear whether they thought it was best to work it out or if they believed that ending the relationship was a better option. I wanted to prevent hearing any excuse they may have found for his behavior, and I also didn't want to hear what a "deal breaker" it would mean to them if they were to go through it. I simply wanted to come to whatever decision felt right for me and for my kids.

It took me a full year until I told my friends about what happened. Around that time, I remember that I'd taken off my engagement ring and wedding band because I didn't want any distractions preventing me from thinking clearly. I wanted my own thoughts and feelings to emerge as I started to slowly rebuild my life post-betrayal. I had no idea what life would look like, and I didn't want to be influenced by anyone or anything.

During this time, about five friends got together for our customary birthday celebration dinners. We'd been getting together to celebrate our birthdays since our children were born, so it's been a tradition for more than 20 years. I remember awkwardly keeping my hands in my pockets when we all gathered together before sitting down, then keeping my hands under the table every time I put down my glass or utensils during dinner so they wouldn't see that I'd taken off my rings. I barely spoke, I had no appetite, and I left as soon as I could. I felt like I had the word "betrayed" stamped on my forehead and there'd be no getting out of there without sharing all of the painful details. I drove home in silence, feeling alone and crying the whole way home.

Finally, and when I was ready, I made plans with one of my friends. My intention was to tell her what had happened. This level of vulnerability was terrifying for me. I was usually the strong one, the one offering a shoulder to cry on for everyone else, and I was shaking like a leaf. My voice cracked, my hands shook, and the moment I shared the news, I cried, and she did too. I was sharing the death of my marriage as I'd known it, and we were grieving together. It was so hard and also incredibly healing.

Once the tears and shaking stopped, she became upset with me. Why? Because she wanted to be a good friend to me when I needed one most, and I was too busy being ashamed while suffering in silence. On some level, she could have also been upset because I betrayed her as well. Our "rule" about our friendship was that we'd be there for each other when we needed it most, and my decision to keep the betrayal to myself meant I wasn't honoring my end of that rule. My decision prevented her from being there for me—just as I'd want to be there for any of my friends. She was also understandably angry at Adam for hurting her friend so deeply. It taught me so many amazing lessons about friendship.

POSSIBLE RESPONSES FROM OTHERS

Now, to be honest, that wasn't the response I got from everyone. Not by a long shot. What were some of the other responses? Judgment, pity, and keeping me at a distance because someone just didn't feel comfortable or didn't know what to say in response to what I was going through were a few reactions. There were even a few who it felt like distanced themselves for fear that what I'd experienced was "contagious" and somehow removing me from their circle would ensure that they'd prevent experiencing a painful betrayal themselves. Unfortunately, betrayal, like any loss, will show you who your friends are. The cream rises to the top, and the others, well, if they can't be there for you when you need them, you're better off knowing, wishing them well, and moving along. By the way, as part of Adam's process of making things right and helping us all heal, without my knowing it, he actually called all of my friends to apologize for who he'd been during that time and the ripple of pain his actions caused. Some *interesting* conversations were had as I'm sure you can imagine.

A few of my friends immediately called me to share their experiences once they hung up the phone. Hearing his remorse firsthand helped them believe he was truly sorry for his actions and conveyed a love and respect for me and the kids as he shared his regret for the pain he'd caused. They also felt that he must have respected the friendships in order to knowingly face these uncomfortable conversations. Of course, they were angry and hurt too, but these talks cleared the air and helped my friends believe that he was on his way to becoming a changed man. He was trying to rebuild a new brick wall with them too, and this was his first brick toward that goal.

MORE EMOTIONAL SYMPTOMS
THAT BETRAYAL CREATES

Confidence and self-esteem take an especially big hit when we've been betrayed by a romantic partner. One study found that 67 percent of betrayed husbands and 53 percent of betrayed wives suffered significant damage to their confidence and self-image after learning about a betrayal. The study also found that 18 percent of betrayed husbands and 21 percent of betrayed wives suffered with a sense of not belonging and a feeling of abandonment, making them feel as if they lacked value within the relationship.[2] Self-worth, emotional security, and a sense of commitment are all compromised too when a partner discovers that his or her partner has been unfaithful.[3] In a nutshell, betrayal is damaging on every level—to the body, mind, and spirit.

Humiliation can be a common response too. It's a painful by-product of betrayal because humiliation involves the perception that we've been treated in a way that exposes us as inferior or ridiculous.[4] For example, people who have been betrayed may feel that they were the last to know, that they were discarded for someone more physically attractive, or that they're being judged or gossiped about or the target of self-pity.[5] Humiliation and the sense of powerlessness that goes along with it can also bring about feelings of hatred.[6] It's the sense of injustice and how morally wrong the action is that evokes such intense anger.[7]

COMMON PHYSICAL SYMPTOMS AFTER BETRAYAL

Researchers have found that people experiencing high-betrayal trauma were more likely to experience pain symptoms, including soft tissue pain, diabetes, chronic fatigue, bladder problems, pelvic pain, headaches, irritable bowel syndrome, chronic pain, and asthma.[8] The trauma of betrayal can even impact how quickly we age. Leukocyte telomere length, a potential marker of cellular aging, was studied over a 40-year span in people who had experienced childhood trauma. It was found that telomeres shorten with time as a result of oxidative stress, highly stressful events, and negative health behaviors.[9] Betrayal is the type of stressful event that has the ability to shorten telomeres.

Now let's talk about diabetes, which is also more common in someone who's been betrayed. Chronic stress elevates blood glucose and insulin levels. Betrayal definitely elevates our level of stress. So those elevated levels due to chronic stress (especially if we obsessively review and reexperience our trauma) is the perfect recipe for diabetes. In fact, one study confirmed that people who've been betrayed were more likely to have diabetes.[10]

Here's what betrayal can also create. As adults, it's been found that those who've experienced betrayal as children are at an increased risk for alcohol and drug use, aggressiveness with intimate partners, risky sexual behavior, issues with anger, anxiety, and depression.[11] People who've experienced these traumas also have an elevated risk for revictimization because of an altered ability to make accurate decisions about trust in their relationships.[12]

All of this isn't meant to depress you. It's meant to motivate you. It's meant to move you toward action as you come to see that the betrayal impacted you in one way and you're keeping it alive through your response. Of course, I understand how painful it is and how it's virtually impossible to "get over it" without support, a strategy, and time, but I want you to get the full experience around what giving it extra attention can cause.

OUR RESPONSES TO BETRAYAL

Here's what I want you to begin to see. As if the betrayal wasn't bad enough, it's our response and reaction to it that makes it even worse. So now imagine that your betrayer completely blindsided you and that, on top of that, your prolonged response is making you struggle with painful physical, mental, and emotional symptoms. Left without a plan, these symptoms are making you sick, sad, stuck, overwhelmed, anxious, exhausted, and unhappy. They're preventing you from enjoying aspects of life available to everyone. They're holding you back from healing and forming new and deeper relationships (with the person who hurt you or someone else) because you're drowning in obsessive thoughts of what happened that can't be undone—no matter how hard you try. So, here's what we do. We're running this poisonous loop of going over the shock and trauma a few more times as if it will give us some new understanding that the last million times couldn't provide. (I'm saying that with love because I get it, I did that myself.) You see, making sense and meaning out of our experiences is healthy and even helpful when it doesn't take over your life. But when the loop can't be stopped, when it gets caught in its own circular motion, it's called ruminating and can lead to anxiety or depression or a new feeling of being stuck in a moment. The thoughts no longer serve you and serve only the loop they find themselves caught in. At those times, it might be helpful to seek professional help.

When we fully understand what a profound impact betrayal can have on our overall functioning and well-being, we can better see why it's so important to give ourselves the time and space to heal and transform. When I interviewed the Fab 14 for my study (whom you'll meet soon), I gave each one a survey called the Posttraumatic Growth Inventory (PTGI), which is a measure of growth following any type of trauma (such as the death of a loved one, a disease, a natural disaster, or a tragic accident). One section of the PTGI focused on how we relate to others after a traumatic experience. The questions in that section centered around knowing we can count on people, a sense of closeness with others, a willingness to express emotions, having compassion for others, putting effort into relationships, learning how wonderful people can be, and accepting that we need others.

Because betrayal involves so many different factors that require healing—like rejection, abandonment, trust, self-esteem, self-worth, and more—it was easy to understand why most of my study participants received a low score in this section. Understandably, people who've experienced a betrayal have lots to overcome in order to have healthy relationships again. That's exactly why moving through the stages from betrayal to breakthrough is so important. You're about to meet the Fab 14 (I'm sure you'll have your favorites), but before you meet them, let's talk about two emotions that are really common too, and these are the ones felt by the betrayer. They're guilt and its cousin shame.

Guilt is an emotion that shows us the pain the betrayer feels as a result of the distress the experience has caused. Shame, on the other hand, is self-focused and creates the need to hide, escape, or retaliate from the situation. The pain and guilt over the betrayer's actions can be a catalyst to encourage them to show remorse and the desire to restore the relationship after betrayal.

WHAT HELPS THE BETRAYED REBUILD WITH THEIR BETRAYER?

Here's what the betrayed person sees when the betrayer feels guilty and remorseful. It's in the sincerity of an apology that implies that the betrayer feels guilty. Studies have found that guilt is felt when the betrayer sees a threat to a relational bond.[13] Guilt is an important element to forgiveness after betrayal too because it sends a powerful message to the betrayed that the relationship and commitment are still important to the betrayer.[14] It's the pain of guilt that often motivates the betrayer to attempt to make the betrayed feel better.[15]

Researchers O'Malley and Greenberg found that guilt serves the "down payment" effect, which somehow helps the betrayed partner feel compensated for their suffering.[16] Studies also found that when we're betrayed, we felt better when the betrayer feels guilty, as if some of the pain that we've experienced was somehow transferred from us to the betrayer.[17] Here's what studies also found, so, if you're the betrayer, read this carefully. First, it's important to say that forgiveness really has nothing to do with the other person and has everything to do with us, which I'll be diving into much more deeply later on. However, when it comes to forgiving the person who betrayed us, it's been found that there's an increased willingness to forgive when the betrayed sees that the guilty party is distressed from his or her actions.[18] What does all of this mean? It means that even with guilt, remorse, and forgiveness, it takes effort and persistence for the betrayed to feel valued and for trust to be restored.

So now it's time to meet the Fab 14. You're going to be traveling on your own healing journey, but here's what I'd like you to do. See which ones you resonate with and relate to. You're going to learn about their betrayals, specifically how they happened and what these experiences led to. Then you're going to learn what they did to move forward and heal. It's through their brave and honorable contributions that the Five Stages of Betrayal to Breakthrough were discovered and that there's even such a thing called Post Betrayal Syndrome and also how we now know that healing from betrayal can lead to (and *will* lead to if you do the work here) an amazing state called Post Betrayal Transformation. I have such a special place in my heart for these amazing women. I want you to know that they all shared the same three reasons as to why they wanted to participate in the study too. The first reason was that they had a desire to contribute. The second was that they wanted to pass on hard-learned lessons to others so that they may avoid or prevent some of the same pain and pitfalls that they experienced. The third was that they wanted to share what sped up their growth and healing so that you may benefit from their experiences. Don't you just love them already? I can't wait to introduce you to them in the next chapter. I'll meet you there.

· 3 ·

Introducing the Fab 14

So, are you ready to meet these amazing "s'heroes" who openly told their stories so that we can extract some golden nuggets from the information they shared? While they haven't all reached that state of Post Betrayal Transformation (remember, my interviews with them are what led to the discoveries I'm sharing with you in the upcoming chapters), they all bravely told their stories so you'd benefit from them. I won't keep you waiting a minute longer. Here they are.

LYNN

Background

Lynn is a consultant and is single. She mentioned growing up with verbal and emotional abuse, the hurt stemming from her brother being favored by her parents and her role as a scapegoat:

> That was very damaging in terms of my self-worth. I still struggle with where my boundaries should be, but on the other side, I've been so willing and motivated to change myself, whereas no one else in my family really has, though I see the blessing in that. I was doing this work, and similarly, I attracted my boyfriend who had the same attitude as my family, which was that the problem was me.

Lynn described betrayal as "promises broken or misleading someone, tricking someone," and shared the story of betrayal by her boyfriend.

Betrayal Story

Lynn was dating her boyfriend who was originally from another country and moved nearby. They dated for a few years, and Lynn believed she was in a healthy relationship. Her boyfriend's father came to visit, and when he left, "It's like he switched. It's almost like a switch went off and he became more dissociative." For two years, Lynn waited for him to "snap out of it" until one day he said, "I'm seeing someone else. We're not getting together anymore." She never saw him again.

The Aftermath

Lynn felt tricked, and this betrayal triggered a series of betrayals she was ready to face within her family. "Basically, within a few years, every single person that had said that they loved me had betrayed me because I was no longer willing to put up with some of the things that have been going on." She felt exhausted, explained the physical pain in her chest area she considers the physical and energetic pain of heartbreak, discovered a noncancerous lump in her throat she suspects was due to stress, and believes she'd been living in a state of denial for years. Lynn described feelings of shock leading to sadness, anger, a sense of abandonment, and feeling used and tricked.

Lynn found the spiritual component of her Catholic faith helpful in beginning her healing journey along with hot yoga, reading books on spirituality and personal development, massage, meditation, and a kitchen timer she used daily to declutter her space as a strategy to help declutter her mind. She also found a therapist, a mentorship program, a spiritual coach, and new friends from her mentorship program who are all committed to their healing and "operating at this higher level" as important components in her healing, along with inundating herself with healthier thinking.

Where Lynn Is Now

Within a five-year period, Lynn describes having more discipline over her thoughts and feeling lighter due to weight loss along with less physical and mental clutter. Certain people have disappeared from her life because she's no longer willing to tolerate what she had previously accepted. She enjoys her decluttered space and simple routines. Lynn recognizes she's still in a grieving process and struggles with losing faith in others yet believes that with the family she came from, this was an inevitability. Learning that she was not alone and how others navigate a similar situation could have helped her too. She still struggles with moments where she realizes she may never be married or have a family yet feels stronger, enjoys the support from friends, and has a better quality of life. Lynn recognizes that her background failed to teach her healthy boundaries and is learning to let go of her ego as well as improve her communication with others.

CLEO

Background

Cleo is a surgical coordinator, is divorced, and has two children. Her mother left her father when Cleo was eight years old, and she reflects that she was a "very unhappy child." She describes betrayal as "someone making a promise and disappointing you where it sucks the life out of you." Cleo's betrayal story is from her boyfriend of six years, and the betrayal occurred six months before we met.

Betrayal Story

There were signs along the way, but Cleo was in love, so she ignored them. She wanted the relationship to work, but she knew something wasn't right. One day, she saw a conversation on her boyfriend's phone between him and another woman. She was crying and devastated, and when she confronted him, he remarked that they would discuss it when they returned from a trip they were on. By the time they got home, the conversation had been deleted from his phone. He told her it was nothing and was not going to explain himself, saying, "I know it's unfair to you but too bad."

The Aftermath

She described the moment of betrayal as "your arms, your legs, everything goes numb and tingly. Your heart races, you're hyperventilating.

My hands were shaking, I was in shock." Cleo was angry, sad, and hurt. Physically, she had digestive and sleep issues. She felt confused, and it was hard to function at work because she was trying to put all of the pieces together, realizing she had "put her head in the sand" for a long time.

Cleo went to an astrologer who confirmed why she and her boyfriend weren't a match and found that confirmation helpful. She then joined a meditation class and started researching how other people felt who'd been through a similar experience and started journaling to put her emotions into words. While she loves reading, she finds it challenging to focus and retain what she's read.

Where Cleo Is Now

Cleo joined a singles group where members meet to enjoy activities together. She's feeling better about herself, is feeling more positive, and realizes that her breakup "shouldn't have to suck away enjoyment from my present and my future." Cleo lost 40 pounds, is off sleeping pills as well as pills for acid reflux, and notes that she is sleeping better and has no more digestive issues at all. "That whole acid reflux thing, it's gone." Cleo monitors her thinking and is proactive about having positive influences in her life. Her strategy for healing is not to replace her boyfriend with a new one but "to feel better about me." Looking back, she believes that more support from friends and family would have helped her but is grateful for her renewed appreciation for the family she has. About friends, she states, "I'm realizing now, if you're not a positive influence on me anymore, I keep you at arm's length. It's like it's opened my eyes to the true friends in my life."

Now that she sees things clearly, she wishes she would have ended her relationship sooner once she realized she was ignoring the signs that the relationship wasn't working. Going forward, she plans on being a stronger, better, happier, and more positive person who keeps her eyes open to much more. As she begins letting go of the anger and moving toward forgiveness, she acknowledges that she did the best she could at the time. Cleo believes that her childhood experiences encouraged her to "make excuses when people weren't treating me well. You have a higher tolerance, I think, because you're used to not having it be perfect."

ANNE

Background

Anne is a nurse. Being the oldest of five children, she has always had the role of caretaker of her family. She recently lost two sisters and three close friends. Her father was an alcoholic, and as we were talking, she remembered a traumatic experience where her father struck her mother. She has two children and has been married for 35 years. Anne was betrayed by her husband. She describes betrayal as when someone "has broken my trust and has broken my heart."

Betrayal Story

Anne was pregnant with her first child and remembers being "trusting and naive." During the pregnancy, her husband started acting differently. She remembers making excuses and blaming herself for his changing behavior until she slowly began to notice more obvious changes: "He told me he was going someplace, and he didn't go there. He told me he was with this friend of his, and he wasn't. All of a sudden, things started clicking." Anne blamed her pregnancy and her hormones and would not believe what her intuition was telling her, so she suppressed it, justifying what she was seeing as "everyone is entitled to make one mistake." Her focus was on having a healthy baby, and she suppressed her suspicions of her husband having an affair whenever it arose.

The Aftermath

After a while, Anne noticed,

> I had severe abdominal pain; I thought I had appendicitis. I went to the emergency room. My white blood cell count had tripled, but they couldn't tell me if it was appendicitis or not. I started to think maybe this is all stress related because I was under so much stress. I was so depressed. But I said this is normal, this is a normal grieving process.

Anne also had a series of tests conducted because she was exhausted. One day, she went to a psychic who suggested she get tested for Epstein-Barr, which was confirmed through testing. While she felt a sense of pain and loss, she didn't feel confident raising her son on her own and tried to put the affair behind her, choosing to keep the experience to herself due to her upbringing of staying "happy on the outside, keep your business behind closed doors" and not wanting to jeopardize her husband's relationship with her friends and family. She was angry at the world and angry at God because she was "a good person, going out of her way for everyone," and couldn't understand how something like this could happen to her. She would cry herself to sleep. Anne did all she could think of to overlook her husband's affair. She became interested in photography, painting, and reading books on spirituality. Her husband had a second affair.

Determined to become financially independent so she could eventually leave the marriage, she began seeing a therapist. She had an emotional wall up due to the affairs as well as two physical attacks. Anne buried herself in cooking, cleaning, caring for her children, and working full-time. She lost 30 pounds unintentionally, started drinking, and became emotional during our conversation as she remembered her sons saying, "Mom, we love you, and we want you to get well." She went to a rehab clinic for one month. Within those same few years, one day at work, Anne experienced numbness, thought she was having a stroke, and told a coworker to call 911. She was taken out of work on a stretcher, placed in an ambulance, and realized, "I can't allow his actions to make me sick. I'm just not going to let that happen. That's when things changed, big time." Over time, the depression lifted, her energy came back, and her focus was on seeing that her sons were financially able to go to college. She became "a lot tougher around the edges. I wasn't as sensitive as I was. I wasn't as trusting with a lot of people. And it was sad because I was always very trusting." She started praying and saw her friends to help distract her from her pain.

Where Anne Is Now

Anne started becoming more self-reliant, self-sufficient, and independent, realizing that "the only person I can change is myself. It took a long time to get here, but it took the second betrayal to push me." Anne now meditates, does yoga, and is preparing herself financially for when she feels she has enough money to leave. She believes a woman's group would have helped her along with speaking about it to her friends. She also believes meditation would have helped better manage her thoughts. As far as she and her husband,

> We do things together for the sake of the family and because my son's wedding is coming up; I'm just stuck in this toxic environment. I have my own space now; I have my own room, which makes me feel better. I take it day by day. I don't really feel that we're meant to be together forever, but I'll just do what I need to do.

As she starts doing things for herself, she notes, "It's about me now." She says she knows when he is lying yet doesn't get as upset about it as she used to. Anne considers being able to talk freely about her experience a gift.

JULIANA

Background

Juliana is the director of public relations for a company she loves. Having lost a sister and having another sister with special needs, Juliana was always told to be grateful for being alive and healthy and, as a result, did not feel comfortable expressing her needs. She is divorced and has two children. The betrayal Juliana shared was from her ex-husband. Juliana explains betrayal as when "something looks the right way but really isn't."

Betrayal Story

Juliana's husband had back surgery and became addicted to OxyContin. She noticed changes within the family dynamics:

> I felt like I was the only one doing the work. It was like a Hollywood set. When you walked around the back, there was nothing. It was not as it seemed. It was not as it appeared. When all the smoke went away, you saw the ugliness of it.

Juliana remembered her husband telling her that he was laid off, and when they were out celebrating their 25th anniversary, she noticed her husband's coworkers nearby. When he went to the men's room, she walked over to say hello, and they said, "Oh, it's nice to see you two together. It's just so sad of what happened. I'm so sorry." Juliana said, "What do you mean?" They told her that he was fired because he lunged across the desk at his boss, the owner of the company, and tried to strangle him. He was told, "Don't come back. Don't ever come back."

The Aftermath

Juliana felt nauseous, her head was spinning, yet she kept it to herself because she was taught, "You never ever showed other people what was going on in the house. What happened in the house stayed in the house." She described the experience as a movie where everything began spiraling; she started questioning every thought that entered her mind and everything he said, and she felt "like somebody had reached into my body and pulled out all my innards." Her husband's behavior got worse until one day he tried to overdose on his medication; the kids found him, and he told the family he had nothing to live for, lunged at Juliana, and was taken to the hospital. Even though it was possible that his behavior was due to his addiction, she felt hurt, sad, upset, confused, and very angry, trying to find out what she may have done wrong. When something went wrong within her marriage in the past, she was always told, "It's because of you," so accepting blame was something she'd grown used to. She also had painful colitis attacks that brought her to the hospital each month, hormonal changes, hair loss, and neck and shoulder pain. Juliana didn't know where to turn. Previously, she felt let down by her church, so she chose not to seek help there again. She turned toward spirituality, herbology, and aromatherapy.

Juliana divorced her husband and started reading books on spirituality and reaching out to friends: "I didn't want to share brokenness, but I started talking to people that I trusted. I started asking for and accepting help."

Where Juliana Is Now

Once divorced, Juliana noticed that the "noise" in her head started to dissipate and she doesn't have to have the TV or music on. She enjoys the quiet and is beginning to enjoy her own company. She still reads personal development and books on spirituality, journals, and notices it took approximately five years to feel a sense of peace. She's more forgiving, grateful, appreciative, and less judgmental of others: "I see somebody good, bad, and ugly and accept them good, bad, and ugly." She hasn't had a colitis attack in three years, her hair is growing back, she feels more positive, and she attributes much of her changes to becoming more spiritual, not allowing toxic people into her life, and having the support of strong friendships, which she wished she had had when she was experiencing her betrayal.

Juliana learned that she doesn't have to take the blame for everything, saying, "That's a me issue, that's a you issue." Juliana also noticed that she's lost interest in material possessions, preferring time with friends and family instead. She's less reactive and calmer while also being more present with those she's speaking with. She's also healthier and has stopped having seasonal migraines. She doesn't want her betrayal to have her give up on trust and the possibility of another relationship. She also sees the goodness of others and chooses to look forward.

PATTI

Background

Patti is divorced, has two children, and is a children's librarian. She wanted to be a clinical psychologist but thought she wasn't smart enough. Patti is divorced from her husband, who was 25 years older, and said, "I was looking for stability." Patti explained her childhood as follows: "It was just darkness. I just was always with babysitters. I don't remember my mom too much. There was no attachment. I grew up without that and I was always seeking it and being let down." Patti's mother divorced her father when Patti was born, then remarried a stepfather Patti was afraid of. She feared her babysitters too and said, "I lived in fear my whole life." Her betrayal is from her mother, and she describes betrayal as "trusting somebody and being let down big time."

Betrayal Story

Patti shared many experiences of trusting her mother and stepsisters, then finding that they shared Patti's secrets with one another. She felt neglected and overlooked and grew to expect betrayals from her mother:

"I never meant anything or enough to her to keep my secret or protect me." In adulthood, wanting to keep her two children close with their extended family, Patti chose to "shut down" after each disappointment as her way to keep the family together. A therapist diagnosed her with persistent mild depression, and Patti explained,

> I think that had to do with me just shutting down all the time. It was kind of flat. I didn't want to go either way because if I went up, it would be a total disappointment for me because I would always know that I'm going to crash. I couldn't go too far down because then I feel like I would drown, and I wouldn't be able to get back up. That's how I maintained it, but I was living a joyless life. No fun, just work.

At her mother's funeral, Patti discovered that her mother had cut Patti and her children out of everything:

> There was a certain resignation about it. It was a confirmation, a confirmation of what I felt my whole life. That was like the truth for me. I never wanted to believe it. I couldn't believe it. I went to therapists, and they would say it sounds like your mother is jealous, and that to me was too crazy. It just was like I was in such denial about it my whole life.

The Aftermath

Patti felt disbelief, then felt angry, drained, defeated, and sad: "I just felt like all my energy was just taken, wiped out." She struggled with either forgiving her mother or mentally cutting her out of her life. At the funeral, years of betrayal from her sister gave Patti a sense of freedom:

> This set me free. I didn't have to put up the facade anymore. I didn't have to do all that. I also had a loss because, still, I wanted to look forward to doing family things, but now I had none, so it was really down to zero.

Patti turned to spirituality, reading, groups, support, and workshops, which brought her to a state of acceptance, saying, "I've just learned to accept that that's the way it is. It's not my fault, but I still live with the repercussions of me thinking it's my fault that I'm not worthy enough. It still creeps up."

Where Patti Is Now

Patti carried stress in her neck and shoulders, which is now gone. She finds she is now able to appreciate things such as a positive conversation or interaction. Patti said that it took approximately two to three years to start feeling better. She mentioned a sense of clarity at the realization of what her relationship with her mother really was about. She tries to meditate and is learning to listen and trust her inner voice, which she said she ignored and didn't trust in the past. Patti also sees a spiritual adviser.

Patti mentioned having more patience; being more authentic, whole, and spontaneous; and being willing to try new things yet maintaining a distance with friends. Pattie believes she hasn't fully healed yet but is heading toward healing with an intention of learning about love and trust now. She believes that without the ability to trust, healing is impossible. That premise brought Patti back to church to reestablish her connection with God, which she believes is much deeper and different now than it was before, believing that "God is in everybody and in everything."

DENNY

Background

Denny is divorced and is a supervisor at a biotech firm. She has two children and strong friendships that have lasted more than 30 years. Her father was killed in a car accident on her sister's fifth birthday. Denny was betrayed by her husband, and she recalled that while she was "living day to day" and the marriage was never exceptionally happy, she "wasn't going anywhere," believing that as their children got older, they would have more time together and the relationship would improve. She describes betrayal as "when you have 100 percent trust and then having that trust broken."

Betrayal Story

Denny said that after being home for seven years with her children, she began working part-time. Years later, her husband was acting differently, which caused her to become suspicious. After a few instances and to confirm her suspicions, she followed him one evening and found him leaving a restaurant and getting into a car with another woman. Denny followed them to where they were going, and when they got out of the car, she confronted them both:

> Right then, my heart just sank. It was a rush of shock and disbelief. When you're in that situation, your head is spinning. You can't even get control of the thoughts. It's like somebody speaking another language. You can't understand what's going on.

The Aftermath

Denny found that she couldn't stop crying, she was exhausted, and she had constant diarrhea. She felt overwhelming sadness, depression, anger, and stress. Denny remembered panicking and thinking, "How am I going to do this? What am I going to do? Where am I going to live? How am I going to survive this? What can I do?" She went to church and prayed daily for strength. Her husband had no remorse and offered no apology. Denny went to a therapist who put her on Lexapro and Ativan to help stabilize her moods. "I would pop one, and then the crying would just stop because it shuts your emotions." Denny's son advised her to tell her mother, and when she called, her mother said, "Well, did you really think he was working all those hours? Stop it. Nobody works that many hours. You have to take better care of yourself." Denny hung up the phone and cried. Her friends were supportive, and Denny found comfort in hiring a private detective, analyzing the phone bill to answer unanswered questions, and reading "every book I could find on betrayal, divorce, and cheating husbands" to confirm her feelings and experience. They continued to live in the same house for another four years, and Denny filed for divorce two years into the four-year period. It was when she filed for divorce that she noticed improvements in the way she felt.

She meditated, went to therapy, and walked for an hour and a half each evening with a friend, which she found very helpful. Denny lost weight, started feeling more independent, and took a full-time job, which increased her confidence. Feeling torn between "doing what I needed to do" and breaking apart a family was a challenge, but physical abuse started after she filed for divorce, which confirmed she'd made the right decision.

Where Denny Is Now

I look back at it as the biggest learning lesson in my life. What I take out of that is, I've made a pact with myself that I will never give more than I get out of a relationship. It has to be a two-way street.

Denny is learning to trust again. She values her independence and her close friends and believes she should have left the house sooner despite her lawyer's advice. She feels strong, a sense of freedom, growth at work, yet sadness that her dreams of raising children and grandchildren with her ex-husband will not be realized.

SUZANNE

Background

Suzanne is divorced and has two children. She described her mother who "nipped away at my self-esteem" and a neighbor who sexually abused a few of the girls in the neighborhood, including Suzanne. She believes it had an impact on her self-esteem, so when she met her husband, she believed it was a path to a happier future. Slowly realizing her husband was a "con artist and master manipulator" yet busy raising her children, she chose to ignore the signs of his cheating and drug dealing. She was betrayed by her husband and ultimately divorced him.

Betrayal Story

During their marriage, many instances had Suzanne questioning her husband, and there were many nights he would come home after 3:00 a.m. The moment she remembered vividly was when he woke her at 1:30 a.m. to say, "I just wanted you to see that I didn't stay out so late." Confused, she realized, "I've got nothing to work with here." She describes feeling helpless, hopeless, nauseous, and a sense of despair yet realized she needed to take action for the sake of her two children. She wondered, "How on earth did I get here? How on earth did I allow myself to be with a man who doesn't value me, my kids, and his home?" He was "far gone," and she realized that the part of him she fell in love with was fictitious. She realized, "If I remained the victim, my kids would have no shot at having a good life."

The Aftermath

Suzanne described feeling sadness, heartache, ugly, rejected, and unwanted. She vividly recalled her husband being disgusted with her body after the birth of her second child. She smoked cigarettes, cried, and felt lost and foggy-headed:

> I knew that I had to get out. I had to fix myself. I realized I was a huge part of the equation. I could blame him for many things, but I let him into my life. I had two children with him. I own that.

Suzanne started surrounding herself with other women in a support group and realized her low self-esteem prevented her from taking action sooner. She divorced her husband, and within one year after her divorce, she noticed her body feeling better, she lost interest in smoking cigarettes, her coloring improved, the fogginess lifted, and her digestive system improved. After the second year, she started exercising and became more interested in getting dressed and putting makeup and perfume on and realizing she deserved to take better care of herself. She remembered thinking, "I cannot allow this to take me down" and recalled the feeling of lifting her head up and opening herself up to possibility. She started teaching at the group she went to for support, went to therapy, read books on spirituality, and accepted a full-time job.

Where Suzanne Is Now

Suzanne now sees that her determination to not be a victim enabled her to heal. She has also had conversations with her father, who shared, "I think your mother may be jealous of you," which Suzanne has made peace with. She has learned to be very selective with whom she lets into her life, and while she is a naturally warm and open person, she finds herself more guarded, hardened, intolerant, and cautious. She values honesty and integrity, wants to help other women, and believes she wouldn't be as strong as she is now had she not had that experience.

JO

Background

Jo is separated and is a mental health professional with two children. She knew she was meant to work with children because she remembers growing up as a quiet, depressed, sad, and angry child and always wanted to help other children because of how she felt during her childhood. Jo never went to college and went from her parents' house to her own home when she got married at 20. She was a wife, mother, and caretaker, yet she always had a feeling of disappointment in herself that she was meant to be, do, and experience more. Feeling guilty that she was not satisfied with what others saw as a beautiful life, she suffered from postpartum depression, guilt, and frustration and took mood stabilizers and antidepressants. She decided to go to school, work, and then night school to accommodate her work schedule, and that was when she discovered her husband had a problem abusing drugs. Her husband betrayed her when he began using drugs behind her back and lying about it. She describes betrayal as "what you think is supposed to occur, doesn't."

Betrayal Story

Jo described her experience: "I remember completely being frozen like an out-of-body experience, seeing my future and thinking, 'I don't belong here.'" The betrayal felt compounded when Jo learned that her brother knew of her husband's drug use. She felt as if "the wind, the rug was ripped out from under me." The pattern of lying, hiding, and then Jo finding out continued for years. She felt sad and angry and put a wall up to prevent others from getting close to her. She knew she was meant to be traveling a different path and distinctly remembered a "24-hour period of time where I couldn't control what internally I was feeling, but I was getting physically ill from it and emotional for a full 24-hour period. I knew what I had to do." She left.

The Aftermath

Jo saw a therapist, which helped, and noticed a "great divide" between friends who advised her to stay and other friends who gave her the support she needed to leave. She dove into helping children, fitness, and slowing down her "mind chatter" through meditation and spirituality. Slowly she realized, "This is good. This is what you should be doing. This is the right decision. This is the right choice. This is the path you're supposed to be on." She started feeling stronger, needed less approval from others, and began to experience calmness and a sense of clarity. Jo described the chatter as going from "mind chatter to direction." She stopped taking the mood stabilizers and antidepressants and noticed a deepening of her praying, transitioning from robotic to receiving the messages she was seeking.

Where Jo Is Now

Jo believes she is off the "emotional seesaw" and feels calm, happy, and strong. She feels that surrounding herself with like-minded people, along with therapy, a life coach, and "listening to my inner self," has enabled her to create a new life for herself. Work opportunities have dramatically improved, and she is now in a relationship she describes as one that is so "healthy, normal, and natural," a relationship she was only able to "paint in her head." She does not use the word "friend" freely anymore and believes relationships are bidirectional as opposed to one person always giving. Jo wishes she had listened to her inner voice earlier and left sooner but realizes she was afraid. She wants women to know that "fear is always going to be part of your life, but you can definitely move forward through it. Once you get to the other side, the fear starts dissipating."

DJENA

Background

Djena is separated, is a teacher, and has two children as well as grand-children. She recalls being an insecure child, believing it may have been due to her parents leaving Djena and her sister in Haiti for a year while they came to the United States to find work. Although she doesn't remember that time, she believes it had an impact on her. She shared that she remains in a neglectful marriage and "should have gotten divorced 20 years ago" but remained married due to her religious beliefs. She developed an emotional affair with Paul, whose family was very intertwined with hers. They saw each other often until one day everything changed, and Paul betrayed her. She describes betrayal as "when rules are purposely broken."

Betrayal Story

Djena and Paul saw each other every week for five years. One day, Paul said, "You're making this up. I never said that I loved you, you're suffocating me." She said he also became very verbally abusive. Djena was in shock; she didn't understand what was happening: "He changed the rules and was making up new rules." She felt vulnerable and angry, had panic attacks, struggled with diverticulitis, and became depressed. "I was very disappointed and angry at myself."

The Aftermath

Djena continuously tried to work on the relationship until "I finally woke up and realized I had to love me." Slowly over a five-year period, she started meditating, going to spiritual classes, and reading books on spirituality while focusing more on learning to love herself. She began losing weight, exercising more, and taking better care of herself. The spiritual classes encouraged a growing sense of gratitude. Djena's healing had begun once she made a decision:

> I started feeling better once I made the decision that my life was better off without him. It's not that I didn't feel sadness that he was gone, but it was almost like a weight had been taken off my shoulders. The feeling of freedom felt better than the pain.

Where Djena Is Now

Djena attributes her growth to a shift in her thinking from the spiritual classes:

> Through the spiritual classes, I have such gratitude. I know that it sounds weird, but there are times, when I will be just sitting there, and I'll just say, "Oh, God, thank you. Thank you for it all. Thank you for the sky." Or I'll see a little bird, and the bird will chirp; I will look at the bird, and I'll go, "Aww, thank you." I really do have

such an appreciation for life. I really, genuinely, do. I'm so grateful. I'm really grateful. It's not that things don't get me down. It's not that I don't get upset. It's not that my life is perfect, but underneath everything is just this gratefulness.

Djena feels a sense of great peace, has forgiven Paul, and feels that his actions stemmed from his level of ability at that time. Djena believes that her experience helped shape who she is today. Because she's feeling better, she enjoys her work and her students more and enjoys a better quality of life. She's learning to take better care of herself and "not feel bad or guilty about it," as she now lives a life where she is not being "verbally abused, manipulated, or put down."

DANA

Background

Dana experienced multiple betrayals from family, friends, and partners. She had grown used to betrayals from her sisters, whom she said her mother turned against her by saying things like "Why can't you be more like Dana." Dana says she was a poor student but pretty and her sister was a good student, so, as she explained, "She felt ugly, I felt dumb." She remembered many experiences of inappropriate behavior and abuse from boyfriends, a teacher, her grandfather, her father, and her husband. "These men who you love and adore, and they're supposed to adore you—especially your mate, and then they are the ones who hurt you. There's no greater betrayal than that." After a lifetime of betrayals, the biggest one was at the hands of her husband.

Betrayal Story

Dana recalled a father who did things that were sexually inappropriate, which caused great confusion because, as she says, "Your father is supposed to protect you, so when he doesn't and you need to protect yourself from him, your self-esteem is affected. So, I attracted men who were hurting me." One day as Dana and her family, including her father, were sitting at the table for dinner, her mother asked Dana if her father had ever done anything inappropriate to her. Dana denied it because she didn't want her mother to have trouble within her marriage, yet as she denied it, she looked squarely at her father conveying the unsaid message of "I'm saving you and your marriage, now you'd better stop." The message was understood, and he never did anything like that again. Her parents eventually divorced, and he died at 52. Dana believes his death was from the guilt of his actions. Dana always had digestive issues, food intolerances, congestion, and allergies. She was angry and felt frozen during times of abuse, often feeling guilty that she was somehow responsible.

She left home at 18 and got married at 19, remembering, "I felt old already." She married a man who was physically abusive and living a double life she didn't know about. The physical abuse began when she was four months' pregnant with her first child. She chose not to tell anyone about the abuse, feeling that

> the hardest part is not feeling like a liar. I always felt like I was exaggerating what was going on in my life because it was so freaking bad, and I felt like if I told anybody about it, they would think I was lying.

Dana didn't want to talk about her experiences with anyone, feeling she was protecting everyone by keeping the abuse to herself.

The Aftermath

Dana began going to a group for battered women and began helping women within the group. Philanthropy and helping others served as fuel to help herself, and she realized she needed to be strong and find a way to care for herself and her children. After attempting to leave three times, she finally left and divorced her husband. Her decision went against the wishes of her mother, who didn't want Dana's children to be children of divorced parents as Dana had been. Dana's mother may have given her different advice had she known what was happening within their marriage. It was over a 13-year time period where Dana slowly started believing in herself.

Dana began supporting her mother as well as her own children. She was angry and focused on survival, denying any fear: "It was all about doing, going forward and tackling the world and taking it on and making money and taking on challenges. I was pretty fearless." Dana felt empowered about being so busy working yet struggled with not seeing her children:

> I felt a little torn, and anger was constant. Everyone was annoying to me. "Get out of my way. If you're not going to help me, get out of my way." I was on a roll all the time. I didn't like it. My family didn't like me.

Over time, Dana saved enough money to feel financially secure. She bought a house for herself and her kids. Once there, she got very sick. It was at that point that Dana left the work she'd been doing and realized she wanted to help people, which was a major turning point in her life. Over a period of years, Dana mentioned that what helped her heal was trauma hypnotherapy; EMDR (eye movement desensitization and reprocessing) to release the physical trauma from the attacks from her husband; EFT (emotional freedom technique); AET (accelerated empathic therapy); yoga; meditation; Amma therapy, which is a type of acupressure; following the work of spiritual and personal development teachers; and Ho'oponopono, the Hawaiian mantra meditation.

Where Dana Is Now

Dana feels a deep connection with God and admits that besides her faith in God, she struggles with not being able to rely on others, believing that we should be able to rely on what others say and do. The more anger she releases, the better she feels. Dana believes she should have released relationships sooner because she "always gave others the benefit of the doubt at her own detriment" and did not "honor her soul's voice," which she believed created weakness in her body as well as illness and disease.

She has become a prolific writer, is highly intuitive, and has learned to trust her inner wisdom. She believes that what may have helped her would have been someone to speak with about such painful and deeply personal topics. Dana now helps others heal from trauma. She's forgiving, tolerant, compassionate, and empathetic yet still struggles with her self-esteem, believing that unless she heals that final piece, she won't be unable to enjoy a deeply loving relationship.

MARIE

Background

Marie is a first-generation Cuban American and the youngest of five children. She's divorced and in transition from her previous position as the student life director at a university. Her father cheated on her mother, and her mother stayed in the marriage, which Marie struggled with until she was able to forgive her father years later. Marie met her husband, who had a child she became very close with. Her husband was involved in many of the activities Marie planned with her students. While there were signs that he was going to be unfaithful and Marie was suspicious since the beginning of the relationship, she was dismissive whenever those thoughts arose. He'd cheated, and she'd forgiven him once before until she experienced what she called "a double betrayal." Her husband had an affair with one of her students, one she was particularly close with. She describes betrayal as a "manipulation of loyalty and trust."

Betrayal Story

Marie came home after an exciting meeting where she was eager to share her experience with her husband. As she walked up to her front porch, she saw a license on the front stoop. It was the license of the student she had been mentoring who must have dropped it when Marie wasn't there. "I felt like they punched me in the stomach." She was sad and disappointed and realized she needed to think of herself: "I had to put myself first. This was about me now, and I started to think about how do I approach this." Marie's relationship with her stepdaughter was of great concern and one of the reasons she didn't react immediately, although she wondered how she'd allowed her relationship to continue with her husband for as long as she did. Marie stated, "I did my own ass kicking. I'm a good ass kicker for myself, I would do that consistently for quite a long amount of time."

The Aftermath

Marie divorced her husband. She immediately started losing weight and had what she called a "spiritual crisis" as she pulled away from the church yet strengthened her spirituality. Marie went to a holistic healing center run by one of her students and dove into studying the chakras along with journaling and a 20-minute meditation practice, which "just straight changed my life." Marie also found comfort in a Robert Frost poem as well: *The Road Not Taken*. She described her world as changing while breaking apart at the same time. Marie noticed she was becoming more compassionate and began a yoga practice, which she began to love even though she did not like yoga in the past. She also saw a therapist, but Marie noticed great healing resulting from a spiritual coaching certification program where she worked with a coach, explaining that "the healing that came from that program was exponential." Marie also began going to a women's group every Saturday and found it healing to be with other women. She described healing as follows:

> It's that day you wake up and you're suddenly aware it's not there. You're not carrying it anymore. It's gone. It's dealt with. That was a huge part of my spiritual emergence, a huge part of what gave me better direction as to where I'm supposed to be going in my life. There's no denying I'm not supposed to be where I'm at right now because I'm not comfortable. I think that, that's what was happening at that time. Things around me were not supposed to make me feel comfortable. It was supposed to make me act.

Marie remembered a radiant glow to her skin developing and a growing desire to simplify her life along with appreciating simple things:

> I felt good. I feel grounded. I was sleeping differently. I was falling asleep earlier and waking up much earlier. I've come to appreciate that. The quiet morning and the ability to be able to see the sunrise.

Marie also discussed having to make peace with her student's betrayal, which originally caused her to leave teaching. She returned, though, believing it was what she was meant to do and attributes many of her changes to an "attitude adjustment."

Where Marie Is Now

Marie acknowledges a growing awareness and commitment to her healing. She has noticed a certain vulnerability about sharing her experience but is able to manage it because she knows how it helps her heal, although she would have benefited from a group of like-minded women going through a similar experience:

> There wasn't a structure or model to follow or a group to go to and talk about—that didn't exist. And it was also a very personal process, and you kind of get embarrassed by it to an extent. And there's a lot of nonsense that goes around that shame, embarrassment—stupid, I feel stupid. It's a shared experience, and I find that what helps people in my experience move through things is to feel they're not alone in it. It's not like misery loves company; it's to understand this isn't exclusive to you.

When looking back, Marie wishes she had ended the relationship sooner, although she feels it "cured her of savior syndrome." She felt she needed the safety and "safe haven" felt when being alone for a while but is now striking a balance, which includes more time with new friends. She knows she's much stronger than she thought, she has more empathy, and she has improved her relationship with her family. With her new confidence, she finds she's able to take more calculated chances in her life.

ARIELLE

Background

Arielle is divorced, has two children, and is a business owner. When asked about her personality years ago, she described herself as a busy working mother who went to work, cared for her children, and felt exhausted and unhappy most of the time. Arielle described how she felt as "not happy but not taking the steps to change it." She believes her decision to stay in an unhappy marriage was due to the pain she experienced from her parents' divorce when she was 18. Arielle also remembered thinking she might be making a mistake by getting married but chose to ignore her instincts because she loved her husband, felt lonely, and wanted to be loved.

Arielle, her husband, and children lost their home and all of their belongings in a house fire. Her father-in-law perished in the fire as well. Losing everything, Arielle, her family, and her mother-in-law moved into a neighbor's house that had extra room to spare while they were recovering from their traumatic experience. It was during this time that Arielle discovered her husband having an affair with the woman whose home they had temporarily moved into. She describes betrayal as "an expectation that you have, whether it's that the world is fair or that you'll be safe, and something happens to knock you down and make you start all over."

Betrayal Story

Arielle discovered an e-mail between her husband and the woman who was hosting Arielle and her family after the fire. "I was completely surprised. I had no clue. I knew they were friends, but I never thought, ever, that he would do that." Her husband and the woman claimed that the e-mail she found was sent in error, and both denied that they were having an affair. She described being "obsessive" about reading their e-mails after that discovery because "they never said, they never apologized, they never admitted" and compared finding out about the betrayal to the sense of panic that can overcome someone when they lose their child in a crowd. She remembered feeling "shock, disbelief, anger, surprise, literally every feeling all at once." Arielle recalled being sad, angry, and upset simultaneously.

The Aftermath

Arielle and her husband divorced. Arielle recalled physical issues arising during that time:

> During this whole period, I had stomach issues—a lot of physical issues. I . . . got a lot of cold sores, headaches, just every possible physical way that my body could show me I was not in a good place.

Arielle's husband asked for a divorce, and while she was very upset, she remembers a sense of freedom, although her main concern was the well-being of her children. She began therapy and noted that therapy had helped her sort out her feelings. She realized that her need to own a home was driven by the need for security, which she didn't feel within her marriage. Exercise also helped along with support from her community, and over a period of five years, Arielle felt much stronger. She described her life as becoming "much broader" when she met new people, made new friends, and became involved in giving back to the community that had helped her after the fire. These changes, along with the strength emerging from overcoming her experience, gave Arielle the confidence to date again and start her own business:

> While that was very tough, somewhere in me because of what I had already experienced, that's why I started a business. I don't think I ever would have taken the risk or the perceived risk to do that. That was a huge change.

Where Arielle Is Now

Arielle said she is a "completely different person" who now expresses her feelings and needs more than she had in the past. She is more compassionate and willing to try new things and notes a more positive way of looking at life. When looking back, Arielle mentioned that having close friends to lean on for support would have helped her, yet she was grateful for the people who took care of her and her children after the fire and betrayal. When describing herself now, she feels she is "an incredibly strong person," she is more accepting of others, she chooses to be selective about having only positive people in her life, and she describes her changes as follows: "It's a real metamorphosis. I was such a shy, introverted, unhappy person. I blossomed, essentially." Arielle attributes being in a committed relationship, her new business, new friends, and positive outlook as outcomes of her experience.

NANETTE

Background

Nanette is a licensed social worker who is remarried and has two grown children. When she was 10 years old, her parents were in a car accident that killed her mother. She remembers her father neglecting her after that, and Nanette spent her time being watched by friends and family. Within two years, Nanette and her two brothers had moved in permanently with her aunt and uncle, who had five sons of their own. She loved this time with her brothers and "cousin brothers" until they all moved to a remote location when Nanette was in her junior year of high school. Another car accident soon after that killed her cousin and left her brother temporarily in the hospital. One of her brother's friends stood by her side during this difficult time. She and her brother's friend eventually dated, married, and had two children.

Nanette's aspirations were to become a wife and mother. A few years into the marriage, she expressed concern to her aunt that she thought her husband may have been having an affair. Her aunt replied, "God forgive us for having such evil thoughts." Each time Nanette sensed trouble within her marriage, she was dismissed by her aunt and eventually believed her suspicions were incorrect. She noticed, however, that whenever the families got together, her husband spent lots of time with the wife of one of her brothers, Nanette's sister-in-law. Nanette's suspicions were confirmed when she discovered that they were, in fact, having an affair. She describes betrayal as "when you trust somebody and put your faith in them and then they turn around and betray that trust that you put in them."

Betrayal Story

Nanette remembers the problems they had in the marriage before the affair was discovered:

> I had a clean house, I took care of two children. I did all the correct right things. How bad could I be? Maybe I wasn't meeting his emotional or intimate needs or whatever in his mind, but to me it was like, even if that was the case, it's not like I'm neglectful.

At the same time, her brother had been having challenges in his marriage but chose not to speak about it with anyone. One day at a family event, Nanette mentioned her suspicions to her brother about her husband and her brother's wife: "Something doesn't seem right, I feel like there's something going on." Nanette remembered the look on her brother's face: "I just confirmed everything that he was thinking, and it just all came out." Her brother then said, "Oh my God, it *is* true, it wasn't my imagination, there's something going on." Soon after that conversation with her brother, her husband left. Two months after that, her sister-in-law left her brother. Nanette remembers a painful comment made by her sister-in-law after discovering that Nanette and her brother had that discussion with each other: "What are you telling your brother? Just because you can't hold on to your husband, don't blame me." She remembers that comment as one of the most painful moments of the betrayal. Nanette explained that not only was her husband blaming her for not being a good enough wife, but she was being blamed by the sister-in-law he was having an affair with. She was also frustrated by not getting the support she needed from her aunt. She found the strength to finally divorce her husband.

The Aftermath

Nanette remembered being "shaky upset," crying, sick, angry, and hurt: "Probably every negative emotion there can be I experienced at that point." She had stomach issues and a "sick feeling" because her life dream of raising her family with her then husband had just been "pulled out from under her." She also felt conflicted because, according to her faith, she wasn't supposed to have "evil thoughts" that her husband was cheating, yet she felt frustrated because her suspicions were correct. Due to this conflict, Nanette pulled away from her church. She also remembered another painful moment of her husband telling her then five-year-old son that he was leaving. Her husband said, "Everything is going to be alright," and her son replied, "No it's not, how would you like it if your father left you?"

Having her brother who was going through the same experience was helpful in that they were able to offer each other support, although Nanette was fearful:

> Suddenly, I'm single. Now my whole world was shattered. I was a homemaker and two years at college never really worked full-time. For the past nine years, I'm taking care of kids at home with no means to support myself. What am I going to do? What am I going to do with my life now? My homemaker life was just pulled out from under me, the whole thing. I had to figure out what I was going to do.

She used the small amount of money she had to learn practical skills at a school for women returning to work and learned how to type, learned business skills, and more. Her brother would watch her children while she was in class, and in exchange, she would take care of some of his household errands and chores. Nanette was eventually offered a position at a university and spoke with a staff psychologist there, which she found helpful. She also saw a priest, another therapist, and a social worker whom she found especially helpful. Nanette eventually found work that included health coverage and other benefits. Once there, she saw a career counselor who ignited Nanette's passion for social work, which she eventually pursued. Her approach was to focus on one day at a time to prevent becoming "overwhelmed, upset, or depressed." She learned to focus on what she was able to control at the moment and find success in the accomplishments of each day.

Where Nanette Is Now

Nanette has become a strong and independent woman. She's learned to trust herself and realizes that "you have the strength and you get through anything, and sometimes you just have to get through one day at a time." She feels proud of her ability to support herself, own her own home, and have the ability to purchase whatever she chooses, adding, "I'm not going to take any crap from anybody," which is an attitude she also attributes to her experience.

MONICA

Background

Monica is the daughter of Holocaust survivors and shared how her mother's life has "caved in on her" due to tremendous fear and loss resulting from her experience. She described her father as an angry man who lost his family in the war. Monica has an older brother and was told that when her parents found out they were pregnant with Monica, her father asked her mother to have the pregnancy aborted. After a failed attempt by her mother, her father said, "Just put her up for adoption or something." Her mother refused, and Monica remembers an unhappy childhood, where she was often left with friends or relatives while her parents were traveling. She remembered feeling unloved and neglected as a child, so she tried to fill that need through the many men she became involved with. Monica felt betrayed by her parents for not loving her the way she needed, which she believes brought about a series of betrayals, including the sense that she betrayed herself. She felt pressured by a boyfriend to get married at 19, then had an affair with his best friend: "Subconsciously, I was looking for a way out. I betrayed myself. I betrayed my husband at the time." Monica had many unhealthy relationships where she felt used and betrayed, looking at her experiences now and realizing that

> I was in my own victimhood. Subconsciously, I was attracting it because of everything that I was vibrating and radiating, but I couldn't see that. I was so engrossed in my own crap, my own shit, that I could not see that I was actually attracting this. "Here we go" the universe says, "you want to be unloved, you want to pick men that are going to hurt you, this is what you are asking for, so I'm going to give it to you." I had no idea.

Monica describes betrayal as "someone that I would have trusted like my father. I would entrust him to love me, to embrace me, and to always nurture that little girl that I was, but he betrayed me and that trust." Her betrayal story is the result of a series of betrayals she now sees clearly.

Betrayal Story

Monica's low self-esteem led her to become involved in a series of unhealthy situations and relationships:

> I was an attractive young woman, and I had no identity. I was drinking too much, and men would take advantage of me, and I allowed that. It was horrible, and I would feel awful. I would just absolutely feel miserable every time the next day. That's men betraying me and not seeing this hurt child and respecting me and saying, "Look, you need help." But instead taking advantage of my sexuality, taking advantage of somebody who is weak at the time, psychologically, who wasn't able to fend for myself, didn't have the psychological or physical at any capacity to really stand up for myself.

She mentioned having a "few abortions" due to her experiences and mentioned, "I would never think I was good enough, pretty enough, smart enough." Monica remembered feeling "horrid, so miserable. I felt so dark."

The Aftermath

Monica remembers never loving her body because of these experiences: "I would sometimes beat on it like girls cut themselves, I would actually beat or pull my hair or do something just to get out of my skin because it felt so foreign or creepy or something." When I asked her why she was hurting her body in those ways, she replied,

> Low self-esteem, I was not feeling good about myself. I had no self-worth, I didn't amount to anything, I felt I didn't deserve anything. I was unlovable, and I was unloved. I felt so unlovable. What was the point of finding anything really good?

Feeling "horrible, empty, and depressed," Monica started drinking and taking Quaaludes, "anything to numb the pain. To numb myself and just get out of that pain." She didn't feel she could turn to her parents, had no supportive friends, and didn't feel a connection to religion or spirituality at that time. Feeling she had to do something, she went across the country to see relatives who followed a spiritual practice, which she found therapeutic and healing. This practice enabled her to grieve her past as she began to see her experiences through a newer and healthier perspective.

Monica found that once she became spiritual, it was spirituality that always helped her "climb back up." Within two years, Monica noticed she was sleeping better and had more energy and attributes dance as a positive outlet that possibly prevented her from illness. She was vigilant about changing to a more positive way of thinking as well and found herself saying "cancel" approximately 200 to 300 times each day whenever she noticed a negative thought arise. Monica found that a new way of thinking was beginning to emerge. She became completely immersed in spirituality, asking for guidance, support, and direction. Monica meditated, journaled, and maintained her commitment to a new way to think and feel.

Where Monica Is Now

Monica is involved with many women's groups that she finds very supportive and helpful. She immerses herself in spiritual retreats, personal development books and practices, and "staying in her power and staying authentic." Monica attributes many of her changes to Julie Cameron's book *The Artists Way*, which taught her to write three pages in her journal first thing in the morning. At 61, she believes she's finally on the right path, and while she feels afraid of the unknown, she feels that she's being led in a healthy and inspired direction: "I'm more alive, more authentic, and more real, and opportunities—I see things starting to manifest, and I'm creating it, I'm envisioning it." Looking back, she notices, "I created it all. It was a drama that I created, a story, a movie. I was the queen bee actress of this horrific drama. This crazy life that I lived, I turned my mess into a message."

Monica believes that what would have helped her would have been support from other women. She believes that "just the support, the camaraderie, the collaboration, anything I think is just so helpful." She also believes that having supportive parents would have made a significant difference as well. Monica has learned to ask for help and attributes much of her healing to her ability to forgive. She has more patience and a greater understanding of her past as well as of the path of those who've hurt her and knows that she was doing the best she could with what she knew at the time. It was those decisions and experiences that made her who she is today, which, she believes, present themselves in order to heal ourselves and then others.

The experiences Monica shared have made her more compassionate, empathetic, and forgiving and enabled her to find opportunities to help other women by "paying it forward." She understands now that there are patterns and conditioning that have us seek something familiar. She's learned to change her thinking and now loves herself, which she believes is a fabulous gift emerging from her experiences. She understands now that she must love herself in order to love others and that it's an "inside job." Monica admits that the most challenging lesson for her is viewing others who have hurt her as protagonists, giving her opportunities to heal areas within that needed healing. She finds comfort in nature and loves reading, being alone, and enjoying the silence "where spirit lives."

So now that you know their stories, let's talk about how you can turn your betrayal into positive life change. I'll meet you in the next chapter.

• *4* •

Turning Betrayal into
Positive Life Change

*N*ow that you have a good understanding of how betrayal affects us and why, how do you turn betrayal into a positive life change? In addition, is that even possible? Not only is it possible, it's predictable. I never would have believed it myself if it didn't personally happen to me and my clients and if I didn't see it daily through members in our signature *Betrayal to Breakthrough* online program and with students in our *PBT Academy Membership Program* who I'm privileged to serve every day.

First, let's get a baseline for what "positive life change" even means. For some, it can mean simply being able to get out of bed after their betrayal had them so depressed they could barely function. For others, it can mean feeling comfortable and safe enough to trust again. While there's a wide-ranging spectrum of what you might consider positive life change, we're aiming for something specific: Post Betrayal Transformation (PBT). That's our ultimate goal.

POSTTRAUMATIC GROWTH

Before we get to PBT, let's talk about a few steps on the road to reaching that goal. First, there's posttraumatic growth (PTG) and resilience (which is what I was studying before PBT was even discovered). PTG involves features such as the following:

(a) An acceptance of the reality of an individual's experience
(b) Finding support

(c) Recognizing the positive elements discovered as a result of the trauma

(d) The writing of a coherent narrative either literally and/or figuratively where the experience becomes a part of the individual's story as opposed to his or her entire story

(e) The appreciation of the new life being lived as a direct result of the trauma[1]

When you've experienced those features of change, you can officially say you've experienced PTG, and you can congratulate yourself because healing from trauma isn't easy. Now, that's not to say you won't get upset about your traumatic event anymore; rather, it's that even though you may still feel sadness and pain, you can appreciate all it has taught you. What can these changes look like?

It can look like changes and improvements in personal strength where you feel more vulnerable yet stronger. These changes also impact how you relate to others, which can lead to a greater connection to other people, along with the ability to be more compassionate. Your priorities often change as well. A change in priorities, along with a new philosophy about what's meant to be valued and considered important, often happens too. What was considered unimportant or maybe something you didn't give much value to in the past, such as time spent with a loved one, can become a much bigger priority post-trauma as you experience a greater appreciation for life.

RESILIENCE

Now let's take a look at resilience. PTG is different from resilience, although both are potential outcomes after a traumatic event. Resilience can develop after an accumulation of challenging events, or it can be centered on a single event.[2] With resilience, you're able to still function well, go about your daily routines, and work through your feelings, although you may have challenges with your normal sleep routine and may find yourself spending lots of time thinking about an event. With resilience, you've maintained your physical and psychological functioning and are able to weather the storms better than if you did not have resilience. Yes, the event angered, frustrated, or upset you, but it's not compromising your physical and/or mental health to a large degree, which has a lot to do with hardiness.

Hardiness, a personality trait that promotes well-being, isn't really tested under normal circumstances but helps us during highly stressful events. It's because of our level of hardiness that we're better able to respond to stressful events and bounce back from them. The more we can do that, the more resilient we are. How can we increase our resilience? Studies have found that positive emotion and laughter can help.[3] We also build resilience when we accept that change is a part of life and when we see a challenge as something we can handle as opposed to something too difficult to manage. Building resilience happens when we take the time to nurture ourselves and when we try to solve problems as they arise instead of assuming that a challenge is too hard to deal with. We can also increase our resilience when we take action, which helps build our confidence. Finally, seeking support from like-minded friends and feeling a sense of purpose are also helpful ways to boost resilience.

POSTTRAUMATIC STRESS DISORDER

While there are many differences in resilience and PTG, one of the biggest differences is that with resilience there is a lack of posttraumatic stress disorder (PTSD) symptoms following a trauma.[4] What's important to know is that resilience helps us in our daily lives. It helps us manage, adapt, and adjust to life's challenges, big and small. Transformation however, is what can happen after a significant crisis like betrayal, and, unfortunately, a painful betrayal has the ability to leave us with various PTSD symptoms. Some symptoms can include hypervigilance, behavioral changes, feeling anxious, experiencing flashbacks and nightmares, avoidance, and reexperiencing the event when reminders present themselves. You can find yourself having difficulty concentrating, remembering, and experiencing physical responses when you're triggered by something you think, feel, or see.

Before my betrayals, I thought PTSD symptoms were "reserved" for those in combat or a possible result when experiencing or witnessing a violent act. I learned firsthand that betrayal qualifies as a type of crisis that can leave someone with PTSD symptoms that need healing. (If you're experiencing any of these symptoms, seek support from someone qualified to help you.)

RESILIENCE VERSUS TRANSFORMATION

Whether your betrayal left you with painful symptoms or not, complete healing means you need to rebuild what was torn down. Do you remember my analogy of the brick wall when it comes to trust? In that analogy, I mentioned how trust can't be *repaired*; rather, it needs to be *rebuilt*. It's the same thing when it comes to rebuilding ourselves. Whether you're rebuilding with the person who hurt you or not, there are aspects of the self, such as confidence, worthiness, and self-esteem, that have been impacted. These parts of ourselves don't just need to be patched up. To make sure they're solid and strong, they need to be rebuilt. The good news is that betrayal sets the stage for a complete rebuild if you're willing to use the experience as an opportunity to do just that. You see, nothing has to be rebuilt unless it has been destroyed. But if it is destroyed, it can be rebuilt to become much better, stronger, and more beautiful. To better understand the difference between PTG and resilience, let's use the analogy of a house.

Let's say your house needs a new boiler, so you get a new boiler—that's resilience. Let's say your house needs a paint job, so you paint it—that's resilience. Let's say you need a new roof, so you get a new roof—that's resilience. Now, here's transformation:

A tornado storms in and levels your house.

A new boiler isn't going to fix it. A new paint job isn't going to fix it. A new roof isn't going to fix it. In fact, all three aren't going to fix it. Now let's be clear. You have every right to stand at the lot where your house once stood and say, "This is the most horrible, terrible, awful thing that's ever happened!" You'd be right. You can call all of your friends over and say, "Look at this! Isn't this the most terrible, horrible, awful thing you've ever seen?" They'd agree. You could mourn the loss of your house for the rest of your life, and no one could fault you for it.

However, if you choose to rebuild your house (and remember, you don't have to do anything), why rebuild the same house? Why not give your new house everything the old house didn't have? You see things so clearly now, so why not make this house so much better and more beautiful than the last one? That's PTG.

THE ROLE OF RELIGION AND SPIRITUALITY IN HEALING

Spiritual and religious changes can also be an important part of growth along with a greater sense of meaning, purpose, and satisfaction when someone experiences PTG.[5] Spirituality plays a big role for some in helping people cope with traumatic situations. It can contribute to resiliency through the understanding that while the event can't be undone, spirituality can bring meaning to it. Through spirituality, there's also the belief that there's a greater force at work that can bring comfort and help us adapt to where we now find ourselves after betrayal. Through challenging times, spirituality (through religion or on its own) can be a means to offer much-needed support as well, giving us explanations and a sense of control when we can feel as if a sense of control has been taken from us.[6] Spirituality, something accessible to people of any belief system, is an important part of meaning making and coping too and helps make PTG possible.[7]

So how is spirituality different than religion? Many people enjoy the spiritual aspects *within* their particular religion, but that's not what I'm referring to. What I'm talking about here is the type of spirituality that's not tied to any specific religion. Maybe you've heard people say, "I'm spiritual, not religious." That type of spirituality is independent of a specific religious belief. It encourages self-discovery and is based on love, not fear. It encourages you to trust in your inner wisdom and create your own unique path based on what feels right for you. It unites, enabling everyone to feel that we're all connected versus believing that someone's status somehow positions them to be more important than another. The biggest difference I see in spirituality when compared with religion is that there are no rules or dogma. Questioning is encouraged and not viewed as something wrong or bad.

Personally, spirituality played a huge role in my healing as well as with many of the Fab 14. Spirituality seemed to serve a few purposes. Betrayal can have us feeling so overwhelmed and alone. We can feel like we've been blindfolded and then thrown into the deep end. During this time of intense confusion and uncertainty, spirituality can help us feel as if we're not alone by giving us a greater sense of connection. That's definitely what it did for me. Spirituality also plays a big role in rebuilding trust (I know, I promised to teach you my four steps to rebuilding trust, and it's coming). It also helped to give the experience a different meaning and to give me the hope that, while I wasn't able to see it, there may be something bigger going on behind the scenes.

THE INNER GUIDE VERSUS THE INNER CRITIC

From a completely human and ego standpoint, betrayal was an absolute, nonnegotiable deal breaker. There wasn't one cell in me that felt that betrayal was acceptable or anything I should go along with. Here's where spirituality kicked in because it encouraged me to ask different questions, such as these: What if this trauma was meant for a bigger reason? What if we actually did somehow "plan" this so that we could both crash and then rebuild in order to be the people we're meant to be? What if the people who hurt me the most are actually my greatest teachers and in some way (although my ego would be kicking and screaming) I'd be grateful for the lessons learned? What if everything really is divinely orchestrated, and instead of tirelessly swimming upstream, I surrender to what my experience and growth can lead to? What if . . .

I wrestled with these questions endlessly because on a spiritual level they sounded great and made perfect sense. Then the nasty voice of my ego would chime in, saying that those ideas were insane and that if I listened to the voice of my highest self versus the voice of my inner critic, I was setting myself up for only more heartache. My ego/inner critic was trying to convince me that it knew best and was only trying to "protect me." My inner critic (who, to me, has a very distinct sound and feel) used every tactic possible to determine my next move as I heard things like "Do it to him so he knows what it feels like!," "You're going to accept that? What's wrong with you!," "What's everyone going to think of you?," and the one that always hit me right in the gut: "What kind of mom are you, and what are you teaching the kids if you give him another chance?" The ego was giving orders and instructions in that constrictive, low-energy feeling way, just like the bully on the playground.

Yes, the ego can be pretty ruthless if you give it time, attention, and a platform to tell you how wrong or lame you are. By the way, your highest self—the voice of your soul, source, God, divine energy, or whatever you want to call it—never speaks that way. It'll never fight for your attention over the abrasive chatter and noise of the ego. It'll never put you down or bully you in order to get your attention. It'll also never use fear as a motivator to act. Messages from your highest self, what I call "supernatural secrets whispered in your ear," speak in brief words, images, or flashes of insight that leave you with a comfortable knowing. Be open to them, and you'll strengthen that muscle so it becomes a stronger voice and what really helps make the decisions that best serve you. I'll be sharing much more about spirituality later; I just wanted to give you a glimpse of something to consider from where you are right now.

MAKING MEANING OUT OF YOUR EXPERIENCE

Reflecting on and reviewing your experience are ways to find meaning and make sense out of a traumatic experience. When it is not entirely negative, attempting to make sense and actively think about what occurred creates a greater likelihood of healing and growth.[8] In fact, studies have found that when people think about what happened, not in an exclusively negative manner but as a means of coming to an understanding and making meaning from the event, they are more likely to experience PTG.[9] As I mentioned earlier, however, think about it too much, and it turns into marinating, and that's when you drown in your own pain and negativity. I've also found with our program members that the longer you hang on to your story, the harder it is to leave it behind because after a while it feels very familiar—so familiar that it becomes almost like a comfortable old sweater you've worn for so long you don't even know it's on. It feels like it's become such a part of you; you can't imagine taking it off because your identity now includes that ratty old sweater. I'll be walking you through the Five Stages from Betrayal to Breakthrough, and this is something I typically see in a classic "stage 3." Don't worry, I'm going to show you what to look for so you'll know if you're doing this. You'll also know why it's been feeling so hard to move forward and heal. More important, I'll teach you how to gently put that old sweater down for a stylish new jacket that suits you so much better.

While you don't want to hang on to your event for too long, going over your experience in order to give meaning to your negative event is important. When you do, it can increase your ability to relate socially to others, and it can even be measured on something called the Perceived Benefit Scales. The Perceived Benefit Scales consist of eight subscales:

(a) Lifestyle changes
(b) Material gain
(c) Increases in self-efficacy
(d) Family closeness
(e) Community closeness
(f) Faith in people
(g) Compassion
(h) Spirituality

Based on the type of negative event, along with the severity of the event, the scales compare the relationship between the trauma and the perceived benefit.[10] While these traumas and the benefits they can bring can be measured through scales like the Perceived Benefit Scales, gender differences in those with PTG can be measured too. It's been found that there's a big difference in the number of women versus men who experience PTG, with women reporting higher levels when measured by the PTGI.[11] So there's some amazing potential here. Women experience more trauma, and they also experience more growth when they're willing to heal from the very experiences that caused so much pain.

The key to coping and adjusting after trauma requires a shift in meaning around how that trauma is perceived. It also involves a more positive view of yourself and how you view the world based on what you've been through and who you're becoming. It is not that the negative experience is forgotten but rather that a new inner world that we can find comfort from is slowly being created.[12]

POST BETRAYAL TRANSFORMATION: HEALING SPECIFIC TO BETRAYAL

Now, PBT takes it a step further because we are not only rebuilding what was lost as a result of our crisis but also rebuilding aspects of the self so brutally destroyed. We may rebuild after a loss (which can be a feature of PTG) for example, but after betrayal, we also need to rebuild our self-esteem, confidence, self-worth, ability to trust, and so much more. There are aspects of ourselves, as well as our circumstances, that need to be tended to and healed in order to move forward.

While the growth from betrayal could be called PTG, the specific aspects of healing from the pain of betrayal would be missed. PTG is more of a general term describing healing after trauma, but it wouldn't fully encompass the breadth of repair to ourselves that's required to feel fully healed and transformed after an experience with betrayal. Here's why. When we lose someone we love, for example, we're sad, we miss them, we grieve, and we mourn the loss. We typically don't question the love. We're definitely not the same, and we need to re-create life without that person in our physical presence anymore. It's a huge shift and adjustment, but we usually don't question the person's love who is no longer physically with us.

I remember so clearly when my mom passed away years ago. The grieving process was deep, painful, and real. It took a long time to stop automatically picking up the phone to call her when my kids did something cute, when I needed to talk, or when I wanted to share things that only a mom would care about. There were many moments when it just didn't make sense that she was alive one day and gone the next. I remember many moments during that time of grieving that were so painful to get through, such as milestones, holidays, and everyday seemingly insignificant details.

I was in the store buying new towels because we were having friends stay at our house. In the towel section, I saw and overheard a mom and daughter spending what seemed like a tremendous amount of time and effort to make sure the lavender towels the daughter chose would go perfectly with the rest of the bathroom decor. It was such a simple conversation and one I would have loved to have had with my mom. The pain of her loss hit me hard, and I raced out of the store, tears flowing from my face. While I missed her terribly, however, I never questioned her love or myself.

WHY PBT IS A DIFFERENT TYPE OF HEALING

When it comes to betrayal, because it feels so intentional, we take it very personally, and that's why it feels like a complete attack to the self.

We question the love along with ourselves, our sanity, and the world around us. Nothing makes sense, and in one blinding moment, we can feel alone, rejected, and abandoned. That brutal attack we feel to the self can crush our confidence, self-esteem, sense of worthiness, sense of belonging, desirability (if it's a romantic betrayal), trust—it goes on and on. That's why this specific type of growth resulting from healing from betrayal needed a new term, now called PBT.

This term captures the elements and transformation possible when we heal specifically from everything that was impacted by the betrayal. PBT captures all of the physical, mental, emotional, and spiritual transformations possible when healing from the trauma that this type of experience can cause. PBT expresses the full nature of change that's required when aspects regarding our worldview, self-perception, and self-worth are all brought into question. It represents the complete breakdown of what was known and familiar and the birth of a stronger, wiser, and more empowered self, earned through a rebuilding of ourselves after an experience with betrayal.

PBT expresses the emotional trauma, the physical complications, and the mental processes all impacted when someone we trusted and felt close to violates the spoken or unspoken rules within a relationship. It causes a need to relearn how to navigate and negotiate relationships, while there is a reprioritizing of needs that may have been neglected before the betrayal was discovered. It causes a complete shift in our worldview regarding our beliefs, our sense of safety, and trust. It causes a dramatic shift in how we move through other relationships going forward because of the wisdom and personal healing of the self that were earned through this type of traumatic experience. PBT builds on PTG, acknowledging the same changes that signify growth while also incorporating the additional aspects of the self that are in need of attention that PTG doesn't address.

Here's another exciting element of PBT: it creates an opportunity for a completely new type of relationship with others and ourselves to emerge. This new type of relationship is based on an entirely new set of criteria, as we're able to use our experience to create deeper and more meaningful connections as a result of what we've been through. Here's an example of aspects of the self that are impacted by betrayal, using one of my study participants, Juliana.

Juliana experienced a betrayal by her husband when he lied to her about being laid off. She found out the truth when they were out celebrating their 25th anniversary. Her husband had gone to the men's room when she noticed a couple of his former coworkers at a nearby table. She walked over to say hello, and they said to her, "It's just so sad what happened. I'm so sorry." Confused by their sympathy, the co-workers revealed that her husband hadn't been laid off after all. He had lunged across the desk at his boss and tried to strangle him, after which he was fired on the spot—and lucky he wasn't arrested.

The lie her husband had told her destroyed not only their relationship but also Juliana's trust in others and herself. Juliana went on to divorce her husband, this final lie serving as the last in a series of lies she was no longer willing to tolerate. She noted a dramatic difference between the pain of betrayal and the pain of other traumas, such as the death of both parents and that of miscarriages. She noted that the death of a parent can be anticipated, even if the timing comes as a surprise, yet the shock of betrayal is not anticipated. "Betrayal starts by making you think you're crazy," she explained. "That you're not enough. You start to believe their press about you. You make excuses and take the full blame regardless of truth. You do so to keep the calm. Make it easier on others and make it easier on yourself for that moment. But all it does is prolong the inevitable." Another study participant, Djena, said something similar: "With something like a death, it's sad, but you don't take it personally. With betrayal, you take it personally."

To say that self-esteem is impacted by betrayal was an understatement in Juliana's view: "It works on every part of you: your body, heart, mind, and soul. You lose your trust in others, but worse, you lose trust in yourself. You question everything. In the process, you lose yourself."

To help her heal, Juliana turned toward spirituality, herbology, and aromatherapy. She started reaching out to friends she trusted and began asking for and accepting help. She said it took about five years before she regained a sense of peace, but once she did, she was forever changed. And the things she turned to in order to get through the experience have become a permanent part of her life. She still voraciously reads books on personal development and spirituality. She journals regularly and has a different relationship with many of the people in her life. She considers herself more forgiving, grateful, and appreciative and less judgmental of others. At the same time, she no longer allows toxic people into her life, instead relying on the strong friendships she's built when she needs support.

Juliana shared, "Betrayal strips you naked and unfairly forces you to rebuild. It puts all your memories into question. It tarnishes everything. Some can and do rebuild. Some will never. No one gets their innocence or memories back intact, and all are forced to contend with the dirty baggage this trip left behind."

Betrayal can cause us to question everything and everyone we knew. It can impact our health and sanity. Rebuilding our lives *and* rebuilding ourselves following something like that is no small order. The good news is that you're about to find out exactly how to do it. Remember, Juliana shared her story, and it's her story and others that shorten *your* learning curve and allow you to heal so much faster. Because of the contributions of the Fab 14, we know exactly what prevents our healing and what helps us move toward PBT even faster.

I'll never forget one woman in our PBT Institute Membership Community who said, "Oh my God, having this program available years ago would have saved me 20 years of pain," or "E," who shared, "Your session about betrayal spoke to the deepest parts of me. For three years, I've struggled with a friend betrayal—I don't want to spend another year ruminating on this betrayal because it is gradually ruining my identify, my life, my relationships, and the good things I still have. I can personally speak to the symptoms—the 'foggy' brain, weight gain, bad skin, digestive issues, shattered worldview, irritability, achy body, extreme emotions, and 'stuck' feeling—I look in the mirror and don't recognize who is looking back at me. I've confided in friends and my husband and, currently, a therapist. Your session was eye-opening and articulated everything I have been feeling in my mind, body, and soul for the past few years. No one has ever articulated betrayal the way you have! I am so happy to have found your video and hopeful that your program will help to improve my quality of life!"

Or V.T.: "After being hurt deeply, I tried everything to heal. Nothing worked, and I had pretty much given up on healing until I heard Debi Silber describe what happens to your mind and body after a betrayal. I knew this was for me. I'm now healing and growing and have a new dream and vision for my life! So grateful for Debi and this betrayal work! It's life changing!" Or, finally, Linnet: "WOW, this is so powerful and the most comprehensive explanation of the transformation process I've heard at age 78. It looks like a lot of work but I'm excited and hopeful after many programs, years of therapy and even working as a psychotherapist to gain freedom to embrace and hold onto ME. Thank you for doing your work and going on to inspire others. You are deeply appreciated. Grateful."

Now it's your turn. There's absolutely no reason to wait another minute. I know I'm preaching to the choir here because you, brave one, are doing the work to heal, and with that intention, that's exactly where you're headed.

I'll soon be sharing the Five Stages from Betrayal to Breakthrough, which I'll walk you through, one by one. As you read through them, you'll be able to see exactly where you are on your healing journey and what you need to do to move forward. Before we dive into each stage, here's a little preview of each stage, along with common themes that we experience during the different stages too.

A PREVIEW OF THE FIVE STAGES OF BETRAYAL AND THE FIVE THEMES

It was so interesting to me to see the stages slowly emerge through the study. While each participant had their own healing time line (remember, they were sharing their journeys before we knew what you're learning here), regardless of their circumstances, the participants who fully healed went through the five stages. They'd come to the end of one stage, and as they did, there would be a certain amount of overlap as they slowly moved on to the next. They didn't skip stages or change their order, but the amount of time spent with each stage varied from person to person. It also wasn't like they exchanged one stage for another; it was more like they outgrew the stage they were in as they slowly entered into the next one they were ready for.

I saw other really interesting and common themes that most of the participants experienced too. These themes didn't have a specific order or timing like the five stages, but they were themes that made themselves known as each participant gained confidence and clarity around their betrayal experience. The themes were different from the five stages because they'd appear at different times, within different stages, and were more fluid and subtle than the five stages. However, whenever they managed to show up, these themes were common to almost every participant, so

I want you to know what they are so you know you're not alone if you experience them too.

THREE REASONS WE STAY STUCK

Now, while of course the intention is to move you from wherever you are now to a place of PBT, I want to make something really clear. Not everyone heals. In fact, there were three groups in the study that didn't heal, and I want you to know about it because if you're doing this, it's going to affect your healing too.

You may think that people who have less to overcome heal the most or the quickest because they have the least to heal from, meaning that the ones who are the hardest hit by their trauma would grow the least because they had the most to overcome. That's what I thought. That had absolutely nothing to do with their healing. In fact, some of the participants in the study who came from the most challenging scenarios healed faster and more fully and reached that state of PBT while others did not. I found three reasons why, so be on the lookout in case you're doing this.

Numbing/Avoiding/Distracting

Are you numbing, avoiding, distracting, or doing things to avoid feeling and facing your betrayal? If so, you're keeping your healing at bay. When we use things like food, drugs, alcohol, work, TV, keeping busy, reckless behavior, or anything else to distract ourselves from "facing it, feeling it, healing it," we're doing ourselves a huge disservice. Now, I understand that betrayal and trauma are hard to face, but without dealing with them, they'll follow you around like a shadow. If you're unsure if you're numbing, avoiding, or distracting yourself, ask yourself these questions:

Am I numbing, avoiding, and distracting? If so, how?
What am I pretending not to see?
What's life going to look like in 5 to 10 years if I keep this going?
What could life look like in 5 to 10 years if I change now?

I know those are challenging questions, but transformation begins when you tell yourself the truth. Sure, using those "methods of mass distraction" may make the day a bit easier to get through, but they're also keeping everything you want and deserve at a distance.

Refusing to Accept Their Betrayal

The next reason I found for why people don't heal is because they refused to accept their betrayal. They hung on to it for dear life, clinging to it and refusing to accept it in order to move forward. Accepting their betrayal would have set the stage for them to begin rebuilding a new life post-betrayal, but they just weren't willing to let it go. Remember when I shared the story of the house that gets leveled by a tornado? Not accepting the betrayal is like staring at the lot where your house once stood, yelling, screaming, raging, and more, as if anything you could say or do would somehow undo the tornado and all it left in its wake. Refusing to accept where betrayal leaves us prevents our healing and keeps us tragically stuck in Stage 3 (which you'll learn about very soon).

No Consequences for the Betrayer

Finally, there was one more group that didn't heal, and in fact this group suffered with the most physical symptoms. This was the group that didn't heal because the betrayer had no consequences to their actions. What does that mean? Whether out of fear of breaking up a family, financial fear, religious reasons, or any other reason they may have had, these participants did their best to "get over it," "suck it up," "put it behind them," or "turn the other cheek."

This response hurt them for many reasons. They were betrayed by the very person they gave their heart, loyalty, and trust to, and in one soul-crushing moment, it was revealed that their betrayer took complete advantage of that trust and love. From this painful and broken place (we're never really broken, we're bent, but you get the idea), it was somehow the betrayed person's responsibility to keep moving through life as if nothing had changed and as if their heart wasn't broken in a million pieces. As if that weren't bad enough, they were also influenced by the opinions of others, an outdated belief system, or low self-esteem that kept them somehow believing this was all they could expect or hope for. This scenario was so damaging and overwhelming for their body, mind, and spirit.

DEATH, REBIRTH, AND THE BEST TIME
TO MAKE DECISIONS

There are only two options here that help you heal. One option is that the relationship as you've known it comes to an end and you re-create an entirely new relationship with the same person (if you read my story, that's what I did with my husband). The other option is that you rebuild yourself and move forward without that person in your life or at least not in that same role or capacity (that's my other betrayal story and what I did with my family). That death of the old allows for the rebirth of the new and takes you from one stage to the next (specifically, it's one of the things that takes you from Stage 3 to Stage 4). You deserve so much more than accepting poor or abusive behavior out of fear or a belief system that doesn't support you, and while I'd never tell anyone what to do, it's my intention to show you what you're doing so you can make decisions that serve you best.

One last thing. I've been coaching thousands of people for close to 30 years, so with that experience under my belt, here's one thing I definitely recommend. Don't make any decisions from a low place. The decisions you make now may be very different from the decisions you'd make when you feel healthy, healed, and whole. For example, I remember a client who came to see me because she wanted help getting back together with her boyfriend. I was really clear that my work was in helping her heal—whatever that would lead to. Sure enough, by the time she felt physically, mentally, and emotionally better, she had completely lost interest in him. She wanted someone who was so different, and to be with him at this point would have felt like settling.

What I'm saying is that you really can't predict what will happen, but in being open, receptive, and willing to do the work, you'll see your best self emerge, and that's the version of you who's best at making your decisions. Of course, if you're in danger, your safety is most important, so make decisions that serve you best in that moment. If a decision can wait until you're in a better mental and emotional place, however, it's best to wait.

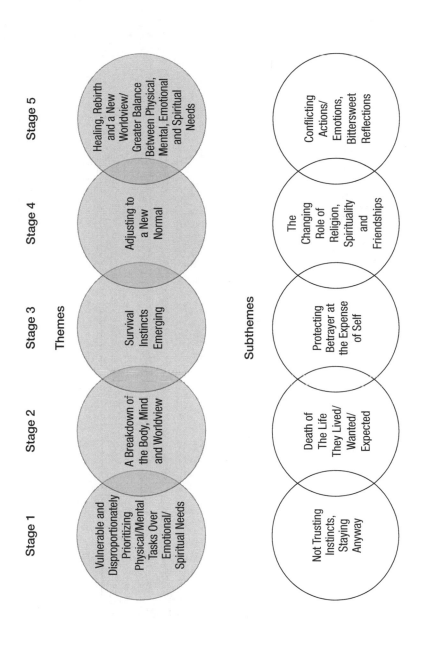

Stage 1   Stage 2   Stage 3   Stage 4   Stage 5

Themes

- Vulnerable and Disproportionately Prioritizing Physical/Mental Tasks Over Emotional/Spiritual Needs
- A Breakdown of the Body, Mind and Worldview
- Survival Instincts Emerging
- Adjusting to a New Normal
- Healing, Rebirth and a New Worldview/ Greater Balance Between Physical, Mental, Emotional and Spiritual Needs

Subthemes

- Not Trusting Instincts, Staying Anyway
- Death of The Life They Lived/ Wanted/ Expected
- Protecting Betrayer at the Expense of Self
- The Changing Role of Religion, Spirituality and Friendships
- Conflicting Actions/ Emotions, Bittersweet Reflections

II

THE FIVE STAGES FROM BETRAYAL TO BREAKTHROUGH

Stage 1

Physical and Mental versus
Emotional and Spiritual

*I*magine a table. When it's resting on four strong legs, it's stable and grounded. Now imagine a table with only two legs. Without the other two legs in place, the table is shaky and unstable. In that position, it's easy to see how the table can topple over. We're the same way. We have four "legs," which are physical, mental, emotional, and spiritual. Yet for so many of us, we're spending the majority of our time on the mental and physical legs (thinking and doing) versus the emotional and spiritual legs (feeling and being). While this strategy allows us to get plenty of things done, it comes with a price.

This doesn't mean that being busy is a setup for betrayal. It does mean, however, that every one of my participants (myself included) was too busy doing it all to pay attention to the signs that something wasn't quite right. So as you dive into this chapter, pay attention to any similarities you may find here to how life may have looked for you before your betrayal discovery. It's my suspicion that you'll be nodding your head in agreement while you're realizing that you're not crazy and you're not alone.

THE SETUP

Most of the participants said that they had low self-esteem, which they believed enabled them to make the choices that they made or allowed them to stay in a relationship they would have left if they had a more positive view of themselves. Suzanne remembered thinking, "I didn't value myself enough to say, wait a minute, this doesn't make sense."

In addition to having a low self-esteem due to a variety of factors, many felt they had too much responsibility at an early age. Dana remembered, "I felt like I was responsible for the whole family, like the weight of family came on me," and Juliana recalled caring for her sister with special needs: "Since the age of seven, I was responsible for taking care of my sister and always had to put her needs before mine."

Many experienced something traumatic in childhood, like Anne, who had an alcoholic father; Cleo, whose mother left her father when she was young; Marie, whose father was unfaithful; Lynn, whose parents had mental health issues; Monica and Patti, who had parents who were unloving; Dana, whose father was sexually inappropriate; Nanette, whose mother died in a car accident in a car her father was driving; and Denny, whose father also died in a car accident when she was 10 years old. Suzanne and Patti were both told that their mothers' coldness and harsh criticism, which contributed to their low self-esteem, was due to their mothers being jealous of them. These types of traumas had a profound impact on each participant, and each believed these situations played a role in shaping them as adults.

It was scenarios like these that had many of the participants feeling that they weren't ready but wanted to leave their childhood home, believing that leaving their childhood homes early would help them create a happier future. Dana, Monica, and Nanette all left their childhood homes and were married by 20 years old. Dana shared, "I got married at 19. I wanted out, and I guess I just, I married the first boy who asked me. I felt like I was old already." Monica remembered, "I didn't want to get married. I was 19 years old. I just lost my father. I didn't even want to get married. I really didn't love him, but he was constantly badgering me to marry him, and I just gave up and said all right, I'll get married."

Nanette shared her experience of marrying at a young age: "We got married, we had a baby the following year, we bought a house the next year, we had a baby the following year. We didn't have a lot of money. I guess it was stressful. Suddenly I had all this responsibility, and I was only 23 at the time with all that. What do you know at 23? I mean at that time, I didn't think I was young. I think because of my background, I just wanted to be married and have a family of my own and have my own life."

Jo was married at 22 and shared her experience: "I was married at 22. I was not even 23. I was going to be 23. What do you know then?

You're still in a growth pattern in your mind. You have no real good life experiences. I never went away to college. I was never able to experience outside groups except for my family or my cousins. Those were my friends. It was this new experience. Okay clap, you're an adult. In a house, maintaining, taking care of it, doing what was expected of me from everyone else, but always internally saying, 'This isn't really what I want. This isn't really where I'm supposed to be. I'm supposed to be doing more. I should be in college. I should be in medical school.' It was this constant video in my head of what I could be, yet my life was moving in the right direction. House, cars, kids, career. Everything looks so perfect, but my self-talk was always, 'You really weren't supposed to be here. You really should've been doing more. You really should be experiencing more.'"

While each story was different, it seemed that a combination of youth, a low self-esteem, being pushed into adulthood too soon, and too much responsibility at an early age created a level of vulnerability, leaving all of the participants open and trusting to relationships that seemed better than those they had grown used to.

Most of the participants also said they didn't feel they had a sturdy foundation on which to make healthy decisions or create healthy boundaries. Lynn expressed that growing up with a foundation of unhealthy boundaries led to issues regarding trust: "There was no reason why I should trust or feel okay. I had gone through so much abuse." Monica expressed the impact of growing up with an unhealthy foundation, which led to finding circumstances that felt familiar: "This is familiar. Oh, you remember that. That feeling's good. You can go there."

While physical, mental, emotional, or sexual experiences in childhood impacted in some way many of the people studied, even those participants who experienced no childhood trauma felt a certain level of unworthiness or unhappiness or felt consistent negative emotions, such as sadness, anger, or fear, that left them vulnerable to a situation or relationship they perceived may help them feel better. Jo remembered, "I absolutely was a very, very, very depressed, quiet child always full of anger." Cleo recalled, "I was a very unhappy child," and Arielle said, "I think I was depressed and stuck for most of my life even as a child. Nothing specific happened as a child, but looking back I think I was definitely frequently unhappy."

THINKING AND DOING VERSUS FEELING AND BEING

When I asked each of my study participants what their lives were like before discovering their betrayals, they were all busy working and/or raising their families. They were doing what they thought they needed to do in order to be their definition of a good partner, parent, worker, child, or friend. Many considered themselves "on autopilot." This was a period of their lives when they rarely considered their own emotional or spiritual needs and instead spent their energy on "getting it all done." Many maintained their homes, raised families, worked full- or part-time, and rarely took time for themselves. If they weren't raising families, they were building their careers and spending their time between work, home, and relationships.

At this stage, considering their own emotional, religious/spiritual needs wasn't a priority, and every participant recalled feeling chronically exhausted, not particularly happy yet not knowing how or feeling the need to consider a major change. Can you relate to any of their experiences?

TURNING DOWN THE VOLUME OF OUR INTUITION

Many admitted that there was a level of vulnerability allowing them to enter or stay in an unhealthy relationship, and they were physically and mentally exhausted. During this time, however, they remembered often ignoring their instincts and chose to be dismissive when suspicions arose. Because this is the stage where we find we may have turned down the volume on our intuition, we're faced with questions like "I never saw this coming—how could I be so blind?"

Arielle recalled, "I suspected something was happening but I ignored my instincts." Suzanne recalled, "The red flags were there. I chose to ignore them." Marie said, "I would be a liar to myself if I didn't say there were nuances even then, that he wasn't going to be a 100 percent loyal. I was dismissive of them." Cleo remembered, "There were little things all along that I've thought were a little suspicious, but I let it go." Denny said, "Something was in the back of my mind." Anne recalled, "I had a feeling, an intuitive feeling, but I just kept putting it aside."

Juliana shared, "Something was going on there. I didn't know what it was, but you know when you feel it inside," and Nanette remembered trying to speak with her aunt about her suspicions. Her aunt immediately responded with, "God forgive us for having such evil thoughts," so Nanette dismissed her instincts as well. Looking back, each of them clearly remembered feeling that something wasn't right yet chose to ignore their suspicions for many reasons.

Many of the participants said that they were dismissive of their suspicions because they were determined to stay married. Arielle was determined to stay married because she remembered the pain she experienced when her parents divorced when she was 18 and didn't want her children to experience the pain she felt during that time. Djena stayed in an unhappy marriage due to her religious beliefs. Dana's mother pleaded for her to stay married because she remembered her own pain of being a child of divorced parents. Dana recalled that this plea from her mother prevented Dana from leaving her marriage sooner. Denny said, "We didn't have an exceptionally happy marriage. I wasn't happy, but I wasn't going anywhere." Nanette admitted, "Growing up the way I did, I would have stayed in a miserable marriage. I don't think that I would have ever left."

Whether they would have stayed in an unhealthy marriage believing they were protecting the well-being of their children, due to their religious beliefs or due to their upbringing, most of the participants now saw that although they didn't trust or listen, their instincts were guiding them all along. Looking back, they all recalled the subtle and quiet voice within that, at the time, they didn't trust and chose to ignore.

Anne remembers herself as being "trusting and naive" during this stage. She was pregnant with her first child when her husband started acting differently. She remembers making excuses and blaming herself for his changing behavior until she slowly began to notice more obvious changes. Until then, Anne blamed her pregnancy and her hormones and would not believe what her intuition was telling her.

Another study participant, Denny, ignored her intuition for a few months before her suspicions about her husband grew too strong to ignore. One evening, she followed him and saw him leaving a restaurant and getting into a car with another woman. She continued to follow them to where they were going, and when they got out of the car, she confronted them both. Her intuition had been correct all along.

STRENGTHENING OUR CONNECTION
WITH SOMETHING BIGGER

This is also the stage where you certainly don't trust your betrayer and you hardly trust yourself. That's why it's the perfect time to begin learning how to trust again by strengthening your connection with something bigger than you. Whether that means God, the Universe, source, spirit, divine energy, or whatever you want to call it, I'm going to show you how to begin to strengthen and trust that relationship. I'm also going to teach you how to hear and interpret the subtle messages you'll start receiving as this relationship begins to strengthen and grow.

Creating and deepening this spiritual connection is going to play a crucial role in your ability to move forward as you begin to make sense out of your situation. This new or renewed relationship becomes invaluable, serving as the perfect testing ground to begin rebuilding something precious that was lost—trust. Also, I'm going to share some simple yet effective ways to connect that will suit your personality. It may feel odd in the beginning, but this relationship is the perfect place to begin because it will be one of the most important ones you will ever have, now and going forward.

I remember one of my mentors who said that our gut instinct is 10,000 times more perceptive and spot on than our minds, meaning trust your gut more than your head. If that gut instinct is so much more spot on, why don't we listen? Here's what happens. We get a gut feeling, an intuitive response, and if we don't act on it immediately, the ego/mind chimes in and talks us out of it. Have you ever noticed this happen to you? You get a gut feeling about something, then start talking yourself out of it, coming up with reasons, justifications, excuses, rationalizations, and all kinds of "logic" that have you feeling like it's wrong or a bad idea. So even though you got a strong feeling about something, you ignored it or overrode it and didn't listen. What happened next?

If you're anything like me, here's where you slap your hand to your forehead and say, "Ugh, why didn't I listen?!" Yes, the intuitive message was subtle yet clear, but it'll never shout over the noise of your ego. It'll patiently wait until you eventually realize that its messages are always in your best interest if you'd only listen and pay attention.

Take a minute to think back to how many times you may have done that, and you'll find that instead of putting your higher self in the driver's seat, it's as if you gave the keys to a little bully that doesn't know how to drive. You gave it the keys not because it deserved it but only because it demanded it. So how do you begin to strengthen and trust that intuitive muscle?

First, let's start with understanding that you're usually better off trusting your intuition over your mind. Unfortunately, our minds have become so polluted and poisoned by outdated beliefs, judgments, criticisms, and so many other negative perceptions that drive and guide our thoughts, behaviors, and actions. It's so constant that we don't even notice it. Unfortunately, that becomes the lens you're seeing through. It's like we're wearing some type of weird, distorted goggles that make everything look a certain way, and just because we're wearing them, we think that's how things really are. It's not, but it's as if we forgot we put those goggles on in the first place. If we know or remember we're wearing the goggles and then take them off, we'll look at things a whole new way. It's time to take off those goggles so that you see things differently.

HOW TO START TRUSTING YOUR GUT

So instead of trusting your mind, you're going to begin trusting your gut (which you can also call your BS meter.) The more you strengthen it, the more protected, guided, and safe you're going to feel. To do that, first think of something that feels positive for you—maybe it's a scene in nature, maybe it's when you were laughing with someone you love, or maybe it was when you just had a moment of joy and peace. Close your eyes and get a real sense of what that felt like for you. Bring up all of the emotions that went with it. Now notice where and how you feel it. Does it feel open and expansive? Do you feel it in your heart? What does that peace, love, and happiness feel like for you? Get a rich emotional and physical feeling that perfectly relates to the experience. Have it? Now lock it in so you know exactly what love/peace/joy/trust feels like for you.

Now, think of a time that felt awful. Maybe you just pictured D-Day (Discovery Day) or some other moment that was painful for you. Think of how that experience "landed" on your body and the emotions it brought up for you. Does your body feel tight and constricted? Is there a dark or heavy feeling? Are the emotions anger, sadness, or pain?

Whatever the physical and emotional feelings are, get a clear feeling that correlates with the experience. Have it? Now lock it in so you know what negative experiences feel like for you.

So now that you know what positive and negative experiences feel like physically and emotionally, that's a great start. It's those bodily sensations along with the emotions they go with that you can begin to trust. Those are your specific reactions and responses to those types of situations and feelings. Slowly start using that measuring system with everything—from the way it feels to interact with certain people to the outfit you choose to wear for the day. How do those people or that outfit make you feel? What are the emotions that go along with that physical feeling? Identifying these physical sensations and emotions may be subtle at first, but it's because it's a muscle that hasn't been strengthened. The more you work out that muscle, the stronger it becomes, and this is one that's crucial to strengthen.

Now let's use that "inner GPS" (which will always guide you appropriately and always has your best interest in mind) to help you learn to slowly begin to trust again. After a painful betrayal, trust is shattered, and while so many people choose to never trust again because of how painful their experience was, it also prevents them from ever forming deep and intimate relationships. That's not fair to you. The betrayal was bad enough; keeping everyone at a distance to prevent potential future pain is like having one bad meal that gave you food poisoning and swearing off delicious food forever just to prevent it from ever happening again.

So with your intuition slowly becoming strengthened by testing it with just about everything throughout your day, here's my four-step process to begin trusting again. This process works if you're willing to commit to it, and, let's face it, there really is no downside to any strategy that'll help rebuild what the betrayal destroyed.

THE FOUR-STEP TRUST-REBUILDING PROCESS

Let's start at the very beginning because betrayal demolishes our entire worldview. Our worldview is our mental model. It's how we interpret the world. It's formed by our culture, beliefs, perceptions, relationships, interactions, exchanges, and more. Our worldview is how we understand the way the world works. It gives us a sense of order, and it's the lens we see through. So, when our worldview is shattered, it needs to be rebuilt so that we can create a new level of order. That's why our "trust-rebuilding project" starts there.

The first step is to start trusting in the most simple and predictable aspects of life, such as trusting that the sun will rise each day or trusting in gravity—throw something up, it's coming down. Choose something you feel you can count on that's as simple yet predictable as that. Have something in mind? Now for the next few days, test it. Unsure the sun will rise each day? Look out your window every morning and watch it (with the understanding that even though it's a cloudy day, that sun is still doing its job behind the clouds). Whatever you choose, question it beforehand: "Is the sun really going to rise? Can I trust that?" Notice that while you may have been unsure, over time, you can see that you can trust in the simplest of things again. Once that's in place, let's take it to the next level.

Next, we need to rebuild our trust in God, the Universe, source, divine energy, our intuition, or whatever you want to call it. When we do, we don't feel alone. Instead, we feel connected and supported. The shattering of trust can have us feeling abandoned, rejected, alone, and forgotten. So, strengthening this connection reminds us that we're never alone and we have the support we need to help us get through this challenging time. Here's where that work to strengthen your intuition comes in handy because now you're going to learn to interpret those messages you're receiving and trust in them. Do you get a gut feeling to do or say something (remember, that means it's coming from your highest self and not your ego) and you trusted it? How'd it go? Start using your inner GPS to guide you with everything and notice how well it works when you trust your gut. Do it so often that you slowly but surely learn to trust it over the voice of your inner bully. Also, as you learn to trust and strengthen your intuition, take the time to be proud of this new wisdom you're gaining. It's something that may be unfamiliar to you, so recognize and appreciate your changes along the way.

So with a newly emerging trust in the simplest things in life (like the sun rising) and with your faith in something bigger, your intuition slowly being strengthened enough so you begin to trust in that too, let's keep going. Now it's time to slowly rebuild trust in yourself. Why does that need to be rebuilt? Because with betrayal, we question everything, including ourselves. I'm sure you found yourself asking questions like

"How did I not see it?," "How did I not know this was happening?," "How could I be so blind?," or "I'm a smart person; how did I not know anything?" If it's a self-betrayal, you may ask questions like "Why do I keep doing this?" or "What's wrong with me?" and lots of other questions that only cause pain and confusion. It leaves us on shaky ground with trusting ourselves, and that's why trusting in what we think, see, and do needs to be rebuilt too.

Here's where you're going to start using a bit of self-discipline because you're going to give yourself an instruction and then make sure you see it through. Maybe you tell yourself you're going to go to the supermarket and then you do, you're going to drink that glass of water and then you do, or you're going to call that friend and then you do. Maybe you tell yourself you're going to wake up 10 minutes earlier than usual so you can meditate or journal and then you do or you're going to go to sleep 30 minutes earlier so you can feel more well rested. You say it, then you do it. You get the idea. Give yourself these instructions over the next few days and notice how you can begin to slowly trust that if you say you'll do something, you do it. This small yet powerful act slowly rebuilds trust in yourself.

Here's where this takes us so far. You're now trusting in the simplest aspects of life. You can count on these things, and that gives you some sense of safety in how the world works and the "rules" that make it happen. The foundation of a new worldview is slowly being reconstructed. Next, you're learning to trust your gut and in something bigger than you, and that gives you another level of safety. Finally, you're learning to trust in your own word, judgment, and ability to do what you say you'll do. Put these together, and you start to feel stronger and more confident that you have a support system around you. This support is so important as you slowly begin to realize that you're not alone (for example, there's something bigger than you at work that allows the sun to rise, the grass to grow, and the seasons to change). Whatever you choose to call it, it can always be counted on. Think about it: did you ever notice that all day, every day, your heart beats and your lungs breathe whether you're aware of it or not? Learn to trust and count on the idea that there's more at work than you're aware of, even if you can't physically see it.

You're also learning to trust your intuition and yourself, which, together, truly act like invisible bodyguards. These two elements give us a sense of support and protection, allowing us to feel safe, which we need in order to move to the fourth part of rebuilding trust: rebuilding trust in others.

So now that you trust in the simplest aspects of life, you trust your intuition, and you trust yourself, you're ready to move onto the hardest part: trusting others. It's likely that this would have been near impossible without harnessing trust in those other areas, but with the other areas of trust being rebuilt, we can slowly and cautiously move on to trusting in others.

Having said that, you may always be cautious, careful, and hesitant. That's okay. Here's an analogy that'll show you the difference between never trusting again and slowly rebuilding trust. Imagine you've been burned by a hot stove and you want to be sure it's not going to burn you again. Never trusting again is like getting burned by that stove and swearing off cooking forever. You've decided that the burn is too painful, and instead of taking the chance, you'd rather not use the stove for any reason ever again. Sure there may be delicious dishes you'd be missing out on, but you got burned, and you don't want to take that chance. You're swearing off using the stove, and you'd just rather not have those foods that need to be cooked on a stove at all.

Or you can take the approach I'm teaching you here, and using the same analogy, it's a bit different. Yes, you've been burned by that hot stove, and it hurt. You even have a nasty scar to prove it. You also know that there are lots of delicious meals you'd be missing out on if you stopped cooking and you're not willing to give up those foods just because you got burned. Going forward, you're going to be careful, you're going to make sure you have your glove on so you're protected (just as you're protecting yourself by learning the first three elements of rebuilding trust), and you're going to slowly and carefully approach the stove so you can cook and enjoy all of those delicious meals you're excited to create.

With all of the other trust-building elements in place, you're going to carefully start to trust in others again. If you're rebuilding with the person who hurt you, it's as if each trust-building interaction and exchange serves as a brick being used to build a new brick wall of trust. Throughout your day when you're interacting with anyone, you're still going to use these same elements, especially your intuition. Have a gut feeling about someone? Trust it. Someone saying one thing but their energy or mannerisms are saying something else? Trust it. Now, just to be clear, if you experienced a romantic betrayal and you want to start dating again, I still caution you to wait. The version of you starting this journey is going to be a totally different version that emerges by the end of this book. Healing takes time, and you want to be sure that it's your highest and best self that's deciding who's worthy and deserving of this healthy, healed, and whole version of you.

I promised early in the chapter that I'd share some ways to connect with something bigger, whether to you that means God, nature, energy, source, or whatever, and in keeping my promise (because I want you to trust me too), here are a few ideas. Of course, everyone has their own tools that work best for them, so try a few on and see what fits.

STRATEGIES TO HELP YOU CONNECT

First, start with committing to a daily practice. That means every day (the same time is best), you're going to do whatever you feel helps connect you the best. Morning is typically a great time because there are fewer interruptions and it's less likely that your routine will get bumped for errands or other obligations that may creep up throughout the day. So once you've committed to a daily practice, it's also important to choose an amount of time that is doable and not overwhelming. Even a few minutes every day is better than an hour twice per week.

Next, choose a strategy—maybe a simple practice of breathing, gratitude, meditating, praying, or journaling. If you're meditating, is it a guided meditation, using a mantra, Transcendental Meditation, walking meditation, music, or the sounds of nature? If you're journaling, is it free flowing, are you using a sentence prompt, such as "What do I need to know today?" Or are you journaling an improvisational type of dialogue with your highest self? If it's a simple gratitude practice, are you writing down five things you're grateful for or saying, "Thank you for another day" before your feet touch the floor in the morning?

As you can see, there's no limit to what may work best for you. These suggestions are the tip of the iceberg, and we go into them in much greater detail within the PBT Institute Membership Community. For now, choose what intuitively feels right at the moment. The only bad choice is not getting started.

So, with an understanding of what Stage 1 looks like, along with your new plan to slowly rebuild trust and some strategies to help you feel connected, it's time to move on to Stage 2. You'll see why the shock of your discovery impacted you the way it did, and you'll also hear some incredible stories from the Fab 14. Of course, learning about this next stage will give you all the validation and confirmation you need to know that your betrayal hit you hard and that's why you've been feeling the way you do. But don't worry, that's all about to change. I'll see you in the next chapter.

· 6 ·

Stage 2

Breakdown of the Body, Mind, and Worldview

The shock of betrayal affects us on every level. In this chapter, you'll learn about the physical, mental, and emotional symptoms betrayal creates. Knowing these symptoms will explain why you may have been feeling the way you do, and you'll also know what's needed in order to heal.

This is the stage where there's complete mental chaos. It's challenging to wrap our minds around what we've just learned because, up until now, it may never have even crossed our minds that the person we trusted, felt safe with, and loved would ever hurt us. Because of that, we gave our time, heart, loyalty, and trust. Discovering a betrayal is like having that person—the one we *thought* we knew so well—take off a mask and reveal who they've really been this whole time. That's overwhelming to learn, and it has us frantically question everything, including ourselves, as we ask questions like "How did this happen?" and "How did I not know?"

A breakdown of our worldview is also common during this stage. Our worldview is our mental model, our own personal philosophy that explains how we perceive the world based on our ideas, attitudes, beliefs, experiences, relationships, personality, culture, and more. Being blindsided by someone we trusted shatters that mental model in an instant as we learn that the rules and beliefs we've constructed no longer hold true.

This second stage is the scariest for many of us because life as we've known it no longer exists and a new model hasn't yet been created. The bottom has dropped out from under us, and we don't yet have any solid ground to regain our footing. Those frightening circumstances are what ignites the stress response and leads to a cascade of physical, mental, and emotional responses. In fact, there's a collection of symptoms so common to betrayal that it's become known as Post Betrayal Syndrome. At the PBT Institute, we offer a quiz (https://ThePBTInstitute.com/quiz) to help people see if and to what degree they may be struggling. In tracking the data from thousands of people in every age-group and from many different countries, we've found that the following:

- More than 76 percent feel a loss of personal power.
- 72 percent are hypervigilant and on guard to threats and danger.
- Almost 90 percent experience mental, emotional, or physical flashbacks.
- More than 60 percent suffer from physical ailments: low energy, difficulty falling or staying asleep, or extreme fatigue/exhaustion.
- More than 50 percent suffer from mental ailments: feeling overwhelmed, disbelief, being unable to focus, shock, foggy-headed, and being unable to concentrate.
- More than 50 percent suffer from emotional symptoms: sadness, anger, stressed, feeling hurt, anxiety, feeling rejected, feeling disregarded, feeling taken advantage of, fear, feeling a sense of abandonment, feeling as if you got punched in the gut, irritability, and depression.
- 89 percent say that certain events, people, or places trigger the physical, mental, and emotional feelings of the betrayal.
- 80 percent are hesitant to trust again.
- 67 percent prevent themselves from forming deep relationships because they are fearful of being vulnerable and hurt.
- 84 percent find it hard to move forward.
- 90 percent want to move forward but don't know how.

Do you fit into these statistics? If so, don't worry, I did too before I healed, and the good news is that we know exactly what it takes to keep you moving forward.

What symptoms are *you* currently struggling with? The best way to see to what extent you may be struggling with Post Betrayal Syndrome is to take the quiz. You can find it here: https://ThePBTInstitute.com/quiz. Taking the quiz will give you a great baseline for understanding where you are right now. It'll also show you exactly what your particular betrayal has left in its wake and the areas of life where it's impacting you the most. In a way, it's comforting because it allows you to see how everything you've been feeling makes sense. It's also an important step to take because you can't change what you're not aware of. And by the end of this book, after you've used the strategies, tools, and exercises designed to help you heal, you'll be able to look back and see just how far you've come.

Let's start with how betrayal often shows itself physically. In every participant I studied, the stress displayed itself in physical symptoms and illnesses. For many of the participants, physical illness soon followed the initial shock of the betrayal. Arielle described the shock of betrayal as follows: "Have you ever lost a child in a crowd for a minute? Like that. A combination of panic and everything all at once. Like a rush of whatever." Djena remembered, "I was in shock." Lynn: "Shock. I was in shock for a long time," Jo: "Completely the wind, the rug was ripped out from under me," and Cleo: "Where your arms, your legs, everything goes numb and tingly. Your heart races, hyperventilating. physically, it's like someone had electrocuted me. I was shocked." Juliana: "I felt like somebody had reached into my body and pulled out all my innards." Marie: "I felt as if they punched me in the stomach."

After the initial shock, most participants felt they were in a daze, foggy, and cloudy-headed. Djena remembered being "not able to think." Arielle: "My thoughts were such a jumble." Juliana: "My head started to spin." Juliana: "Everything in my head was spiraling around." Lynn: "I'd been living in a daze." Suzanne: "I was in a fog. This awful, awful, awful fog." Denny: "When you're in that situation, your head is spinning. You can't even get control of the thoughts. It's like somebody is speaking another language. You can't understand what's going on." Each participant explained how this sense of fog prevented them from thinking clearly, leaving them feeling dazed, confused, numb, and overwhelmed. I distinctly remember those exact feelings. It was as if I'd just entered a black hole where nothing made sense and time was moving at a warp speed. I felt dazed, confused, and uncertain about everything I thought I knew so clearly right before that life-changing discovery.

Along with the feeling of being dazed and foggy-headed, many experienced extreme fatigue, sleeplessness, and exhaustion, which made perfect sense because as stress hormones increase, the sleep hormone melatonin decreases. In addition, they shared that the stress they felt drained them physically, mentally, and emotionally. Anne remembered, "I've always been full of energy, I go 24/7 nonstop. I didn't want to go out, I didn't want to do anything. I had no energy, I was exhausted." Denny: "Exhausted. I would nap a lot." Patti: "I just felt just like all my energy was just taken, wiped out." Lynn: "I felt exhausted." Jo: "I was so emotional and so sad that I would not want to function for days at a time." For me, it felt as if I were walking through mud and against the wind all day. Everything felt like an effort, and my body just didn't have the strength I needed to do the most basic of tasks. It was as if my life force had been completely drained out of me. Did you experience similar symptoms too?

One of the most common health challenges following the shock of betrayal for participants was digestive issues. Some participants who experienced childhood trauma already had variations of digestive issues before their betrayal. After the shock of betrayal, however, many of the participants shared that one of the most notable health challenges they faced involved digestive issues.

Cleo was taking medication for acid reflux. Anne remembered, "I had severe abdominal pain, I thought I had appendicitis." Arielle: "During this whole period, I had a stomach issue." Djena: "I wanted to throw up. I also got diverticulitis." Juliana: "I had really bad colitis. I was, on a monthly basis, going to the hospital where I was outrageously in pain." Denny: "I completely lost my appetite. I had a lot of diarrhea." Dana: "I had stomach problems, I had a spastic colon, food intolerance, constipation." Suzanne: "I was so nauseous."

Here's what I find really interesting about the gut. The gut is known as our "second brain" because the enteric nervous system is so smart that it operates on its own and without needing impulses from the brain. A healthy gut has so much to do with how well we're "processing," "absorbing," and "digesting" what we take in. Think about that for a minute. Besides the nutrients we ingest each day, we're also processing, absorbing, and digesting feelings and emotions. The feelings and emotions tied to betrayal are intensely painful. Is it any wonder why it's difficult for us to process, absorb, and digest these things and that our gut is struggling to accept them too?

Also, think about how we describe our intuition as a "gut feeling." With almost everyone in my study, myself included, we turned down the volume on our intuition. This means that something didn't feel right but we were too busy to stop and question it. So, all of the messages that our "gut" was trying to tell us was getting squelched and "backed up" for a period of time. It sensed something was wrong so much more effectively than our brain, yet we chose to ignore and override its messages. Can you see how perfectly it shows itself physically by creating physical issues in our gut? This is really another example of symptoms starting from an emotional issue, then manifesting in a physical issue—if for no other reason than to get our attention.

Other physical issues manifested for many of the participants as well. Arielle summarized her physical response to her experience as "Every possible physical way that my body could show me I was not in a good place." Suppressed immune function; cold sores; viruses; respiratory infections; back, neck, and shoulder pain; hair loss; skin conditions; headaches; migraines; congestion; allergies; weight; and hormonal changes were all mentioned as well in addition to extreme fatigue and digestive issues.

Within this theme of a breakdown of the body, mind, and worldview, "not knowing what to think" was common. This change in thinking was due to a breakdown in their previous worldview. Participants expressed how their previous ways of thinking had broken down yet a new way of thinking had not yet been formed. The rules and expectations they had previously known, believed in, or lived by no longer existed, yet a new set of rules and expectations had not been developed at this point. This uncertain and unstable ground causes a great deal of fear. For some of my participants, this process was too challenging to take on, and they remembered disassociating or shutting down. Lynn: "I was so dissociated, it's hard for me to really know what I felt." Monica: "I just shut down." Patti: "I went to my go-to defense, and I just shut down." For me it was a bit different.

I didn't shut down; in fact, for me, it was the opposite. I was desperate to understand how the mind works, why people do these things, and how I could heal. That search led me to want to understand betrayal at the PhD level, where I registered as a new PhD student in transpersonal psychology (the psychology of transformation and human potential). That search led to the study, its discoveries, and what I'm thrilled to share with you here. It was all so intuitively guided too. When I learned about the program, it almost felt like I didn't even have a choice. I felt like I had to enroll. Of course, my ego was saying things like "Are you crazy? You're too old to go back to school," "It's too expensive, and you don't have the time," and "You think you can do

all that schoolwork and manage your family and work too? No way!"
I kept ignoring that "advice" because although I didn't know what going back to school would lead to, I decided to trust in my highest self
instead, and I'm so glad I did.

Everyone has their own way of processing these painful emotions.
What I know for sure is that as long as you keep moving forward, you'll
continue to heal. It's when you numb, avoid, or distract yourself that
you keep healing at bay. Yes, these emotions are painful, but they need
to be experienced and addressed. When they stay stuck, we stay stuck.
We also manifest all kinds of illnesses, and, as they say, "The issues are
in the tissues," meaning that trapped trauma gets stuck in the body
and shows itself as symptoms, illnesses, conditions, and disease. That's
why it's called "dis-ease." That's also why many study participants and
members of our programs find somatic therapies helpful. What are somatic therapies? They're different types of body-based therapies that
understand the body/mind connection. Some examples are EMDR (eye
movement desensitization and reprocessing), Rolfing, the Alexander
technique, exercise, breathwork, yoga, dance, tapping (EFT [emotional
freedom technique]), acupuncture, Amma therapy, somatic experiencing,[1] sensory motor psychotherapy,[2] and more.

A combination of shock and feeling hurt, sad, angry, rejected,
disregarded, and abandoned were common emotions among most participants during this period of time. Nanette remembered her emotional
state during this time: "Probably every emotion—every negative emotion there could be."

The shock and pain of their experience led to a breakdown in how
they previously viewed the world because the old rules no longer applied and new rules weren't formed yet. This was generally expressed as
confusion and being overwhelmed. Denny remembered, "It was overwhelming." Anne: "How could this happen to me?" Denny: "I couldn't
get a grasp." Juliana: "Everything that he ever said suddenly became in
question." Cleo: "I can't believe this is happening." Suzanne: "How
on earth did I get here? How on earth did I allow myself to be with a
man who devalues myself and my kids and his home?" Djena: "I didn't
know where to go, I didn't know want to do." Nanette: "I didn't know
what to think." Monica: "Why is this happening to me?" Patti: "I can't
believe this is really true." Nanette: "That was my life dream, and he
just destroyed it."

This is the stage of intense fear and the shattering of faith and trust in those who betrayed us. We're also faced with the reality that life as we'd known it no longer exists along with the ending of a picture of what we wanted life to look like or what we'd come to expect. When this happens, there's a certain level of resignation or realization that needs to happen in order to move forward. It's the understanding that the life we had planned will no longer come to pass.

That was definitely something my participants felt. Suzanne remembered feeling helpless, hopeless, and uncertain as to what the future held. Patti: "There was a certain resignation about it. It was a confirmation of what I felt my whole life. That was like the truth for me. I never wanted to believe it. I couldn't believe it." Marie: "This isn't something I could accept or continue to pretend that I even wanted to try working on anymore." Denny: "I was starting to accept the situation and planned how I was going to deal with the situation." Lynn: "I have to accept that I'm at an age that I don't have a husband and I might not have kids." Denny: "I saw us retiring and watching our children get married and be grandparents together. That will all be done separately now. That was a big change. I accepted it as what it is." Nanette: "My whole world had shattered." Dana: "I had to process that my whole entire marriage was based on a lie." This stage of slowly accepting that their betrayals occurred and their lives would never be the same set the foundation for the third theme to emerge.

The best way I know to explain what this stage feels like and how it looks to move forward from this stage to the next is with an analogy. (You're probably seeing how much I love using analogies to explain things, so here's another one that'll explain this stage and what it leads to.) I'd written about this in *The Unshakable Woman: The Workbook*, and it's a good analogy to include here.

When a life crisis comes along that rocks us to our core, we can feel like the wind has been knocked out of us. The way I've experienced it is similar to the feeling of bracing yourself against waves in the ocean. In the beginning, the waves are coming at us so hard and so fast that we're unable to catch our breath and manage them. It's hard to find solid ground, and it seems as if we're doomed to get caught in an undertow that is too difficult to fight. We can barely breathe as the waves continue to take us under. We wonder if we can survive this experience at all.

After some time, here's what happens next. We barely have any strength left, we're exhausted and worn out. We can't think of anything other than preventing the next wave from taking us under. It feels as if those waves are still coming at us hard and fast, but there are brief moments when we're able to catch our breath long enough to brace ourselves for the next strong wave. The waves feel like wave after wave of an unrelenting force determined to knock us off from the feeling of having any solid footing. We keep bracing ourselves, however, and after each wave knocks us down, we're somehow able to survive it until the next one comes.

At some point, if we've made it this far, here's what happens next. There are slightly longer breaks between waves, giving us enough of a chance to catch our breath and start making some sense out of where we are now, even if these periods last for only a brief period of time. Each moment in between waves gives us hope; they show us glimpses of possibility and allow us to see that there's a light at the end of this dark tunnel if we can only keep managing these waves until we're strong enough that they don't keep knocking us over. If we're willing to face and brace ourselves against those powerful waves, using everything we have, we'll start to notice something a little bit different.

We begin to realize that our legs are getting a little bit stronger and our feet a little bit more rooted beneath us. At the same time, we notice that the time between each wave feels like it's getting a little bit longer. The waves still challenge us, but we have enough of a reprieve in between each one to gather our strength, stand strong, and brace ourselves with a renewed power we didn't have before.

If we're willing to and if we have the strength to stick with it long enough, here's what happens next. Eventually, our strength becomes stronger than those powerful waves. We realize the waves will still come, but after what we've been able to get through and how strong we feel, they feel like splashes in the kiddie pool. Our legs, along with our resolve and determination, are solid and strong.

Finally, at some point, we realize we've simply had enough. It dawns on us that we don't have to deal with the waves at all anymore if we choose not to. We're strong enough that we're not at the mercy of the waves at all, and our newfound strength gives us what we need to decide what it is that we want to do next. We've gone from being reactive to proactive. When we're reactive, it's as if we're at the mercy of what life throws our way. When we're proactive, we create and design what it is that we want. This feels empowering, and with this new understanding and newfound strength, we realize our next steps are up to us. We turn around and get out of the water. We're sure-footed and use our strong legs to walk on the soft sand. The rays of sunshine warm us as we find the perfect spot where our lounge chair is waiting for us. We lie down; get comfortable; take a slow, deep breath; let out a big sigh; and enjoy a beautiful and well-earned rest.

So, how can your waves become more manageable? If this is the stage you're in right now, know that it takes time to process these painful emotions. It may seem easier to outrun them, but just like a shadow, they'll only keep following you. There's a mantra I created that can be used for any topic. It's something I told my clients decades ago, and it's still useful today. Whether you're talking about health, relationships, business, or anything else, try it, and you'll see how much sense it makes and how it may help you. Ready? It's this: "Easy now, hard later. Hard now, easy later. Take your pick because it's going to be one of those two!" Want a few examples?

The painful emotions of betrayal are just too hard to process, so you choose to numb yourself at the end of each day with a few glasses of wine (easy now). Now it's a few years into the future. You haven't dealt with the betrayal, and not only are those emotions still lingering, but you're also dealing with weight gain from the wine along with hangovers and more (hard later). Or let's say you need to have a difficult conversation. You made a decision to have that conversation (hard now). Because you spoke up, your message was heard, and there's a new understanding and respect for you and your wishes (easy later). Here's another one. Your highest and wisest self made the decision to invest in your healing, although it would have been so much easier to put it off because you're just too busy. You realize there will never be a time you're not busy, so you invest in this book and your healing (hard now). Because of that, you move through the stages from betrayal to breakthrough with a strength, sense of freedom, peace, health, and happiness you *never* would have experienced had you not done the work you're choosing to do now (easy later). In case you didn't notice, that's also my way of showing you how awesome you are by choosing to do this work. While it's optional and many people simply hope it'll go away (as

I always say, "hope" isn't a strategy), you, brave warrior, are on your way to healing—once and for all.

Okay, since I'm loading you up with analogies in this chapter, here's one more. I love this one because it also demonstrates what complete chaos looks like and what happens when we do the work to clear it. Stage 2 is definitely an intensely chaotic stage, so it seems appropriate to share this here before moving on to Stage 3. My secret goal here is to inspire you to dive into your healing even more, and this analogy will hopefully help.

Imagine a messy garage or room or even a messy drawer. It just feels bad to deal with it, so you do all you can to avoid it. You think it's not vying for your attention, but every time you walk by that space, it just doesn't feel good. You keep avoiding it and avoiding it as long as you can, dealing with it only when you absolutely have to.

One day, you made a decision. This is a defining moment too. People think change takes time, and here's the reality. Change happens the moment you make a decision. Implementing the change may take time, seeing the results of the change may take time, but the change (and eventual transformation) began the moment that decision was made. Back to our analogy. You decide that it's time to clean that room (let's make it a garage, for example). You roll up your sleeves, grab a bunch of garbage bags, and tell yourself that while it may not be fun, you're not coming out of there until it's clean. Think about what happens next.

Once you start diving in, it actually gets worse. It's getting worse because you're creating all kinds of piles and organizing systems. You have one pile of things you're going to donate, another of things you're going to fix, another of things you're going to toss, and another of things you're going to keep. Everything is all over the place, and it's a big mess.

Once your piles are made, you toss and donate those two piles and put the items you want to fix into a big box and into your car that you'll take to get fixed. That leaves the last pile of things you're going to keep. You take a break (after all, this is hard work). You find yourself thinking about how to neatly put back what's left. You go to the store, where you buy some great storage containers and other organizational supplies. You come back home, excited to put all of your new things into the right containers and in the right spaces. Everything is in the perfect spot, and it looks great! You stand back with pride, admiring and enjoying your beautiful and clean space. Sure, it took some effort, but look what it led to.

That's exactly what happens when you "face it, feel it, heal it." It's tough work (as you're likely experiencing). But think of it this way. When you numb, avoid, or distract, you don't heal—just as the room didn't get cleaned when you kept avoiding it. However, when you bravely and boldly did the work by diving in and committing to getting it done, you can stand back and enjoy what you've created. That's exactly what you'll experience here. That sense of accomplishment, that feeling of strength and success, can be felt only by doing the work. You can't feel that if you avoid it. That feeling is earned by taking a deep breath, rolling up your sleeves, and getting it done. Same thing here. You're diving in and doing the work, and the version of you that'll surely emerge has every right to feel insanely proud, empowered, and accomplished.

So what's something you can do now to take you from where you are to help move you to the next stage? Here's where fostering and strengthening that connection with something bigger is more important than ever. Journal, meditate, breathe, pray, or find something that specifically feels right for you. That's so important because you're boosting your sense of connection and regaining a sense of trust.

It's also important to find some type of support. What's so crazy is that this is a time when we need support the most but are the least likely to seek it. Do you have a "trusted other"? That can be a family member, friend, counselor, therapist, or someone who can help you during this difficult time. It's important to find support, but a word of caution here.

Too many times, I've heard from people who've confided in the "wrong" people. While they may have meant well, their intentions may not have been in your best interest. For example, maybe you confide in your mother-in-law about your husband's affair and his unwillingness to change. You need support, but she wants you to stay married to her son, so her "advice" is for you to somehow get over it and look the other way. Or let's say you're not married but you've been dating a few years. You discover your partner's affair. The therapist is untrained in how to specifically work with narcissists, so she's charmed by your partner's smooth talk and crocodile tears. Your therapist urges you to "communicate better" so that your partner won't misinterpret your exhaustion as a lack of interest and fill their need elsewhere. Or let's say your coworker betrays you. You share your experience with another coworker who manages to use it as an opportunity for their advancement and growth.

All I'm saying here is to be careful with whom you confide in. Consider the lens they may be looking through to see why they may make one suggestion over another. Want an unbiased approach? Find a support group (not one that'll keep you stuck but one that'll give you the support you need). In fact, that's exactly why we created our PBT (Post Betrayal Transformation) Institute Membership Community, along with our Certified PBT Coach and Practitioner program. Actually, it was for two reasons. The first is to have these Certified Coaches and Practitioners in every state, in every country, and eventually every few blocks so that at a time when you need it most, you can find people who "get it." The second reason is this. We're much more likely to continue to do the work when we have to "show up." For example, would you hire a personal trainer who was overweight and out of shape? Would you hire a financial professional who's broke and has no idea how to make and keep their income? Would you trust a doctor with your health if they smoked or had other unhealthy habits? I hope not. People who do the work understand what it takes to get and stay there. It may be the perfect next step for you and a beautiful way to open up your heart to others who are just starting out on their healing journey and who'd benefit from all of the wisdom you gained as a result of your experience.

So with that, let's keep the momentum going as we move onto Stage 3. Are you ready? You're doing great. I'll see you there.

· 7 ·

Stage 3

Survival Instincts Emerge

If you were walking down the street and the ground were to suddenly drop out from under you, you'd do all you could to grab on to something so that you'd survive. That's exactly what happens after the initial shock of our betrayal experience starts to wear off. We enter an extremely practical stage, which is all about how we'll survive our experience. We realize that the life we had envisioned is no longer an option and that we need a new plan—ASAP.

In the study, every participant eventually figured out how they would survive. If doing so for their own well-being wasn't enough, the drive to create a safe environment for their children supplied the motivation they needed to pick themselves up and move forward. At this point, overcoming their situation or thriving as a result of their experience wasn't a priority at all. What participants focused on during this stage was (1) surviving the shock and (2) finding practical ways to find solid ground again.

THE DRIVE TO SURVIVE

For example, Nanette was a stay-at-home mom who suddenly needed to find work after discovering her husband's betrayal and their subsequent divorce. During this stage, Nanette started searching for answers through questions such as "What am I going to do? What am I going to do with my life now?" She asked these questions, to which her aunt suggested, "You need practical skills, so you need to learn how to type." She used her savings to register for a six-month course to learn basic secretarial skills, going to school while her children were at school during the day and studying at night. To make extra money, she ironed her brother's clothes so he could pay her instead of paying for a dry-cleaning service. When Nanette completed her course, she found a data entry job, which included medical benefits. It wasn't a job she'd stay at for long, but it was the first step to being able to support herself and her two children. Later, she would find her purpose and pursue a career in social work, which she still enjoys today. But during this stage, she was focused firmly on doing what was necessary to get by.

Although each participant found their own strategies based on what they believed would be beneficial for their individual circumstances, every participant I studied entered and exited this stage with the intention of surviving their experience. The time frames were different for each person, yet the instinct to survive their ordeal remained a daily fuel. Marie remembered, "The first thing that came to mind was that I had to put myself first. This was about me now, and I started to think about how do I approach this. It was a survival-skill mentality."

Similarly, Dana recalled, "I wanted to get the hell out of there. I wanted to get out of the marriage, and I realized that I had to make my own money. He was never going to take care of me, and I knew he was going to come after me. I had to really be strong, and . . . committed to being on my own. I was trying to get to the next day, trying to keep going, trying to make money, trying to take care of myself. I realized that I had to take care of everything. I needed to be the breadwinner. I had a child to take care of. It led me to really being self-sufficient, and I wanted more for my kids. I wanted my daughter to see strength, not weakness."

Anne remembered, "I had a wall up, and I did whatever I had to do to survive." To find answers, Denny asked questions such as "How am I going to do this, how am I going to survive this" in order to reveal the next steps she needed to take to move forward. Suzanne realized, "There was part of me that knew I needed to do something. I have two babies in this house."

Juliana remembered the drive to make money to support herself and her children: "I was working. I was bringing money in. I had, I can't tell you how many jobs. I was making myself sick." If you're in Stage 3, does this sound familiar? Which of the Fab 14 can you relate to the most?

I remember this stage so well too. I felt the "drive to survive," and that's all I could think of. I had conversations with myself about how I was going to deal with my kids while dealing with myself. I thought about how to show up for my clients while I was in so much pain. I considered what I needed, what I'd let go of, how the heck I would also take care of my six dogs, whom could I talk to, and how I could make my heart feel better while making sure I could be there as best as I could for the kids who each needed me in their own ways. I was too overwhelmed to see friends and didn't have the bandwidth to anything but the basics. I also didn't want to share my story or my pain with anyone during this stage. The only people I confided in were my intuitive coach and my psychic friend, who both kept telling me how I'd look back on all of this one day, seeing it as a huge turning point, a blessing and gift for me, my family, and those I serve. I just remember rolling my eyes and shaking my head, thinking, "Blessing? Gift?! Yeah, right. They obviously don't know what they're talking about but . . . whatever."

At this stage, many of the participants felt unsafe and insecure, and many lacked a sense of personal power, yet the drive for survival was greater than their fears, and they searched to find ways to move forward. This was a period of time where regardless of how they felt physically, participants took action. Their survival instincts emerged, and a search for practical solutions began. They were jolted into action as they each struggled to find their best, next steps.

PROTECTING THE BETRAYER AT THEIR OWN EXPENSE

Although the participants were the ones betrayed, during this survival process, they often blamed themselves and protected their betrayer for a variety of reasons. One reason was due to their upbringing. Anne remembered, "I never told a soul. I didn't tell any my girlfriends, my male friends, I told no one. I'm brought up in an Irish family; happy on the outside, keep your business behind closed doors. I blamed it all on myself, everything was my fault. I never told my mom that he cheated on me, but I'm very close to her. She knew. I even think my friends knew something was going on, but I never said it. My brothers would never have forgiven him, I can tell you that for a fact, and even my sisters. I didn't want him isolated from the family. I couldn't tell my friends, I just couldn't do it."

Marie hesitated confronting her ex–husband because of the relationship she had built with her stepdaughter: "I had a big concern regarding my stepdaughter. I was very invested in her." Nanette struggled sharing anything with her children because their father left the marriage to begin a relationship with Nanette's sister-in-law, her children's aunt: "How do I let my kids know? It's okay, love your father without saying he's an asshole, basically. That was my struggle." Patti shared that while she never felt a sense of closeness with her family, it was something she had wanted for her children: "I was keeping up this family thing, that's what I did all the time. I tried to keep the family together, tried to make family memories." Denny struggled with sharing her betrayal due to the embarrassment or judgment she feared facing: "I was too embarrassed to tell my mother or my sisters. I felt like it's a reflection on me." Juliana had grown accustomed to taking responsibility for challenges within her marriage, remembering, "I was owning it. I've done that since I was little, and I couldn't go to my parents because they would have, in my mind, overreacted. I kept everything inside. I didn't share with other people because I didn't want to share brokenness."

Keeping the pain of their experience to themselves was a decision they believed served them best at the time. While every participant I studied realized that support would have been beneficial, at the time they didn't feel ready or willing to speak openly about their betrayals due to shame, embarrassment, judgment, or the decision to protect the betrayer. When they did speak with someone, most often they spoke with a close family member or therapist first, leading to speaking with close friends later and once they felt ready. So, before we move on, does this sound familiar? Is this what you did or how you felt? I'm sure you're seeing how common it is to protect our betrayer and keep all of this to ourselves—unfortunately, at our own expense. I hope you're also seeing that they would have benefited from support, so learn from them and find the support you need.

IDENTIFYING THE SUPPORT YOU NEED NOW

To help you find that support, let's start by identifying the team you'll need to help you through this frightening and unsettling stage. Whether it's a therapist, doctor, healer, trusted family member, financial planner, religious or spiritual guide, mentor, lawyer, mediator, accountant, a support group, or simply a knowledgeable friend who can help, let's put together your team of trusted support to help you find solid ground again. Start by asking yourself what it is that you need right now and who can help you with that. If you're unsure, reread that list of people I just mentioned. Would anyone in those areas help you right now? For example, I remember working with a woman who was struggling with a horrible string of repeat betrayals from her husband. It had been decades of lies and deception with regard to their finances. She would regularly find that although he said every bill was paid, debt collectors would call, money would go "missing," and they didn't have the money needed to pay for their children's next college tuition payment. She carefully squirreled away money she made through her job, yet this money would somehow manage to disappear too. This happened constantly, yet he always managed to say just enough to throw her off track. (This is known as gaslighting, and we'll talk about it more later.)

When she finally realized that she kept getting duped and nothing was going to change, she slowly took action. For her, the first step was a financial planner because the fear and panic of never knowing when the next financial bomb was going to drop was just too much to take, and it was taking a huge toll on her as well as her kids. This first step turned down the panic enough to move toward a next step. See how this works? While you may need lots of support in many different areas, what do you need *right now*? That's the best place to begin.

SELF-CARE STRATEGIES AFTER BETRAYAL

As you know or can remember from this stage, this is still a scary and unsettling time. You're not in that Stage 2 of complete shock, but your body and mind are still in a state of high stress. Left unchecked, this chronic, unmanaged stress is the perfect recipe for stress-related illnesses, symptoms, conditions, and disease, so let's take some immediate steps to reduce some of that stress as best we can.

How can you settle your nervous system, sleep a little better, and calm down even a bit? Anything you do now to take even the slightest bit of care for yourself is a step in the right direction, even if you're reading this, thinking, "Debi, I don't have time to read this book, you're asking me to do even more?" Yes. You are the engine that runs your operation. If the engine fails, everything stops, so let's find some simple ways to settle your nerves in a healthy way.

BREATHING

Here's the simplest strategy I can suggest: breathing. You're doing it anyway, so why not make the most of it? Take a minute to consider your breathing. When we're stressed, it's quick and shallow. When we're relaxed, it's slow and deep. With that, even if you have to set a timer for a few times throughout the day, check your breathing. Give yourself 30 seconds of deep, full breathing a few times a day, and while it seems like it's not helping, it is. It's bringing oxygen to where it's needed, helping your nervous system, your brain, and so much more.

YOUR DAILY PRACTICE

As I've already mentioned, it's an important time to have that daily practice too, especially if it involves meditation, mindfulness, journaling, prayer, and so on. Even if it's for only a few minutes, there have been countless studies on the benefits of meditation and mindfulness. While these practices help us connect and feel more grounded and centered, they absolutely help manage your level of stress. There are plenty of both free and paid apps too that can help you cultivate a breathing and mindfulness practice. Insight Timer, Calm, and Headspace are just a few.

MOVEMENT

Movement is also incredibly helpful during this time. It helps release all of those stuck emotions, and studies have found that a strong body helps create a strong mind. Walking, weightlifting, dancing, running, or even gentle stretching are a few ideas to consider. I've had clients who loved kickboxing because they took out all of their anger on the punching bag, while others have found something deeply healing about the body/mind connection they felt through a regular yoga practice, tai chi, or qigong. Choose something based on your fitness level and what feels like a fit for you so that you can release all of that energy.

NUTRITION

Of course, better food choices will also help. I'm not suggesting that this is a time to overhaul your eating (that's not your priority during this stage), although fueling your body with nutrient-dense, whole, real foods will help your brain, body, energy levels, and digestive system run more efficiently. Eliminating sugar, dairy, gluten, or any other substance that taxes your body reduces inflammation and supports healthier functioning. So, any change you can make will help.

If that's not enough motivation, here's another reason that eating well and exercising are important now. Betrayal has us feeling as if so much has been taken out of our control. Eating well and exercising are two things completely within our control, so getting started with eating better and moving can help you feel like you're beginning to take the reins back on your life a bit. Also, if you experienced a romantic betrayal, your confidence has been impacted. A leaner, healthier body can help you feel better about how your body looks and feels.

SLEEP: HOW TO TURN DOWN ALL THAT "NOISE"

It's also important to do all you can to get the most out of your sleep right now. Sleep is a time for rebuilding and repair, so use those sleeping hours to do double duty for you. Create a more peaceful sleep environment by making your sleep space peaceful, serene, and comfortable. Get rid of the clutter, make sure it's dark enough, and minimize anything that'll prevent disrupted sleep, like watching something stimulating before bed, caffeine, being on social media, and so on. As far as sleep goes, here's a tip that I learned from the late Dr. Wayne Dyer. Before falling asleep, consider the thoughts going through your mind because those are the ones you're going to be spending the night thinking about. Go to sleep with unrelenting, negative, and painful thoughts, and those will be the ones you're spending the night with. Go to sleep with more positive and peaceful thoughts, and you have the night to put those to work too.

Now I know that if you're in this stage, you may need a boost with that, so let me give you a few ideas. For me, nights were the worst because, during the day, I was able to sometimes become distracted with work, kids, and so on. At night, with the quiet of my own mind, every demon and painful thought I could experience reared its ugly head. Listening to music or calm sounds wasn't enough to drown out the "noise," so I had to take it up a notch. I wore a headset to sleep, and all night long, I'd have guided meditations or spiritual books I could listen to. The volume was purposely loud because it helped drown out the painful thoughts. Eventually, I'd fall asleep and figured that even if I didn't consciously hear the books or meditations, they were somehow working on my subconscious mind while I was sleeping.

QUALITY SUPPLEMENTATION

I also took advantage of some health and energy boosts from quality supplements during this time—nothing that I'd stay on for long but enough that would help my nerves, energy, focus, and sleep. It's important to remember that your foundation has been rocked, and these strategies will give you comfort and support as you move through this unfamiliar and unnerving time.

You don't have to do them all. Just get started with any one of these strategies. See if it's making you feel a bit better, then, as that one becomes a habit, include something else. What you're doing is slowly rebuilding a new version of you as you give yourself what you need to heal. Some other suggestions to help during those harder times of the day are these:

- Take a moment to breathe deeply and mindfully
- Have a cup of chamomile or other soothing tea
- Write or type in a journal, getting out the hardest feelings
- Start a gratitude journal and turn to it in negative moments
- Listen to upbeat or soothing music depending on the time of day
- Call a friend or family member

YOUR MIND-SET

Another very important part of this stage involves working on your thoughts. There's a big difference between reflecting on your experience and going over it endlessly without ever feeling better for having spent time and energy on it. Let's start by talking about how to slowly yet steadily break the negative thought/feeling loop that plays endlessly in your mind.

Here's how it works. It starts as a thought. We take that thought and infuse it with feelings. We replay those thoughts over and over again. We attach emotions to those thoughts as we replay them endlessly. Now we've given those thoughts free reign as an endless, negative tape loop continuously plays in our minds. It's like a bunch of five-year-olds running around a classroom because the teacher left the room. It's chaotic and exhausting. We have between 60,000 and 80,000 thoughts each day, and the majority of them are negative, especially when we're struggling to heal from a painful betrayal. If we don't rein in those negative thoughts, it's as if our mind says, "Oh! I see you want me to keep replaying these thoughts. Okay, no worries. You go about your business, and I'll just keep running these like a subconscious program throughout the day." Once this happens, you're not even aware that these are the thoughts driving everything you think, say, feel, and do.

What's even worse is that now this way of thinking is so familiar that you don't even realize you're doing it. It's not that it's good or working for you, it's just so familiar that in a weird way, it starts becoming comfortable. It's like someone who hasn't showered in days. It's gross, but they've become a little comfortable with their own stench. Yuck. Now, since "what we feed grows," here's what happens next.

BREAKING THAT NEGATIVE TAPE LOOP

These toxic, unrelenting negative thoughts now become so familiar and a part of you that you can't even imagine things any other way. Here's where you start attracting situations and circumstances to you that are equally as negative. Why? Because "like energy attracts like energy," and what we feed grows. Your mind will do everything to confirm your beliefs, so if you believe, "This sucks, life will always suck, and I should just get used to it," then your mind thinks, "Well, okay, if that's what you believe, I'll just find some confirming evidence to support your belief." Confirming evidence comes your way, and you think, "See? Life sucks, I knew it!" And on and on it goes. It's not that you're doomed or destined to stay stuck, but that's the exact mind-set that'll keep you firmly rooted in that exact spot. Over and over, you find all of evidence you need to prove your case, yet so often we fail to realize that it's your thinking that's bringing all of that evidence to you in the first place. All that "stinkin' thinkin'" has taken on a life of its own. You've given those negative thoughts momentum and power. It's time to take that power back.

I proved this myself. For years, it always seemed like things were especially hard for me. If it took someone an hour to do something, it would take me three hours. If someone said, "Oh, that's easy, all you need to do is . . . ," I'd do exactly what they said, and it wouldn't work. It got so bad that I even made a joke out of telling everyone of the time that, without fail, a service person would come to the house and say, "Wow, we've never seen that before, I don't know what to tell you"; that the person behind the counter at the post office would say, "Sorry, we've never seen this error message, we can't help you with that"; or that I even had an operation on my foot that "works for everyone" yet left me worse off than before I started. This became one big unfunny joke. There are even the countless stories of bringing a carry-on suitcase whenever I traveled, and without fail, I'd have to check my bag, or I'd be taken off the line to have the bag searched.

One day, I learned that all of this "bad luck" may be somehow linked with negative programming and beliefs in my subconscious mind. I wasn't aware of consciously choosing these things, but I was willing to consider that these beliefs may be running subconsciously. I learned how the mind works and thought that I just may be bringing these situations into my daily life. I worked on my thoughts by first seeing what may be hiding out in my subconscious. Over time, things slowly changed, and now when my carry-on isn't checked, I feel downright victorious.

If I had to identify the most common stage to get stuck in, it's Stage 3. You might be thinking, "Of course I want to heal," but believe it or not, you may be receiving lots of benefits from staying stuck. I know that sounds so crazy, so let me explain.

THE "BENEFITS" OF STAYING STUCK

You may not be consciously doing this, but subconsciously, there are lots of benefits to staying stuck. Here's what I'd like for you to do. Go ahead and grab a pen and a piece of paper. I'm going to list these "benefits," and if any of them resonate with you, write them down. You need to be totally honest here, and no one has to see your list but you. Ready? See if you're receiving any of these "benefits":

- You get a powerful story.
- You get self-pity and somehow benefit from being a victim.
- You get to be right.
- You get sympathy from others.
- Let's face it, staying stuck is easier than changing.
- You get a great excuse for not doing something.
- You get to hide.
- You get to build your case (this happened, then this, and then this).
- You prevent anyone from hurting you again.
- You don't have to do the hard work of rebuilding trust—you just won't trust, period.
- Your ego stays in control.
- You get someone/something to blame.
- You get a target/bull's-eye for your pain.
- You get to feed/fuel your addiction (a "chemical cocktail" is released every time you think about your betrayal, and, like any cocktail, it's addictive).

Pretty shocking, huh? These "benefits" keep us stuck and prevent us from creating the health, body, love, success, relationships, and experiences that make life fulfilling and meaningful. They keep you from creating the life you deserve.

THE BENEFITS OF MOVING FORWARD

Now, here's a list of what you get when you're willing to let those things go.

- You get freedom.
- You get improved health.
- You get to grow.
- You get an improved immune system.
- You look younger.
- You get to put new boundaries in place.
- You get new relationships based on who you're becoming.
- You get new opportunities you never would have access to when you were hanging on to those small self-benefits.
- You get a new worldview.
- You get a clean slate to create something better than before.
- You get a much better story.
- You get to be the hero or heroine of your story.
- You get to be a role model for others.
- You get a new level of confidence—earned by what you're healing from.

A LOOK AT YOUR SUBCONSCIOUS BELIEFS

So, here's what I invite you to do now. Take a look at what those small self-benefits are getting you and check in. How do they make you feel? Are they really worth it? Then, imagine how you'd really feel if you let go of those benefits for ones that are *so* much better.

Now, those small self-benefits are driven by those beliefs and keep you painfully tethered to the past. How can you see what's lurking in your subconscious? Here are a few prompts to consider. Write these down and see what follows:

I'm so . . .
I can't . . .
I'll never . . .

You may find that you have lots of beliefs that don't serve you at the end of those prompts. The good news is that you can slowly change them for ones that do.

As long as I'm giving you a few tools and strategies, here's another one that may help. It's one that's helped so many members of our *Betrayal to Breakthrough* program, and I hope it helps you too.

AWARENESS IS THE FIRST STEP TO CHANGE

During this time, we can have so many toxic, negative thoughts that we're not even aware we're having them, and since awareness is the first step to changing something that doesn't work, it's time to become aware. Let's get started by putting a simple rubber band on your wrist. Any rubber band will do. Next, remember that peaceful scene you pictured in an earlier chapter, the one you imagined along with the peaceful feelings that went along with it? You're going to get that ready because you're going to be using it for this exercise.

Now that you have your rubber band on and that peaceful scene ready, you're ready for the next steps. Here's the idea. It's likely that those negative thoughts will come up. After all, it's become a habit. So, the idea is, whenever you catch yourself going down that rabbit hole of toxic and unrelenting thoughts and you're feeling those negative feelings that go along with them, you're going to do these three steps.

Step 1. The first step whenever those painful thoughts come up is to choose a word that you're going to say out loud or in your head. Choose either "stop," "change," "cancel," or whatever word gets your attention. For me, I'd say or even scream "Stop!" as those runaway thoughts were hijacking my mind. Sometimes it was in my head, and when no one was around, it was out loud. This serves as a "pattern interrupt," where we're stopping ourselves from going down that slippery slope.

Step 2. You're going to snap the band. It's not to hurt you but to remind you to *not* go down that painful path you've traveled down a million times. If you don't want to snap the band, rubbing it is fine too. You just want to remind yourself to consciously choose to not go down that road to more pain and suffering.

Step 3. You're going to picture that peaceful scene along with all of those pleasant feelings and emotions that went along with it. You see, what you're slowly doing is replacing that negative thought stream with a more positive one while you're also preventing yourself from those toxic thoughts that create illness and disease and that don't do anything to help move you forward. Do this often enough, and you'll find that you're slowly losing the emotional charge of the negative thoughts as the more positive scene begins to take over.

Now, I can just hear you saying, "Does this mean I'm avoiding the pain and not dealing with things by doing this?" No. If you've gone over your experience countless times, it's time to walk that line between making sense and extracting meaning from what you've been through while being careful to not have it pull you under. Only you know how long and to what extent your thoughts have been hurting you further, so use your best judgment here.

COMMITMENT AND A PLAN

This takes commitment—mental commitment because it's so familiar and easy to go down that well-worn path, even if it's taking you to a painful place. By making the commitment to (1) stop, (2) snap, and (3) envision your peaceful scene, you're strengthening your mental muscle as you slowly lay down new "tracks" in your brain. It's like water flowing over rocks. The water flows in the same pattern because a path in the rocks has been created over time. You're creating a new path that'll lead to much better outcomes. It just takes commitment and a relentless determination that while you may want to indulge in that negative scene for a while, it'll only lead to more grief. It's like indulging in anything unhealthy that leaves you feeling sick, empty, hungover, and awful the next day. It's time for something better.

So, this was a big chapter with lots of ideas for you to consider. We talked about finding the right support based on where you are right now, how to better manage your stress, and how to get a handle and slowly rewire your mind-set. Take your time here and maybe reread this chapter, committing to choosing one person to talk to, one way to reduce your stress, and one way to see what thoughts and beliefs are lurking in your subconscious.

As I mentioned, betrayal affects the body, mind, and spirit, and that's why they all need your attention in order to heal. It's also important to realize that this journey isn't an easy one, so give yourself credit for embarking on it at all. Every day, so many people tell me how badly they want to heal yet choose not to do anything differently in order to make that happen. They want the reward without the work, and it just doesn't work that way. It's like paying someone to do your workouts for you. Unfortunately, the only way to get in shape is by *you* doing the work. Same thing here. You heal only by *you* doing the work, and that's exactly what you're doing. I'm insanely proud of you. I know how challenging this can be, and I also know that it's the only way to Post Betrayal Transformation, which is an incredibly rewarding state for a job well done. Keep up the great work, and I'll meet you in the next chapter.

Stage 4

Finding and Adjusting to a New Normal: Grieving/Friendships

$\mathcal{I}$magine moving into a new home. At first, you're not quite sure where to put your things. You don't know the best route to get to the store or to work. You're unsure what the neighbors will be like. So many things are new and unfamiliar, yet with time, you believe it's going to be okay. That's what this stage is all about. First, there was the shock of a betrayal, followed by the physical, mental, and emotional repercussions. Then there was the drive to survive the experience. Once practical solutions are found (the ones we talked about in Stage 3) and you feel you can survive your experience, you will begin to feel as if you're back on more solid ground. That's when you will begin discovering, adjusting to, and settling into what will become a new normal.

ACKNOWLEDGING AND GRIEVING YOUR LOSS

One of the elements of this stage involves our own personal grieving process, where we grieve over what we're now able to see more clearly. We grieve over what we believed we had and now don't have. We grieve over what we wanted and what we won't have going forward. We grieve over a certain expectation we had of what relationships should include. We grieve over broken promises, shattered trust, and unmet expectations. Denny remembered, "This was a grieving process. There is a piece of me that died. I don't know what piece that is, but inside, all the way inside in my soul, I feel like somebody just chiseled out a little corner of it."

Patti's betrayal came at the hands of her own mother, who repeatedly shared her secrets with her stepsisters and removed Patti from her will without telling her—a fact that Patti didn't learn about until her mother's funeral. When she got to this fourth stage, Patti remembered the experience clearly: "There was a certain resignation about it. It was a confirmation, I think, a clarity that I received from seeing what my relationship really *wasn't* with my mom. That fantasy kind of just broke down, and it just was like nothing. It just kind of dissipated like the whole relationship."

How can you grieve and then make sense and meaning out of your experience? We'll be doing an important experiential exercise at the end of this chapter called "Writing a Coherent Narrative." I'll ask you a sequence of questions to identify what you've learned, what you've gained, and what you now see so clearly because of your experience. This process allows you to make your experience a defining chapter of your story, not your life's story. Through organizing, sequencing, and understanding the experience, you'll emerge from this stage understanding all that was *gained* through a painful loss. Gained? Yes. I know it sounds crazy, but you'll be amazed at how writing this narrative clearly shows you how the Universe is always conspiring in your favor, even if its intention isn't clear just yet. You also weren't ready for this exercise before this time because you were struggling with the shock, then how to survive your experience. I'm assuming you're working through these chapters and feeling better as a result, making it the perfect time to continue moving forward.

Let's get started by diving into what I mean about the grieving process. This is such an important stage because unless you let go and grieve what's been lost, you can't welcome in the new. That grief is taking up mental and emotional space. It's keeping you stuck and preventing next steps. Everyone has their own time line around how long it takes to grieve and when they're ready for it. There's no specific time it needs to occur, but this is a step that can't be avoided if you want to move forward. It's so deeply healing and cleansing as you energetically let go of all of those lost hopes, wishes, and dreams as it paves the way for something new and beautiful to slowly emerge, even if you can't see what that is just yet. Nanette recalled, "The grief process, it had to come. I now had to live a life that I didn't want to live. My homemaker life was just pulled out from under me, the whole thing."

This grieving process can feel like an adjustment in understanding. Marie said, "I had to make peace with the fact that the betrayal also was from one of my students that I was mentoring. I had to make peace with that because I've dedicated my whole career to education." She also said about the grieving process, "There's a shedding of things around you. When you walk away from a certain lifestyle, there are things that walk away with that." Marie added, "There's a coming to terms with that, because again, that's also challenging old paradigms, what you've been taught. Coming into an awareness, knowing there are just different ways to do things."

Lynn expressed grieving as follows: "I'm still going through the grieving process of losing everyone. It's difficult for me to know, I still struggle with that. I've had to accept. This is the thing, I still have my moments. I've been really angry that I don't have a family, angry that I'm at an age that I don't have a husband and I might not have kids." Juliana was grieving her loss as well: "I have been really working hard not to go back because if I look at the rearview mirror, I'm going to end up stuck in the rearview mirror." Dana expressed her grief over not being able to rely on the men in her life: "I cried thinking about why it is I have never been able to rely on a man not to hurt me." As she grieved, she reconciled with thoughts she now understands more fully: "I understand things now. I see the soul immediately. I see the trauma in the person that's hurting me, and I don't react to it. I'm probably single for a reason. That's the sadness because I have so much to give, so much to love."

Cleo recalled what she did during her grieving process: "I would let a few months go by, then I'm suddenly being happy or sad; that would make me reach out. I want to pick up the phone; I wouldn't, but sometimes, I guess that's what I did." Anne remembered how grieving helped her: "I think it got me out of my slump."

Do you see yourself in any of the Fab 14? Whose story do you relate to? I remember the grieving process so well. It was this realization that no matter what I did, what I said, what I wanted, or what I hoped for, I'd never be able to "undo" the betrayals from my family and my husband. It was like realizing that I'd been banging my head against the wall all this time. All it was doing was hurting me and making me unable to be there for those in my care and reach. That grieving process felt like I'd finally stopped banging my head against the wall as I made the decision to start moving forward from where I was to the new emotional space I found myself in.

There's something else that may come up for you during this grieving process, and it's very common to experience during this particular stage. I want to be sure to bring it up so you're not surprised if it happens. As you grieve all that was lost due to your betrayal, you may also find that you need to grieve the loss of some friendships too.

A NEW NORMAL MAY MEAN NEW FRIENDSHIPS

The grieving process is a time when, as we let go of what no longer will be, we have the space to see other areas of life more clearly. We're creating space for something entirely new, and we want to be sure that everything that's going to be a part of that new space represents the version of us we're ready to become. Since you know how much I love analogies, here's another one.

At the beginning of this chapter, I gave you the analogy of moving into a new house. So, now imagine that you're ready to move and it's time to pack. Yes, you may be sad that you're leaving and grieve all you'll miss as you leave that space that served you so well during the time of your stay. In getting ready for your move, however, you'll find that there are things you want to take with you and other things that are best left behind. Why?

Some of those items don't represent who you're becoming and what's best to have around you as you slowly create the new updated and upgraded version of you. It's not that those items are wrong or bad, you've just outgrown them, and in letting them go, you're allowing space to welcome in something new. So, instead of packing those things and bringing them into your new space, it's the perfect time for some "spring cleaning." Sure, they may have been perfect for you at the time, but they just may not work for you anymore based on what you're ready to create now. Your new start means taking things that support you, that inspire you, and that represent the version of you that's ready to emerge. That means that as you reset boundaries and rewrite the "rules" around what you need and what no longer serves you going forward, it's a great time to do some spring cleaning as it relates to your friendships too.

As you slowly begin to re-create your new life, it's common to be-come very deliberate about who you allow in. Were your friends there for you when you needed them? (That's assuming you reached out and they knew what you were going through.) If not, this is often a time where we redefine what true friendship means.

Jo experienced changes in friendships, explained as follows: "I was frightened at the fact that I wouldn't have all those people in my life, when, now, it feels like they really didn't belong in my life." Juliana changed her rules with regard to friendship as well: "I want to be there for them until it crosses the line where it's going to negatively impact me. I can't allow that anymore. Now I really have really nice girlfriends. They are just fantastic. They have my back. It's a small group. I'm not a propo-nent of having a gazillion friends. I don't call people friends easily lately."

Dana noticed changes within her friendships as she continues to change: "There's been a major feng shui going on for the last year, where old friends are going out and new friends are coming in like crazy, and they're all like-minded." Lynn realized how new friendships help her heal, and those who are unwilling to give as well as take are no longer friends: "I still have my girlfriends from the past, who are great. Gaining these new friends, that are more committed to their healing, has been an even greater support, but if it was going to be an 80–20 relationship or I would not have the relationship, those relationships ended up dying."

Letting go of certain friendships that were not supportive was chal-lenging for many of the participants, yet finding like-minded friends they could speak with was helpful. A crisis gives us an opportunity to wake up and realize what we need. We're unwilling to settle for what no longer serves us, and, unfortunately, friendships that worked only when things were easy is no longer a fit. Also, friendships that were based on who you were are often no longer a fit. In the old you may have indulged in gossip, low energy, or superficial chatter, the newly emerging version of you may find that intolerable. A change in friendships is so common during this stage, and I want you to know about it so it doesn't surprise you if or when it happens. It's not that there's anything wrong with your old group, as you may have energetically outgrown them as you feel a growing need for a tribe that "gets you."

So, as you grieve all that was lost in your betrayal, as you redefine your friendships, and as you write new "rules" around what you will and will no longer accept, it's time for your next transformative activity. This is one of the most important steps during this stage because it turns what may have become your *life* story into a *defining* and pivotal chapter of your story. When you do this, you write your *new* story. To help you get there, let's talk about writing your "coherent narrative."

THE *BENEFIT* OF YOUR BETRAYAL?

So, with this understanding that a grieving process needs to happen and that friendships may definitely change, let's dive into the coherent narrative. Before you do, however, it's important to note how much anger, bitterness, and resentment you're hanging on to. While you may feel justified, right, and entitled to be angry, Dr. Wayne Dyer had a saying I love: "Would you rather be right, or would you rather be happy?" I'm bringing this up because the coherent narrative has you realizing the positives from your experience. Positives? What? Yes.

If you take a minute to think about it with an open mind, you'll realize that the people who hurt you the most are your greatest teachers. They may have taught you what *not* to do, but they taught you nonetheless. They also may have showed you how new boundaries were needed, or they caused you to realize that you're lovable, worthy, and deserving, especially if you never believed that before. They may have showed you how strong you are, or they may even have helped put you on a fantastic new path you *never* would have ventured on had they not done what they did.

There's always a lesson to be learned, and benefiting from that lesson is the least we can give ourselves after we've gone through anything traumatic. If that's not enough of an incentive, this powerful process of writing your coherent narrative has even greater benefits. This process improves your mental and physical health too.[1] In the aftermath of a painful experience, coping can be overwhelming as we move through daily life with a completely altered worldview. The key to coping and adjusting after the experience requires transitioning from a negative perspective to a viewpoint that makes some sense out of the experience while also providing a more positive view of ourselves and the world. It is not that the negative experience is forgotten but rather that a new inner world that we can find comfort from is slowly being created.[2]

WRITING YOUR COHERENT NARRATIVE

So, let's get started. Here are a few questions to start with, and here's what I suggest. Make sure you have the time to do this when you're alone and uninterrupted. Maybe put on some calming music, light a candle, diffuse some essential oils, or do whatever you need to allow your thoughts to flow. When you're ready, write your responses to the questions you'll find here. Don't be fooled by the simplicity of these instructions; this is a powerful exercise, and it's one that members of our PBT Institute Membership Community do and find extremely transformative. Of course, feel free to add any questions that help you and write as much and for as long as you need to. Whatever you do, don't skip this process. It's one of the biggest "needle movers" moving you from where you are to where you want to go. Ready? Answer these questions:

- What did I learn?
- What gift(s) did I receive from this experience?
- How am I better/stronger/wiser because of this experience?
- What new boundaries are in place?
- What will I no longer accept?
- What am I able to see so clearly now?
- How can I use this experience toward my next, best step?
- What has this experience prepared me for?

Were you surprised by anything you wrote? For some, they're grateful and pleasantly surprised by what their experience has taught them. For others, they're holding on to too much anger to even consider seeing any benefit from their experience and find it impossible to do this activity at all. My advice? Take your time here. Continue to do the work and revisit this activity when you're ready. You'd be amazed at how differently you may approach it even a few days from now.

Let's move to another important change that often happens in Stage 4. It's the changing role of religion and spirituality. I'll meet you there.

Stage 4

Finding and Adjusting to a New Normal: The Role of Religion and Spirituality

$\mathcal{T}$here's something else that's common as we're finding and adjusting to a new normal. It's the changing role of spirituality and/or religion. You'll see how important religion and/or spirituality becomes as you continue to heal. The shattering of trust and everything else betrayal creates often creates a spiritual crisis too. You'll see why and how this connection can help take your healing to the next level.

While many of the participants were redefining what they wanted out of their friendships and looking for additional ways to find support during this stage, changes in religion and spirituality emerged during this stage too. Every participant looked toward religion and/or spirituality at some point in their process, especially during this stage, for answers and to find comfort and peace.

Participants had specific ideas about religion and spirituality that changed throughout the phases of their betrayal. Before betrayal, some of the participants were somewhat religious yet struggled with aspects of their religion. Every participant, however, became more spiritual in some way as a result of her experience. This meant a gravitation toward the spiritual side of their religion or abandoning their religion and gravitating toward spirituality alone or even aspects of a different religion.

GRAVITATING TOWARD SPIRITUALITY

Nanette expressed her struggle with her religion because she was made to feel guilty for having "evil thoughts" that her husband was being unfaithful, yet those thoughts were correct. She explained her struggle: "I grew up Catholic. My aunt taught us, 'God forgive us for having such evil thoughts' because we were just talking about what we suspected. Like, oh my God, how could we think such of thing? We were bad. I raised my kids Catholic; it was after that that I struggled with it."

Suzanne's view on religion and spirituality changed as well: "At that time, I really couldn't look at religion or spirituality." Then, about one year after her betrayal, she said, "I read so many self-help books, like Marianne Williamson. All spiritual." Patti remembered, "I don't know, that time I think I just detached because it was something that I wasn't going to understand. At that time, I wasn't deep in my faith. It was a different kind of faith, but it wasn't a deep one. I'm very careful of that today when I pray about something. I don't like to put my own head into it because I will come up with my own answers that make no sense. I went back to church, but it was always like it was a very slow process. I was in and out of that because I didn't trust God. God let me down." Patti also said, "I go to a spiritual adviser, and I don't see the whole thing, and that's why I need her; she goes, 'Do you realize how much you've changed?' I don't. I'm very disconnected, but spirituality keeps me stable throughout everything. I just keep on growing in my spirituality. I think that I'm following more like an inner voice, which has been very difficult for me because I ignored it and I don't trust it. But I'm still pushing ahead. I look at God so differently now than the way I did. I look at God as total spirit in everything, and really, if you're trying to maintain that connection, God is there. I'm the one who distanced myself from God, and when I do, I feel the difference. I don't feel as secure."

Denny originally prayed for strength, sharing, "I don't go to church. I popped into church a few times feeling a little hypocritical like—something's wrong, now, I need you, God. I did start praying religiously every night. I was praying that I have the strength to get through this. That's all I would pray for." Denny's outlook on religion changed too: "I really started praying on a daily basis. I am a spiritual person, but it developed more."

Monica was seeking spirituality and gravitated toward distant relatives who followed the spiritual practice Baha'i: "It's not a religion, it's a spiritual practice. It's all about understanding your inner core, the God within, and to know that it's always there with you." Monica has since deepened her practice of spirituality to include going to local spiritual groups and retreats, which she finds helpful to her healing.

Marie shared, "I was born Catholic and raised Catholic. So, I was having my own spiritual emergence. I was drawn to the mystical component of Catholicism, the nontraditional side of it." After her betrayal, Marie revealed becoming more spiritual: "I went to a holistic healing center and did a study of the chakras once a month and meditation. Deepak Chopra had started the 21-day meditation challenge. Twenty-one days of that just straight changed my life." Lynn remembered, "I feel like I became more spiritual because my grandmother's indigenous, and there's lots of negative things that happened with the church. I had a really hard time, even though I'm Catholic, to accept the Catholic Church. Then, I was teaching at an indigenous school, which is also a nightmare, but the spiritual component of it was really helpful for me. Then, that's been a gateway for me to get back into Christianity a bit. I also started working with a spiritual teacher."

Juliana remembered, "I used to go to church when I was growing up every Sunday. I used to be very religious. That stopped when I got attacked and raped at college, and the church wasn't there for me. It was too much for them to understand, comprehend, and support." Juliana didn't feel supported by her church after her experience in college. After her betrayal, she gravitated toward a more private practice of spirituality: "Anything spiritual I could read, anything I could pick up, anything. Louise L. Hay. It was huge. I also started going to spiritual healing meetings." Now Juliana feels "much more spiritual. Still not religious, it's the spiritual community that I want to be part of."

Jo's betrayal created a need for a deeper connection to find answers to questions she had: "It made me pray and tap into my spirituality much more." The way she prayed changed, however, after her betrayal: "The ability to really start prayer and feel it again, where I think I was for years, just going through the motions and saying the words. Now saying the words, listening, and really getting the message instead of it just being robotic. It was almost the decision was made for me and then I followed it. I listened. That's the spirituality part of it."

Djena remembered turning toward spirituality after her betrayal: "I started going for spiritual classes. I started reading spiritual books, I started meditating." Cleo was not very spiritual before her betrayal. She originally felt "not really that religious, I'm more spiritual." Her perspective changed to "I'm much more spiritual now."

Arielle became more spiritual as a result of her betrayal: "I'm leaning towards being spiritual but not religious." Anne changed her view of religion as well: "I always questioned my religion." After her betrayal, she noticed, "Once that depression started to lift and once I had to pick up the pieces and move on for the sake of my family, then I just prayed to the powers that be." Anne then turned toward spirituality for support: "I was reading spiritual books by Gary Zukav, Deepak Chopra about the soul, about karma."

Dana mentioned struggling with religion since childhood: "I always loved Jesus from the time I was very little, but I always said no to religion. From the time I was five, my mother told me I said that I will not go to church. I stomped my foot that I am not going to church anymore. I always had some sense of my own knowing that church wasn't the place, but Jesus was. I can honestly tell you that I bumped religion forever. Still don't really go there, but as I release the anger, the more anger I released, the closer I became to my authentic self and the closer I became to God."

Many participants were beginning to forge a new path as a result of their betrayal and sought religion or spirituality as a means to help find answers to the appropriate next steps to take. Realizing they could no longer trust their family members or partners and not trusting in their own judgment due to being blindsided by their experience, most participants reasoned that they could still trust in God or a force bigger than themselves. This appeared to be the biggest reason for their changing relationship with religion and spirituality.

SEEING THINGS FROM A SPIRITUAL PERSPECTIVE

Now, to be clear, I'm not suggesting any one spiritual or religious path or practice as the right one. I truly believe that's incredibly personal, and everyone has their own preferences. For me, I can honestly say that spirituality was the glue that brought my "new and awakened" family back together. From a strictly "human" perspective and without any spiritual help, there was zero chance I'd ever try to rebuild a friendship, a relationship, or an eventual remarriage with Adam. From a spiritual perspective, however, it made perfect sense, especially having 10 years of spirituality under my belt by this point. I saw this with Adam and the kids too. Their newly emerging and willing faith led them to trust that "everything happens for a reason," "what doesn't kill us makes us stronger," and "the Universe has our back," even if we don't quite understand what it'll all look like in the end.

Before we leave this chapter, I want to walk you through one last activity. You weren't ready for it earlier when the goal was to survive your experience. Now that things have settled down a bit, it's time. It's another powerful activity that has helped so many of my clients and program members heal. It's a visioning activity, and in this exercise, you'll see who you are at your physical, mental, and emotional best. That vision will become your bull's-eye so that you have a crystal-clear view of what you're working toward. Let's get started with the visioning activity that you're about to learn more about. Ready?

In case you haven't met or seen your best self in a while, there's a version of you who's happy, healthy, empowered, and wise. It's quite possible that that version is hiding beneath a few layers of fear, doubt, insecurity, old habits, prior conditioning, and a few excuses, but that empowered version of you is there, waiting to be unleashed. How do you find, get to know, and *be* your highest self? That's what this visioning activity is all about.

MEETING YOUR WISE INNER GUIDE/ YOUR ULTIMATE YOU

For this exercise, you'll need to have a piece of paper and pen ready that you can put aside for now, but you'll need it soon. Take a nice, deep breath. I'm going to ask you a series of questions, and your job is to create pictures in your mind. Visualize the version of you that matches the questions I ask. Don't overthink, don't judge, and don't critique yourself, just create a visual based on what you're about to read. Okay, now get comfortable, take a deep breath, and start picturing the ultimate you as I ask these questions.

Visualize yourself at your physical, mental, and emotional best, your personal and professional best, and start settling into that space. Once you've settled into that vision, picture your health. What's your health like at your physical, mental, and emotional best and your personal and professional best?

Once you've visualized your health, picture your energy. What's your energy like at your physical, mental, and emotional best and your personal and professional best?

Once you've pictured your health and your level of energy, visualize your body. What does your body look like at your physical, mental, and emotional best and your personal and professional best? See what your body looks like with that level of health and energy when you are at your physical, mental, and emotional best and your personal and professional best.

Once you've visualized what your body looks like with that level of health and energy, imagine what you're wearing. What are you wearing when you are at your physical, mental, and emotional best and your personal and professional best? Is there a certain style, a certain designer? Specific colors? See what you are wearing when you're at your physical, mental, and emotional best and your personal and professional best. What are you wearing with that body at that level of health and energy at your physical, mental, and emotional best and your personal and professional best?

Once you've pictured what you're wearing on that body with that level of health and energy, visualize what you're doing when you're at your physical, mental, and emotional best and your personal and professional best. What are you doing as you wear that outfit on that body with that level of health and energy?

Once you visualized what you're doing with that outfit on that body with that level of health and energy, imagine who's with you. Is there one person, or are many people with you?

Who's with you when you're at your physical, mental, and emotional best and your personal and professional best? Who's with you as you're doing what you're doing, wearing what you're wearing on that body with that level of health and energy? You're at your physical, mental, and emotional best and your personal and professional best.

Once you imagine who's with you, whether many people, one person, or no one, imagine that you're wrapping up whatever it is you're doing and that person or those people are leaving. What are they saying about having spent time with you in this way? What are the words they say and the feelings they have after spending time with you in this way, when you were doing what you were doing, wearing that outfit on that body with that level of health and energy?

You're at your physical, mental, and emotional best and your personal and professional best.

Once you've visualized all of that, imagine that you've wrapped up what you've been doing and you're getting ready to go. How do you feel having spent time in that way with that person or those people while you were doing what it was you were doing, wearing that outfit on that body with that level of health and energy? How do you feel about contributing in that way?

Once you've pictured the boldest, brightest, clearest vision you can, once you can clearly see what you were doing and who you were with, what you were wearing, the body you had, and the health and energy you had, once that vision is bold and bright, vibrant and clear, slowly open your eyes and write down exactly what you saw.

What did you see? How did you look? What were you doing? How did you feel? You never would have seen that version of you if it didn't exist. What you saw is your bull's-eye and the clear target of the ultimate and unshakable you. Do you want proof? Look around at the space you're in now. Every single thing that exists went through three steps.

CREATING AND THEN LIVING AS THE ULTIMATE YOU

First it was envisioned, then it was expressed, and then it was created. It works the same way with you. You envisioned what you want, you wrote it down and expressed it, and now it's just a matter of creating it. Now that you've done steps 1 and 2, how do you get to step 3? Let's track back to see what you have to do to get there so you can take strategic action toward it. Let's say you envisioned yourself as being strong and empowered with a lean, fit, healthy body. For you to have that body, you had to start working out and eating healthier. Get the idea?

What can you do to make your vision real and move yourself toward what you imagined?

This activity helps you become empowered, too, because that ultimate version of you has every answer you need. That version of you knows how to eat, work out, think, act, behave, and react in a healthy way, so why not consult with that vision? Imagine that something comes up and instead of having a typical reflexive response, you think, "Hmm, what would Ultimate (insert your name) do?" How would the highest and best version of me handle this situation or work through this challenge?

I know you may not believe this yet, but you have all those answers, and if you start from this moment forward acting, behaving, and responding as that highest and best version of you, watch how fast you will become that person. I consistently see this happen with my clients. They are blown away with how they show up when they respond from that place, whether they're getting over a relationship, trying to create a new one, changing careers, working on health issues, dealing with an annoying relative, or handling any number of situations. Responding and making decisions as the highest and ultimate version of you is a game changer. The key to becoming your personal best is to envision it. When that vision is crystal clear, it's only a matter of gradual, steady steps consistently taken to get to wherever you want to go.

Just like the others, we covered a lot in this chapter. As you can see, each stage builds on the previous one and continues to make you stronger, wiser and better. Let's move on to Stage 5, a beautiful stage in your healing process. I'll meet you there.

Stage 5

Healing, Rebirth, and a New Worldview:
What Healing Can Look Like

$\mathcal{A}$s a more solid footing, a more stable foundation, and greater clarity begin to emerge, we begin to heal. This healing happens physically, mentally, and emotionally. Physically, we turn down the stress response, so the body stops breaking down and begins to rebuild. Because our old belief system and the way we viewed the world no longer exists, we mentally start to create a new set of beliefs based on what works for us now. Emotionally, we feel less anxious, chaotic, and stressed, which allows us to create a new version of ourselves based on who we're becoming.

Now that we've found a way to survive our experience and have settled into a new normal, we have the bandwidth to focus on ourselves more than we were able to during the previous stages. We're more interested in our own self-care as we realize we deserve nurturing and we're worth it. This sets the tone for Stage 5, which is about healing, rebirth, and a new worldview. Also, remember the table with two legs from Stage 1, which was wobbly and unstable? Now we're much more solidly grounded, focusing on all four of the table legs: mental, physical, emotional, and spiritual.

It's important to understand that moving into this stage isn't a guarantee and happens only when you've done the work to move through the prior stages. So how do you know you're moving forward and healing?

WHAT HEALING CAN LOOK LIKE AT STAGE 5

Finding practical solutions to survive your experience, breaking the cycle of feeding a negative thought/feeling loop, and rewiring your mind for more positive thoughts are signs that you're healing. Making sense and meaning out of your experience along with a willingness to change also represent healing at this stage. You may also notice that while the triggers are still there, they don't carry the same emotional charge that they did in the past.

Other changes may be present as well. You may notice that you have more energy or that you're shedding weight (particularly around your midsection, which is where cortisol, one of the stress hormones, drives fat storage). You may be sleeping more soundly, may feel less anxious, and may have a greater ability to focus and concentrate. You may feel more inclined to be more social, eat healthier, exercise, and take greater measures toward your own self-care. You may notice that your digestive issues improve and that you need less or don't need any medication at all for what you'd been taking it for in the past. You may notice your skin clearing, a stronger immune system, and a more positive perspective.

You may also feel more comfortable removing yourself from a situation that just doesn't feel right while feeling more inspired to try something that may have felt too challenging in the past. You may find that things that bothered you previously seem insignificant now, that you're bolder and more compassionate, or that your tolerance level for anyone or anything that isn't kind, fair, or peaceful just doesn't have a place in your life. You may realize your work isn't fulfilling and it's time to pursue that new venture, or you may experience a level of peace and contentment that you never felt before. Everyone's healing looks different, but what's common at this stage is that the new you that's being birthed is different on every level—it's like "You Version 2.0."

IF YOU'RE NOT HEALING, HERE'S WHY

While these types of changes are common at this stage, there's no guarantee, and here's why. If you haven't taken the time to manage those painful triggers that send you down that path of pain, if you haven't grieved the loss of what you'll no longer have, if you refuse to accept your betrayal, and if you haven't taken steps to move forward based on where you are now, it's virtually impossible to heal. Also, if fear keeps you from making changes to your relationship with the person who betrayed you, if you're unwilling to seek support, and if you refuse to do anything differently, it's pretty obvious that change can't happen either. You know the definition of insanity, right? "Doing the same thing over and over again and expecting a different result." Nothing changes until you do, and betrayal offers a beautiful gift. It sets the stage for transformation if you're willing to use the experience as an opportunity to learn and grow.

WHAT PREVENTS HEALING

I mentioned this in an earlier chapter, and it's important to mention it again here. There were a few participants in the study who stayed stuck, and their resistance to move forward was always due to a handful of circumstances. Some refused to face their betrayal head-on. They found the pain so unbearable and counted on medication, alcohol, or avoidance tactics to ease, numb, or distract themselves from it. While they believed these strategies may have helped them, the study clearly showed that the more something was used to dull, distract from, or numb feelings, the longer it took to heal or the less likely it was that the person would heal at all.

A lack of consequences for the betrayer also prevented healing. If the betrayer was allowed to continue their abusive behavior, they did. Without a consequence powerful enough to shake up the betrayer and encourage change, the only change that occurred was a slow deterioration of the relationship along with the betrayed participant growing increasingly discouraged, numb, frustrated, powerless, hopeless, and physically sick.

Finally, a refusal to accept their betrayal, grieve the change in their relationship, and make meaning out of the experience prevented some participants from healing too. They clung to what they had, refusing to acknowledge that what they had no longer existed. In other words, they refused to grieve the loss. Staying stuck along with an unwillingness to accept their circumstances, fueled by rigidity, righteousness, bitterness, and a powerful sense of injustice, prevented their growth and healing. Of course, they had every right to feel those feelings, but hanging on to them kept them painfully imprisoned.

POSITIVE PHYSICAL CHANGES YOU MAY EXPERIENCE

For those who did move into this stage—which includes me, the majority of participants, as well as most of the clients I work with and members of the PBT Institute Membership Community from all over the world—lots of exciting healing took place. In this stage, most of my study participants noticed changes with their bodies. All lost weight and started to exercise more. Many noticed that chronic illnesses, particularly digestive issues, dramatically improved. One participant, Cleo, reported, "My acid reflux—completely gone." Juliana noticed a drastic change in her colitis symptoms that had previously taken her to the hospital on a regular basis, saying, "I haven't had a colitis attack in three years."

Remember in a previous chapter when I was talking about digestive issues being an inability to "digest," "process," and "absorb"? In Stage 5, we're better able to digest, process, and absorb our betrayals; we've calmed down our nervous systems, and we've strengthened our "gut." Is it any wonder that digestive issues healed once we've done all that?

For other participants, their energy started to come back, and sleep issues simply stopped. Improvements in clarity, outlook, and perspectives were also common. Within this stage, participants became increasingly clear about what they were and were not willing to tolerate in friendships, partnerships, and opportunities. New boundaries were created and maintained. Self-esteem began to increase, as did self-love and self-acceptance. Greater understanding, purpose, and meaning were evident during this stage as well, as participants expressed new priorities and directions based on their new worldview.

Remember when I talked about the small self-benefits of staying stuck? Sure, you may have received sympathy, you had your story, you had someone to blame, and more, but in this stage, we realize how much better the rewards are when we let those things go. We get a much better story that we get to be the hero or heroine of, we get to physically heal, we get freedom, we gain an entirely new perspective on life, and so much more.

OTHER EXCITING CHANGES

Having made it this far, you'll also be rewarded with a renewed sense of readiness to pursue opportunities for self-love and self-care. I'll talk you through some supportive activities that you might want to try, like yoga, journaling, reading, music, cooking, joining a class, learning a new skill, changing careers, and more. What's a fit for you during this stage? I'll give you lots of ideas to choose from. Practice using your newly strengthened intuition to know what's right for you.

By this point, participants adjusted to a new normal, which meant accepting their new lives after betrayal. They made adjustments with regard to their religion or spirituality, which helped them feel supported and safe in placing their trust in something once again. Changes with regard to friendships occurred as well, as unsupportive friendships faded away and supportive, like-minded friendships began to form.

As a more solid footing, a more stable foundation, and greater clarity began to emerge, participants began to heal. These improvements occurred on every level: body, mind, and spirit. During this stage, greater attention was now being placed on all aspects of healing everything that was damaged by the betrayal as opposed to a focus on only certain aspects of themselves. During this stage, a new worldview based on what they had experienced began to form as well. These changes in healing, along with a new emerging worldview, lead us to my favorite stage: Stage 5.

Cleo, Suzanne, Djena, Denny, Lynn, Arielle, and Marie shared changes they noticed with their bodies. They all lost weight and started to exercise more. Monica believed that her love for dance and movement possibly saved her from a multitude of illnesses she would have experienced had she "kept all that negative energy stuck." Cleo said, "I lost 40 pounds." Digestive issues for Cleo, Djena, Suzanne, Denny, and Juliana dramatically improved as well. Suzanne: "I noticed going to the bathroom became more regular."

This stage revealed improvements in physical, mental, and emotional health. New ways in which to view others, the world, and themselves began emerging during this time as well. Before and during their betrayals, greater attention was placed on physical and mental tasks. This stage also revealed a movement toward greater balance between physical, mental, emotional, and spiritual needs. So many great changes happened during this stage, and here's more.

Anne and some of the other participants remembered their energy starting to come back, and sleep issues also began improving. Cleo remembered, "I've always had problems sleeping. I'd have to take a sleeping pill every night. I'm off the pills." Juliana's hair stopped falling out, and she noticed she was getting sick less frequently. Patti's neck and shoulder pain healed. Suzanne and Marie both remember changes in their complexion. Marie was hearing comments such as "Oh my God. You're so radiant."

During this stage, they started taking their own needs into consideration and began taking better care of themselves. Participants noticed other changes during this time as well. Jo stopped taking the mood stabilizers and antidepressants, remarking that she didn't need them anymore. Suzanne stopped smoking and started eating healthier and exercising, remembering, "My body started to feel a little bit lighter. I think all that horrible emotional baggage, as we know, it affects everything. My head started to become a little less foggy. The cloud, the funk all started to lift. I started lifting my head, and things started opening, and I could start to see more of a panoramic view, as opposed to a very tunnel-vision type of view."

Other mental and emotional changes occurred as well. Djena's panic attacks lessened due to taking better care of herself and a tremendous change in her thinking. Anne remembered, "It lightened up with the depression, that definitely started to subside." Cleo found she had a more positive outlook. Arielle noticed she was happier, and Jo noticed clarity as well as an internal and steady calmness: "It's not that emotional seesaw." Juliana remembered, "The noise went away."

These positive changes and growing through their betrayal led to new perspectives and priorities. Some of the participants noted a new perspective in how they view others and how they view the world. They also noted the emergence of a new personal strength. Arielle recalled, "I'm stronger and enjoying being comfortable with myself and building a whole new life. My world became so much broader." Denny now feels independent, which she didn't feel before her betrayal: "I started to feel very independent. I looked better, I felt better, I had more confidence. I was thinking more positive." Nanette became more independent as well: "I've become a very independent woman, and I can take care of myself, and I do not need a man to survive, and I never will, ever."

Djena had an entirely new perspective with regard to how she views the world, now seeing through a lens of gratitude: "I have such gratitude. Peace, gratitude. You start to feel good, and you realize that taking care of yourself and being grateful is what's making you feel good." Juliana noted her growing trust in the Universe, which helped give her strength to continue to heal: "I started trusting the Universe." Patti noticed a growing appreciation and change in priorities to what she'd previously paid less attention to: "I was able to appreciate things around me, little things, a good conversation with somebody, a positive conversation, a positive interaction." Anne noticed, "I started to become a lot more independent and just self-sufficient." Dana acknowledged a growing sense of personal power and strength: "I felt empowered, I felt secure, and I felt so awesome." Monica noticed changes in how authentically she began relating to others as she grew more secure and comfortable with herself: "I'm more alive, more authentic, and more real." Patti shared how her changes strengthened aspects of herself that needed to be healed: "I feel more authentic. I really feel like I am much more whole than I used to be."

Some participants noted being more comfortable with themselves, being alone yet not feeling lonely. They noticed less of a need to have the television or music on as they noticed less "mind chatter" and a growing comfort with silence. Juliana recalled, "I stopped having to have the TV on. I stopped having to have music on. I actually liked the quiet. I liked to be by myself. I started to enjoy my own company. That was bizarre. That was something different."

A NEW ME EMERGING

This was a powerful stage for me as well. I remember feeling a strength and confidence slowly emerge that I never felt before. All of those years of feeling insecure or uncomfortable in certain situations just seemed to disappear, and the more opportunities I gave myself to test it, the more it was confirmed. The situations that used to make me nervous, afraid, or worried just didn't have that tight grip on me anymore. It was almost as if my highest self was saying, "Oh darling, you're going to let *that* bother you? After what you've been through? That's *way* too trivial."

I started making myself—my needs, hopes, wishes, and dreams— a priority. I stopped "should-ing" on myself and started saying no to things more often. I took my spiritual practice more seriously—seeing and feeling the difference in myself whenever I did. I felt more centered, more at peace, and calmer. I started being more deliberate in what I said yes to—if it didn't make me feel good, I just wouldn't do it. I started to better manage my guilt in trying to be everything to everyone all the time. I realized I need and deserve downtime, and if my body needed rest, that's what I gave it.

I also realized that I was highly sensitive and an empath (more about this in an upcoming chapter) and started to understand why I couldn't tolerate superficial conversation and why I needed to recover after being at parties or conferences with all of those personalities and all of that energy. I started spending more time having deeper, more meaningful conversations, and I stopped judging others. That was huge for me as I realized that everyone acts from their current level of consciousness (as Maya Angelou said, "When you know better, you do better") and that, from where they were at the time, that was the best they could offer. It didn't excuse the bad behavior, but my judgment around it fell away.

I started doing things that held more meaning and significance. At the same time, it was the small, seemingly insignificant things that began to mean more. I found myself having a greater appreciation for nature, kindness, the strength of the human spirit, integrity, family, friendship, and love. I started to see a much deeper meaning behind what words couldn't express and saw the hope, faith, and resilience in others.

When it came to my work, new programs, products, and services kept "downloading," and it felt as if I couldn't build this new business and brand fast enough. I started speaking about the topic regularly, and the more I did, the more my confidence grew. It didn't start out the way, though. Early in my healing, I was moving through all of these stages and slowly learning to rebuild trust—rebuilding it just the way I taught you how to do. I was still nervous and uncomfortable, but something shifted soon after my betrayal. It was only six weeks after my entire world came to a crashing halt (the day I discovered my husband's betrayal) that I did my first TEDx talk, an honor that I excitedly yet nervously said yes to. I wasn't yet ready to share my story, but intuitively I knew that this talk was important for me and my healing. People comment on that talk all the time, saying that it impacted them. I was in so such pain and turmoil, but during those few minutes and only weeks after my betrayal, I could feel that a stronger version of me was already under way.

Then going back to school and all of the changes that decision created led to lots more changes as well. While I was happy to share all that the study found, however, I still wasn't willing to be so vulnerable sharing my personal experience with betrayal to a big audience. Yes, I feared judgment, criticism, and everything else that was sure to come my way. That's when my coach (I believe every good coach needs a coach) saw what I'd been doing and called me out on it.

We were on a group video call where all of the members of our mastermind group (an amazing group of health-and-wellness entrepreneurs) were sharing what we'd all been doing over the past few weeks. It was my turn to share, and I was talking about new programs, new talks, the study, and so on. He let me finish then said the words I'll never forget: "Stop hiding behind your *@!#! study already. People can't relate to you if they don't know where you've been!" My stomach sank, and I felt that truth hit me right between the eyeballs. He was right. It was my fear that kept me focused on everything "the study discovered" and not on my own story. I knew that private clients were transforming from me sharing my story with them because it gave them hope and the idea that if I could heal, they could too. I just was so uncomfortable being that vulnerable. I felt my highest self nudge me into this new level of growth, and I knew it was time to share my story with others—not in the "airing dirty laundry" type of sharing but coming from the intention of helping others through my journey.

I sat my entire family down because it was going to affect all of them. After all, this is the type of news that gossip thrives on, and I was about to give people lots of fuel. It didn't matter. The gossip, judgment, and criticism felt petty when I compared it to how helpful this message would be for those who needed it. My family agreed, and I'm so proud of all of them. I was expecting "Really mom? It's *so* embarrassing" or anything else they may have said. They didn't, and instead they rallied, somehow subconsciously knowing it would be great for all of us. Who was my biggest cheerleader and supporter? Adam. I wasn't sure what to expect; I mean, here's a new business and brand built off of the pain he'd caused, and now with a completely new worldview and some serious spirituality under his belt too, he understood things so differently as well. He also knew that while many people will judge, his transformation would give others hope that people can and do change. He also realized that true love means being okay with what's in the best interest of the one you love, even if it's awkward or uncomfortable. Stage 5 is definitely transformative, and the levels of growth and healing can be so life changing—for you as well as for those around you.

This was something I noticed too. The changes that participants experienced weren't always perfectly linear, and, in fact, they often appeared chaotic, muddled, disorganized, and complex. For example, participants who healed to some extent but not fully still experienced healing and growth yet still struggled with issues regarding trusting enough to believe in healthy relationships as Lynn expressed. While many of the participants pursued personal growth books and activities, Denny felt it would help her gain a better understanding of her situation by reading books that would confirm her painful experience. Finally, while many of the participants chose to remove themselves from life with their betrayer, Anne chose to deal with the health consequences she believes were experienced because she chose to stay.

Every participant experienced growth, and every participant eventually found a greater balance between their physical, mental, emotional, and social needs. However, while these changes were all experienced, some participants experienced greater changes and at different rates and extremes than others. It was clear that the "face it, feel it, heal it" mantra was definitely a recipe for healing, while numbing, avoiding, and distracting kept healing at bay. Also, being afraid or preventing the betrayer from experiencing any consequences for their actions not only prevented healing but also created lots of physical as well as mental and emotional illnesses.

Join me in the next chapter, where I'll be explaining two other elements common to this stage too. I'm going to explain two very interesting experiences that seem so odd—until you understand why they're presenting themselves. One has to do with conflicting emotions and bittersweet reflections. This understanding will show you how our new perspective allows for a much fuller and richer way to move through your new life. The second element is about some intense confusion that can feel unsettling—until you understand that it's *that* confusion that serves as your subconscious "think tank," where your next best move can be birthed. I'll meet you there.

Stage 5

Healing, Rebirth, and a New Worldview: Conflicting Emotions/Bittersweet Reflections/ Confusion and Self-Care

$\mathcal{T}$here were two other interesting features I noticed in this beautiful stage, and understanding them will help put your mind at ease if you're experiencing these things too. I'll explain what they are so you're not surprised when you see them. The first involves conflicting emotions and bittersweet reflections, which are common in Stage 5 and give your new life more depth and texture. The other is about an overwhelming sense of confusion that can suddenly appear at this time. That confusion can feel so unsettling—but it's actually something to welcome because clarity, purpose, and a new direction often emerge once the dust settles. Let's start with the conflicting emotions and bittersweet reflections that are common to see in Stage 5.

CONFLICTING EMOTIONS/BITTERSWEET REFLECTIONS

Each of the Fab 14 felt stronger than they had felt before their betrayals, and they all acknowledged growing through adversity. However, there were many conflicting and contradictory emotions that surfaced during this time. Anne, who is a warm and loving woman, felt, "I became a lot tougher around the edges." Other participants noted how they are "loving yet hardened" and "cautious yet trusting." Some of the participants were grateful for their freedom yet sad that their vision of a happy family would not come to pass. Others realized that although they didn't want their relationships to end, they were glad it was over.

Lynn was glad she's healing yet struggles with the idea that she may not have a family of her own. Both Dana and Lynn expressed their disappointment with the realization that while they believe that faith and trust should be expected, both of those concepts present a challenge for them. Lynn believes that "in some ways, it's damaged me to have less trust and less faith in people. I struggle with that. However, based on this lifetime and the family that I grew up in, I feel like it was inevitable."

Participants noticed other conflicting emotions too. Many realized that they still may be fearful, yet they're more likely to move beyond their fears and try something anyway. Some participants noted a sense of feeling a combination of fear and fearlessness at the same time. Some also noted that while it's uncomfortable to ask for help, they've learned to overcome their hesitation and ask for the help they need anyway. They've not only learned to give but are more open to receiving as well. Some felt guilty breaking up a family yet changed the living arrangements in the family anyway, believing that their decision was ultimately what was best.

Some of the participants noticed the desire to react when treated unfairly yet chose to be less reactive when conflicts arose. Some of the participants wanted to punish their betrayer yet realized those actions would punish themselves and their families, so they chose to diffuse their anger in other ways. Finally, many of the participants shared that they experienced a great sense of injustice yet chose to allow forces beyond themselves to right the wrong they felt through their betrayals. I definitely experienced conflicting emotions as well. For me, there was a new level of vulnerability and, at the same time, a new level of courage. There was a fear in not knowing whom to trust yet an undeniable knowing that I could trust in myself and the Universe. There was a fear of the unknown yet a fearlessness about how to approach something new. Finally, there was a sadness of what was lost yet an excitement about the possibilities that lie ahead.

Not only were many emotions conflicting, but there were dramatic changes in emotions from before to after each participant's experience with betrayal. Many began their journey feeling naive yet now feel wise and empowered. Many participants felt uncertain and insecure and now feel certain and confident. Many have gone from perceptions of self-loathing to self-loving, and some participants have changed from being emotionally and financially dependent to being financially free as well as free of another person's opinions of them.

Still other participants have gone from being unhappy to happy, ungrateful to filled with gratitude, and others have gone from feeling restricted to free. Finally, most participants realized that while the pain caused by those who betrayed them was greater than what they ever thought they could handle, they're grateful for the growth and the lessons their experience has provided. As Monica shared with a smile earned through growth, "I turned my mess into a message."

So, what about you? Can you feel the emotions on both sides of your experience? I truly believe that's what makes us so much stronger, wiser, and more empowered after an experience with betrayal. We become richer and deeper as a broader range of emotions have become available to us. These changes allow for a much different perspective now that we've "been there and back." It feels as if we've gone from the little box of eight crayons in the box to the big box with every color imaginable—along with that cool crayon sharpener that comes with it. From this space, life offers so much more depth, color, and texture because of where we've been, what we've learned, and the road we took to get there.

Before I give you some ideas for self-love and self-care that you're ready for if you're in this stage, there's something else that often comes up around this time. I want to make sure you know about it so it's not a surprise if you find yourself here. It's a place of intense confusion and, it's easy to get upset about, but it's actually a sign that you're exactly where you should be. Here's what I mean.

After something like betrayal, we're shattered, we're reeling from our crisis, and then we get to this place of intense confusion. I see so many people getting so down on themselves as they say, "Why am I so confused? I don't want to do what I was doing before, but I don't know what to do now." It's like they had a plan and now can barely figure out what to do next.

WHY CONFUSION IS A GOOD THING

Since you know I love analogies, I'm going to give you a visual reference to help understand this. Imagine you're running as fast as you can in one direction. You're running at full speed, and then all of a sudden you realize, "Oh my gosh, this direction is not taking me where I want

to go." Once you make that realization, you slow down because there's
no point in continuing to run in that direction anymore. Picture what
happens next. You slow down enough to pivot in a different direction.
Now you're facing the new direction, which feels like the one you're
meant to run on. It becomes crystal clear from this vantage point that
the path you're now seeing is the one you're meant to travel. So, now
that it's clear, you get yourself ready to run in that new and completely
different direction that's going to take you to where you're now ready
to go. You start moving in the new direction, which is headed toward
something wonderful. This confusion we may be experiencing is that
same space (the realization, slowing down, pivoting, and redirecting)
right before the new direction is crystal clear.

What the confusion represents is that life as you've known it,
the old paradigm, the old routine, the old way, has come to an end—
whether intentionally or unintentionally. It's not that what you were
doing was wrong because every experience provides an opportunity
to learn and grow. What could that lesson be for you? Whatever your
particular lesson is, that crash leading to that confusion is *your* realization
that that old version, those old rules, and that whole old way no longer
work. You're ready to see, feel, and experience something new.

When the dust settles from all of that, you slowly learn, "Wow,
okay, *this* is what I want. This is what I need. These are the new rules,
and this is what I can see so clearly now." *That's* what emerges from that
confusion you may be experiencing maybe right this very moment. It
looks like confusion, but there's a lot going on beneath the surface. It's
really the end of an old way to think, feel, and act before the new way
is uncovered, discovered, and revealed. That unsettling confusion often
leads to intense and amazing clarity.

I remember this so well. There I was knowing who I was, what I
was doing, and how to go about each day. Then this intense confusion
set in, and suddenly none of that made sense anymore, yet I didn't know
what was next. This confused state is the perfect place to practice your
intuition because you're going to start getting those intuitive nudges that
you'll be able to recognize only if you're paying attention. Wouldn't
you know, that's exactly when I decided to go back for a PhD and con-
duct the study, and, as they say, "the rest is history." This is a time to
be open-minded, listen fully, stay curious, and trust your gut. Messages
will be on the way—just be sure not to rule them out as coincidences

or shrug them off with a simple "Hmm, that's weird." Those are the messages that'll most likely lead you to your next, best step. So, consider that confusion may just be the stage right before a big "aha moment." You've been running so hard and so fast in one direction that's just not in your best interest anymore. You realize it. You stop. You pivot. You're about to run in a new direction based on where you are now. That confusion you're feeling *is* that realize, stop, and pivot right before you take off on a new and exciting path. Trust this process, although it's uncomfortable, it typically leads to intense and amazing clarity.

SELF-CARE STRATEGIES YOU'RE READY FOR NOW

Before we leave this section, let's talk about a few self-care and self-love strategies that may be a fit for you now. While there are many reasons to take good care of yourself, there are a few reasons that you may want to now. One reason is because you now have the bandwidth and interest. When you were figuring out how you'd survive your experience, self-care may have been the farthest thing from your mind. Now that life has settled down a bit, you may find that self-care is becoming more of a priority. You also may want to treat yourself better because you realize you've been through so much and you deserve it. You may also decide that as you create new rules for yourself and others, treating yourself with more love and kindness may just be a new rule that has now become nonnegotiable. If you've been spending more time with new like-minded friends, you may find that self-care helps them stay grounded, healthy, and present, so you want to give it a try too. Finally, self-love and self-care may have become an integral part of your daily routine that's helping to create the healthy, happy, and healed version of you. You're seeing that it makes you feel good and contributes to your healing, so you want to get more of these routines and practices into your life.

So, let's take a look at some of the major categories in your life, possibly health, relationships, work, spirituality, community, education, and so on. You're going to consider every category and see what needs some extra attention. Take health, for example. How can you show yourself a bit more self-love and self-care in this category? Can you start using a meal prep delivery service and create healthy and delicious meals? Can you buy healthier foods, eat less junk food, or drink more water? Can you do more yoga, take more walks in nature, or join a local health club?

With regard to relationships, can you make it a point to call your friends more often, reconnect with someone you lost touch with, or seek out like-minded friends based on who you are now? Can you say no to that draining friend who constantly dumps her problems on you because you're such a great listener but is always somehow busy when you need to talk? Can you deepen your relationships by being more fully present when you're spending time with others? Can you put your phone away when you're with the ones you love?

With your work, can you determine if it's rewarding and fulfilling? If not, can you start moving toward something that is? If you can't leave your current position, is there a way to make it more interesting and satisfying?

With religion and spirituality, can you deepen your practice, read or listen to more thought leaders you admire, or set up a quiet space for your daily routine? Can you get a beautiful journal, crystals, or some type of religious or spiritual symbol that helps you connect more fully? Can you go to conferences, workshops, or online summits where you can learn from leaders you admire?

With regard to education, is there a class you want to take or a certification or degree you want to pursue? Can you commit to reading or listening to more personal development, business, health, or other topics you find interesting? Is it time to learn another language with the intention to visit that country once you're fluent in that language?

It's endless what you can do here. I know people who've moved to a new location to represent a new start, begin a new business, start a health journey, write a book, and so much more. You certainly don't have to do them all—just realize that your new life and everything about it is completely up to you. As the poet Mary Oliver said, "Tell me, what is it you plan to do with your one wild and precious life?"

You've come such a long way! Meet me in the next part of this book, where we take your healing to a whole new level. I'll meet you there.

III

MOVING FORWARD
AS A BRAND NEW YOU

· 12 ·

Forgiveness

Why It's So Hard and So Transformative

This chapter is an extension of the work done in Stage 5, only it's like Stage 5 on steroids. It's next-level healing that everyone needs to experience if they're going to continue to grow and transform. Here's what I've found: forgiveness is just a word—until you're called to do it. It can be one of the most challenging aspects of healing we undertake as well as one of the most transformative. Forgiveness speaks a language that the logical, rational mind doesn't understand. Think about it. Your betrayer said or did something hateful, harmful, or hurtful. If you were to tell anyone about it, they'd likely agree. You were following the rules, and your betrayer, without your awareness or consent, chose to disregard those rules for any number of reasons. The pain is deep, and there may be absolutely no sense of justice, retribution, apology, or even acknowledgment by the person you trusted who hurt you. Forgiveness says, yes that's true, and for *your* sake—not your betrayer's—forgive anyway. Huh?

In this chapter, we'll explore forgiveness on its own and when you may be considering re-creating the relationship with the person who hurt you. For that, we'll talk about the "if–then" rule of forgiving, when forgiving allows us to feel better and when it makes us feel worse. We'll dive into why it takes time to forgive and how closely related the forgiveness time line is to how quickly or slowly we're able to trust again. We'll talk about the unique language of forgiveness, what withholding forgiveness does to us physically, and the profound healing we experience when we let go and choose to forgive.

I'll share the emotions that encourage forgiveness, the "window of willingness" where we go from the most likely to the least likely to

165

forgive, and the false sense of control we may be clinging to in an effort to regain control after an experience with betrayal. Finally, I'll show you how withholding forgiveness (even though you believe you have every right to) is keeping *you* a prisoner in a prison you exclusively hold the key to. It may not be easy—and I'll talk about what creeps in to make it so challenging. But don't worry. You'll learn how to slay those sneaky dragons testing your resilience and strength.

I'll also share two very personal stories. One story involves forgiving and letting go of a very close family member. This person was so toxic that the relationship caused physical, mental, and emotional symptoms like digestive issues, hair loss, skin problems, extreme fatigue, hormonal issues, anxiety, depression, weight gain, insulin resistance, brain fog, sleeplessness, a suppressed immune system, chronic fatigue syndrome, Hashimoto's thyroiditis, arthritis, bursitis, and tendonitis, to name a few. Cutting the toxic tie to this relationship was one of my most challenging yet significant actions that helped me heal. Forgiving was the other action that allowed for complete and total healing. The other story is the one I'm committed to and working on daily: forgiving and rebuilding with my husband. In one of my stories, you'll see what complete and total forgiveness and moving on without the person looks like. In the other, you'll see what forgiving and rebuilding a relationship looks like using a very real example of a hopeful "work in progress." We have a lot of ground to cover, so let's dive in.

WHAT IS FORGIVENESS ANYWAY?

So what's forgiveness anyway? It's been defined as "the 'cancellation of a debt' by the person who has been hurt or wronged"[1] And "true forgiveness, requires the ability to see others in realistic terms (both the good and the bad) and to hold them accountable to natural consequences, yet still be able to feel compassion, empathy, or some degree of positive feelings for them."[2]

Forgiveness helps create a doorway to move past our experiences with betrayal.[3] While not all of my participants chose to forgive their betrayers, some found it a healthy way to encourage greater peace. I know you may have heard that forgiveness really has nothing to do with the other person and has everything to do with you. It's true, but personally, even with that understanding, it doesn't necessarily make it much easier to do. What I did learn, though, was how powerful and transformative it can be.

I remember reading one study that talked about three phases of forgiveness. The first phase is about a new realistic view of the relationship based on what you've just experienced. Next, there's a release of the control over the consequences the action has created. The third phase includes less of a need to punish the person who hurt you. This process allows you to slowly create positive change.[4] Through forgiveness, there can be a lessening of control that the painful experience has on us. There can also be a healing of "inner emotional wounds."[5]

WHY FORGIVENESS CAN BE SO CHALLENGING

Forgiveness is often difficult for people who've been betrayed because of the painful emotions left in the wake of a betrayal. It's the disruption of that relationship by something painful and/or unexpected leading to a feeling of being unsafe and diminished. This is why forgiveness can be especially challenging after a betrayal.[6] It can also be hard because betrayal has us feeling like everything has been taken out of our control. Whether we forgive or not feels like something that we have control over, so we may not be so quick to forgive if we believe we're handing over the little control we feel that withholding forgiveness offers us.

Let's talk about forgiving with the possibility of re-creating a relationship with the person who hurt you. Remember, forgiveness is something helpful to do anyway; for now, we're just talking about using it as a guide with regard to rebuilding a new relationship with the person who betrayed you. Studies have found that we're more likely to forgive when we sense remorse: the admission of wrongdoing and apology.[7] Remorse and apology were found to be the single greatest reasons people grant or withhold forgiveness.[8] This happens because with these actions in place, we feel more valued and respected, which leads to the if–then rule when it comes to forgiveness (with regard to rebuilding with the same person).

THE IF–THEN RULE AND
WHAT WE NEED TO SEE TO FORGIVE

Here's what it is. If the betrayer signals that the betrayed and the re-lationship are safe and valuable, forgive. If the betrayer signals that the betrayed and the relationship are not safe and valuable, don't forgive. Here's why the researchers suggested that. When we forgive and we don't feel safe and valued, it creates low self-respect. On the other hand, when we feel safe and valued, then choose to forgive, as it increases our level of self-respect.[9] I want to take it a step further, and here's what I suggest. To avoid any confusion, replace the word *forgive* with *reconcile* because I believe it's in your best interest to forgive regardless of whether you rebuild with the person who hurt you or not. When I say reconcile, I mean forgiving and rebuilding a new relationship with the person who hurt you. I want you to heal regardless of what you choose to do, and forgiveness helps you do that.

So, if you replace the word "forgive" with "reconcile," then the if–then rule changes to this: If you feel safe and valued, then reconcile (only if you want to, of course). If you don't feel safe and valued, then don't reconcile. Forgiving regardless of what you choose is for *your* sake. Doesn't that make even more sense?

Forgiveness can also be challenging when we look at it as an all-or-nothing proposition, so it's helpful to give ourselves credit for be-ing willing to try. Personally, I was expecting to experience one grand "ta-da" moment, and it didn't quite work like that. With both of my betrayal experiences, it was more like a continual process that happened over a period of time. With my forgiving and moving-on example, the sadness turned to anger and then lessened, eventually turning into com-passion. With my forgiving and rebuilding example, it happened after many interactions and opportunities to feel safe and valued.

Just to be clear, forgiveness doesn't mean that you think what the person did was right, justified, or in any way okay. It doesn't mean that you're some kind of a pushover or weak or naive for letting it go. It also doesn't mean you've forgotten what happened or that you're somehow setting yourself up again for another betrayal because you're choosing to forgive and rebuild (if you feel safe and valued). It's a decision that allows you to let go of the power that pain has had on you.

Empathy is an important aspect of healing from betrayal too because it helps the betrayed person understand that the betrayer is upset over the hurt they caused. It also helps show the desire to continue the relationship and repair the damage that's been caused.[10] While it doesn't always mean forgiveness will occur, it can help reduce negative feelings left after a betrayal.

Forgiveness also involves seeing changes in how the betrayed person views the betrayer; when this change occurs, thoughts, feeling, and behaviors toward the betrayer become more positive. These changes take time to see, feel, and trust, and that's why time is said to be a necessary component and aspect to forgiveness.[11]

THE WINDOW OF WILLINGNESS

So now let's talk about the "window of willingness." Actually, that's my own name for studies that have found that people fall into one of four categories when they do something hurtful.[12] Picture a window that's wide open. Here's where we're the most likely to forgive and have the greatest potential to re-create a new relationship with the person who hurt us. We're going to start from where the window is open the widest to where it's sealed shut.

Starting with the window open the widest, we're at level 1, the best-case scenario after someone hurts us. This level involves sincere remorse, acknowledging what was done, an apology, asking for forgiveness, and restitution. They've taken full responsibility for their actions, and it may sound something like this: "I'm *so* sorry for what I said/did. I know how badly I hurt you, and I want to do whatever it takes to make it up to you." Now with betrayal, that's a good start, but it's probably going to take more than that. At least you have something to work with here. The person understands that what they did hurts, and it's up to you if you want to work with them on rebuilding. Next is level 2.

Here, the person is making excuses. You're hearing reasons, and you know reasons are coming when you hear the word "because." It sounds like "I did it because . . ." The window may still be open, but you can feel it closing a bit here. This level doesn't feel as good as level 1, where they were taking responsibility and you felt like they truly were remorseful for the hurt they caused without making any excuses for their behavior.

You can feel the window closing even more with level 3. With this level, they're justifying or rationalizing their actions and behavior. They can blame you for it at this level too. You know that's where you are when you hear the word "you." It sounds like "I did it because you . . ." This can be so infuriating because here you are, the one who was betrayed, and now you're getting blamed for it. I call this one the "two-sided slap." You're betrayed (slap on one side), then you're somehow blamed for it (slap on the other). Don't believe this one for a minute. It's their inability to take responsibility for their behavior, so they're throwing it to you like a hot potato. I'm not saying you're not supposed to take a look at any responsibility you may have had here; what I'm saying is that their inability to own their actions doesn't make it automatically your fault. You have very little to work with here, so instead of trying to prove, convince, persuade, or any other exhausting activity you're doing to get your point across, don't waste your time (been there, done that).

Level 4 involves complete denial and the unwillingness to take responsibility. Here, the window is sealed shut. You have nothing to work with here, so it's best to forgive (so you take your power back and heal) and move on.

HANGING ON TO A SENSE OF CONTROL

If you notice you're trying to forgive but you're somehow hanging on to it longer than you believe you need to, it can be for these reasons too. Studies found that when it's difficult to forgive and we feel the need to keep reminding the person who hurt us about their behavior, it's often for one of three reasons. The first is to get a sense of the degree of suffering the person who hurt you may be experiencing. Let's be honest: you may not want to see how quickly they bounced back, shrugging off the hurt they caused you, and a reminder gives you a measure of how they're doing with it as you're healing too. It's not that you want to see them unable to function due to deep regret or find them incapable of getting past the realization of what they've done; you just don't want to see how easy it is for them to move forward while you're still struggling.

The second is the readjusting of a power balance. This means that when you see or feel your betrayer getting a little too cocky or confident, you may feel the need to bring up the betrayal as a reminder of where things are now. The third reason it can come up is to serve as a reminder to the betrayer that the transgression shouldn't happen again.[13] Whenever you find yourself doing any of these things, give yourself a little slack. It's your ego at work here, which has been badly bruised, and it's just trying to flex a bit of muscle.

Forgiveness has been shown to lead to less depression and anxiety and to greater hope for the future along with less anger and grief.[14] While forgiveness improves our health, one of the most important reasons that people choose to withhold forgiveness, especially within marriage, has to do with the repetition of the offense. One study showed that 60 percent of unforgiven offenses involved offenses occurring more than once, whereas 30 percent of forgiven offenses occurred one time. Lies, deception, and infidelity were found to be the most devastating betrayals among those unable to forgive.[15] The same study found that shame on the part of the betrayer caused withdrawal, where guilt caused more of an interest in rebuilding the relationship. When the betrayer feels guilty, it's easier for the betrayed to feel as if they care about rebuilding what the betrayal destroyed. It's also important to mention that sometimes getting beyond the pain of withholding forgiveness feels like enough for us, and we may not feel a need to move beyond that goal.[16] Regardless of the option we choose, forgiveness helps us heal—physically, mentally, and emotionally.

TWO FORGIVENESS MODELS

Here are two forgiveness models that involve specific processes. I'm sharing these because sometimes it's helpful to have a framework handy as you work through something that can be challenging like forgiveness. The first is a four-phase process. First, the person who's been hurt needs to fully face and confront the negative emotions and feelings experienced by the event. Next, they need to realize that suffering continues for as long as they're continuing to focus on the painful event for an extended period of time. During this stage, they make a commitment to forgive, and forgiveness is used as the strategy to get them there. In the third phase, they begin their forgiveness work, and there's a commitment to prevent the pain from being transferred to others, including the person who hurt them. In the final phase, the person who's been hurt recognizes the positive benefits from the forgiveness work. They've found meaning in the experiences and recognize that when they let go of the pain and suffering, they heal.[17]

The acronym REACH is used to describe the other forgiveness model. The REACH model consists of five phases. The first phase involves *recalling* the hurt. The second phase involves *empathizing* with the offender in an attempt to understand what they may have been thinking that led to the action. The third phase is called *altruistic*, as forgiveness is seen as a gift the hurt person is able to give. The fourth phase is a declaration to forgive by making a *commitment* to forgive publicly. The final phase is called *hold*, which involves holding on to the decision to forgive when that decision becomes challenged.[18]

Through forgiveness, we can work toward improvements in physical as well as mental and emotional health. Events and actions that have caused pain and suffering can have an opportunity to be reviewed, assessed, and improved when we forgive. While painful events can trigger feelings of injustice, resentment, anger, hurt, and bitterness, forgiveness can be an important element in restoring and healing relationships, especially when trying to heal from the trauma of betrayal.

WHAT FORGIVENESS LOOKED LIKE FOR THE FAB 14

Here's what the Fab 14 did. Some learned that although they struggled with the concept of forgiveness, forgiving anyway set them free and helped them heal. While many of the participants struggled with forgiveness, those who chose to forgive found it was an important aspect to their growth and change.

Anne shared, "I forgave him, but I never forgot." Cleo said, "I did the best I could to have forgiveness for him because I realize I guess he is who he was, and I'm starting to let go of it." Djena mentioned, "I've forgiven him. I've recognized that people can only react to the level of their ability." Dana remembered, "I have so much empathy and so much tolerance. I can see where people get broken so easily, and I don't have any hatred at all. There is no hatred at all." Marie learned about forgiveness during her experience: "Forgiveness doesn't mean you're coming back into my life. Forgiveness means I forgive you, I've forgiven this, I've let it go, and this is where it ends. Forgiveness doesn't mean having to try to reconcile if you don't feel it's there."

Through forgiveness, Marie remembered, "I made peace with myself, and then I made peace with him. After that, just everything was fine in the family. I just really dove into it. It became very cathartic." Monica forgave many of those who hurt her: "Forgiveness is huge, I've forgiven my father, I forgive my mom. I love her, and I forgive her for whatever. I forgive my older daughter, who still struggles. Forgiveness, patience, understanding that they have their journey."

MY JOURNEY TO FORGIVENESS

For me, choosing to forgive was one of the hardest things I've ever done. I wrestled with it constantly. It felt entirely different in both of my betrayals, though. In my family betrayal, which involved forgiving and moving on, it took patience, time, and repeatedly choosing to act from my highest self, even though my ego/inner critic was raging constantly. I struggled with the deep injustice, the lack of taking responsibility, the inability to admit wrongdoing, and the craziness of blaming me for things I didn't say or do. It made me question my sanity at times. I'd switch between the very human and ego-centered thoughts around the unfairness and injustice to thoughts of how sad it was that those were the choices they believed were their best options. Then I'd get angry at myself for trying to overlook the obviously poor behavior, then realize that it's sad that that's how they lived their lives. On and on I'd switch, and it was exhausting. Finally, and when I felt ready, I forgave, and years later, I even had an opportunity to test it.

I actually bumped into this person, and at first, I couldn't believe the Universe would put them directly in front of me around 15 years after I cut ties and worked on healing. Yes, here they were at the same airport, at the same gate, and even on the same flight I'd be taking home from a recent trip I was flying home from. My entire body started shaking, and I eventually found myself walking right up to them. I stood there, waiting to see if they'd acknowledge me. They looked and quickly turned away. I didn't move. I didn't feel any anger or resentment, just peace. I asked, "Do you know who I am?" They responded, "No" and quickly looked away. I asked again, and this time, they responded angrily and in a way that suggested I'd done something to them, they were so upset by it, I wasn't worthy of acknowledgment. (Honestly, I think they were hoping to say that to scare me into walking away and have me think it wasn't them after all.) It didn't work. I still didn't move, and I also didn't feel any anger, just peace. Finally, when they saw I wasn't moving and they realized I wasn't accepting that "no" (which to me meant "If I acknowledge that I know who you are, then I have to deal with the reality of this uncomfortable moment right here and now"), they finally acknowledged me. Then I did the unthinkable. I hugged them, spoke for a few minutes, wished them well, and felt a peace wash over me as if to say, "Good job Deb, you really did do the work to forgive."

Forgiving and rebuilding (what I'm doing with my husband) is an entirely different story. I'd be lying if I said my ego hasn't gotten very involved in the process. It's been an exhausting back-and-forth between my ego and my highest self. Everything about my ego mocked the idea of forgiveness: "What a bunch of garbage, don't bother." "You're just setting yourself up for more pain, don't be a sucker," and "You're going to let him off the hook that easily?" Then my highest self would whisper messages of "You know what's best, trust that." I'll never forget one experience that really showed how powerful my ego was in making sure I didn't fully forgive—until I caught it red-handed.

I had surgery in both feet from severe arthritis (an autoimmune disease I'm convinced was driven by chronic stress). Anyway, from the outside, my feet look fine, but from the inside, I'd worn away the carti-lage, making it hard to walk normally and making it almost unbearable to wear heels because I don't have the cartilage to easily bend my toes. So, I had surgery to help because, well, I just wasn't willing to give up heels (judge if you want, it's the truth.) Whenever I wore heels, I'd be in so much pain the next day, so I always (even after the surgery) have to plan out when and for how long I can have heels on.

Now, it's important to mention that, energetically, foot issues also represent an inability, fear, or unwillingness to move forward. Makes perfect sense after my betrayal, right? So, one night, while Adam and I were pretty far along in our rebuilding stage, the most interesting thing happened. I'd been cautiously rebuilding an entirely new relationship with him, and he'd been consistently and carefully showing me that I'd never have any reason to question anything ever again. During the day, we'd been busy with the kids, running errands and doing normal day-time activities. I remember wearing jeans, a T-shirt, and running shoes (it's important to mention, and you'll soon hear why). We'd gone out to dinner—nothing fancy, just a simple Saturday night out. After dinner, there was the briefest moment where I felt totally safe, as if all of the hurt, the pain, the anguish, the fear, the doubt, and every other emotion that betrayal creates just vanished. I felt an overwhelming sense of freedom, peace, and trust. It was so unmistakable that I remember exactly where I was when this brief but crystal-clear experience happened. The moment ended, it was a nice night, and I went to sleep.

The next morning, I woke up in the most unbearable pain in both feet—it felt as if I'd danced all night long in six-inch heels. It didn't make any sense at all. I'd worn running shoes during the day and flats the night before. There was absolutely no reason that my feet should have been in all that pain. Then I realized that there's always more to things than we often realize, so I used one of the practices I shared with you to help find some answers. I started tapping (that's the emotional freedom technique [EFT] I mentioned in a previous chapter.) Within minutes, I got the clearest message that just made so much sense. I heard, "Your hard stance keeps you in a hard stance," meaning that my hard stance (my rigid and unbending viewpoint in refusing to fully forgive and believe I was safe) keeps me in a hard stance (the rigid, unbending, and painful stance that was keeping my feet, along with the rest of my body and mind, in physical, mental, and emotional pain). I felt and experienced firsthand how withholding forgiveness was keeping me stuck. I was sold and worked to quiet my ego and listen to my highest self instead.

YOUR JOURNEY TO FORGIVENESS

So, what does forgiveness look like for you? Forgiveness can also serve as a beautiful act of self-love. Think about it. When you forgive, you release anger, resentment, pain, grief, and depression, just to name a few. By forgiving, you gain peace, understanding, validation, self-respect, and self-love. You're able to say, "Yes, this happened to me, but I've learned some incredible lessons," and I've turned lemons into lemonade. You're stronger, wiser, more confident, and, most important, free. That doesn't mean you're moving forward with the person who hurt you or setting yourself up for more pain; it just means you're willing to let go of all the small self-benefits that hanging on to that pain was giving you. I love this quote from Mark Twain that sums up forgiveness so beautifully: "Forgiveness is the fragrance the violet sheds on the heel that has crushed it."

I often hear people say, "I'll never be able to forgive them for what they did!" What I hear in that is that they'll never free themselves from the anger, bitterness, and resentment they feel so justified in feeling. You've probably heard that saying: "Holding on to anger/a grudge/unforgiveness is like drinking poison and expecting the other person to die." It's time to free yourself—not for their sake but for yours.

Here's what I'd like for you to do. Grab your journal or a piece of paper and write down the following questions. They'll help you uncover what may be lurking beneath the surface. Take your time with these questions and try to answer them from the energy of your highest self. See what emerges and don't be shocked if you see some incredibly wise responses flow from your subconscious mind and onto the pages. Ready?

- Whom do I need to forgive?
- What is holding on to this pain doing for me/them?
- Can I forgive?
- Am I willing to forgive? Yes/no/why not?
- Can I view this event as a powerful teaching experience or lesson?
- Can I view this person as a powerful teacher?
- Am I willing to look at this event as a powerful teaching experience?
- If I forgave, I'd feel . . .
- If I forgave, I'd believe . . .
- If I forgave, I'd look . . .
- Forgiving would allow or create . . .
- What do I need to do/learn/experience in order to forgive?
- What benefit am I receiving by holding on to the pain of this experience?
- Withholding forgiveness keeps me tied to . . .
- Freeing myself from this pain allows me to . . .
- What needs to happen for me to forgive?

Take the time to do this exercise. You'll see how it really helps catapult you to the next level of your healing. It also helps you regain your health, happiness, and so much more.

As we leave this chapter and move on to the next, consider adding a mantra to your daily practice if you're struggling with forgiveness. It can be something as simple as "Forgiveness sets me free" or anything else that resonates with you. Remember, you're creating your personal healing plan, and it's important to try out a few things to see what may work for you. I was never sold on the idea of tapping until tapping allowed that one sentence to show up ("Your hard stance keeps you in a hard stance"). There's so much wisdom underneath all that pain, and these tools and strategies allow for that wisdom to be uncovered.

What else can you do to signify that you're forgiving and moving on either with or without the person who hurt you? You can tell them about your decision, you can write a letter (that you may or may not send), or you can even put a letter in a bottle and send it out to sea. You can tie a letter to a balloon and watch it float away, create an official forgiveness ceremony, or do something specific to commemorate your decision to forgive. To make it even more special, you may want to do or buy something meaningful so that you connect your forgiveness to something additional that brings you joy. Find what works for you and notice how your decision to forgive makes you feel.

Meet me in the next chapter, where we're taking your healing to another level. We're diving into the topics of empaths, energy vampires, narcissists, and so much more. You'll see why you may be a magnet for energy vampires, and you'll understand why you respond to experiences the way you do. Having a better sense of who you are allows you to further understand what you need, what you want, and how to protect yourself in order to improve your health, well-being, and sanity. I'll meet you there.

· 13 ·

Energy Vampires and Empaths
The Perfect Storm

$\mathcal{A}$n empath is "a person thought to have the ability to perceive or experience the emotional state of another individual."[1] This is different from empathy, which is the ability to comprehend or imagine what another person might be feeling. The empath doesn't just understand what another person may be feeling; they're able to understand it so deeply that they literally feel that feeling too. Because they have the ability to feel how painful it would be to intentionally hurt someone, they're not as likely to act in a way that would intentionally cause harm. Assuming that others feel this way too is one of the reasons that empaths are particularly susceptible to being blindsided by a betrayal. (Of course, you don't have to be an empath to experience betrayal; anyone can be betrayed at any time. There's just something about empaths that seem to serve as easy prey for a betrayer.) Now, whether you are or aren't an empath, you'll still get value from this chapter, so don't skip over it. Empath or not, you're a kind person who's been hurt. It's likely you've been doing most of the giving and never expected to be betrayed, so you need some tender, loving care.

Here's what we're going to cover in this chapter. I'm going to talk about the blessing and curse of being an empath and how the empath often finds themselves mercilessly intertwined with an energy vampire and someone capable of intentionally betraying them. (To be clear, just as not all empaths experience betrayal and not all people who are betrayed are empaths, not all energy vampires betray. Having said that, however, the empath/energy vampire combination is all too common—and exhausting.)

We'll explore why the empath is drawn to the energy vampire in the first place and how those relationships quickly become toxic and exhausting. We'll also cover what the empath in particular experiences after a betrayal yet how their undeniable belief in humanity, healing, and the power of love sets them up to bounce back even better than before. Here's where it's more important than ever to sharpen your BS meter by strengthening your intuition. This way, you'll be better able to sniff out an energy vampire before you're in their powerful web going forward. We have a lot to do, so let's get started.

In Dr. Judith Orloff's book *The Empath's Survival Guide: Life Strategies for Sensitive People*,[2] empaths are described as highly sensitive people who easily absorb other people's emotions. There are many types of empaths too. Some are keenly aware of the emotions of others, and some can feel another person's physical pain as if it's their own. Some have a high sensitivity to animals, others can easily sense the mood change when someone enters a room, and still others are highly intuitive. While empaths have the gift of deeply feeling what others are experiencing, they're also prime targets for energy vampires. There are many types of energy vampires too.

THE NARCISSIST

A narcissist is a type of energy vampire who expects you to put them first and has a deep need to have their egos fed. Some energy vampires drain and intimidate through bullying, others through shame or guilt, and others through drama, feigned helplessness, and more. Dr. Christiane Northrup in her book *Dodging Energy Vampires*[3] explains how energy vampires prey on empaths. Sensing their compassion, desire to help, and willingness to give, the energy vampire drains the empath due to their need for control, drama, attention, and/or recognition. Instead of healing what's lacking inside, they use the empath's love and light to help fill the void of what hasn't been healed within themselves. Energy vampires relentlessly take rather than give, and over time, this one-sided relationship leaves the empath feeling exhausted, manipulated, powerless, and depleted. The tactics used by the energy vampire also leave the empath never feeling good or worthy enough while having them question themselves and their sanity.

WHY BEING AN EMPATH CAN BE EXHAUSTING

Regardless of the type of energy vampire someone is, this type of person drains an empath of their energy because of their focus on themselves. With the empath giving without replenishing their vital energy reserves, it's easy to see how this setup can quickly become physically, mentally, and emotionally exhausting. Now take it one step further. If you've been in relationships with energy vampires, you're already starting out in a compromised position because you're most likely mentally and emotionally drained while possibly having lots of stress-related symptoms, illnesses, and conditions too. So, it's easy to not feel your best, which you may have gotten used to as being your new normal. Then you're blindsided by a betrayal that totally took you by surprise, impacting you on every level. Can you see why the experience affected you as much as it did? You may have felt a bit off kilter to start with and in that weakened state got completely knocked over. While we can't undo the betrayal, let's at the very least equip you with the information you need so you're rock solid going forward. Let's keep going.

While many people can easily set boundaries to protect their energy and well-being, empaths give to a fault and often find other people's pain intolerable. Empaths also go to great lengths to help when someone appears to be struggling. They become so emotionally entrenched in someone else's challenges that they can feel them as if they're their own. Possible unhealed wounds of the empath can also lay the groundwork for even more giving, and they can easily misinterpret the energy vampire's attention as true friendship or love. The energy vampire knows this and uses the big heart, compassion, sensitivity, and devotion of an empath as food and fuel. So, what does this have to do with betrayal?

Because an empath is so aware of the feelings of others, they understand how a mean, selfish, or harmful act would hurt someone. They're very conscious of how their actions impact others, and they often assume that others share that same philosophy. As an empath, I live by a simple rule: "If it's going to hurt someone, don't do it." Seems simple enough, right? That rule makes life easier because it encourages me to consider my actions before I do something and prevents me from doing things that would intentionally cause harm. While I can't speak for other empaths, it's always surprising to me that other people don't live by that same rule and have the ability to intentionally manipulate or hurt someone. That's one of the biggest reasons that betrayal can be so shocking and especially damaging to an empath. Between the assumption that others are on the same page, coupled with the intention to help and heal the energy vampire, it's easy to see how betrayal can blindside an empath. Of course, betrayal is a big shock to anyone, but to the empath, hurting another isn't typically an intention or in their realm of consciousness. So, finding themselves in the web of the energy vampire and then being betrayed by the very person they gave their trust, love, time, and attention to is an incredibly huge shock to the body and mind because it's something so completely inconceivable.

ARE YOU AN EMPATH?

Before we go further, let's first see if *you* are an empath so you can make peace with all of those years of not understanding why it was so hard to sit through a scary movie, why certain types of art or beauty take your breath away, why you feel great when you're out in nature, why you gravitate toward the healing professions, and why you cry watching sappy commercials. (I get it, I do it too.)

Let's get started with the Empath Self-Assessment, designed by Dr. Judith Orloff.[4] What I love about Dr. Orloff's assessment is that she asks a series of questions that confirm exactly why you may respond or react to things the way you do. The assessment asks 20 questions about how you react when you're in crowds and if you absorb other people's emotions and even identifies how you feel physically after an argument. I remember taking the assessment, feeling like I wasn't crazy after all. My reactions to certain types of energy were due to the fact that I was a full-blown empath (I answered yes to 16 out of the 20 questions!). If you're curious, take the quiz too.

Now, while I'm the first one to say if you don't like something, change it, being an empath may be challenging, yet it's also a beautiful and extremely rewarding quality. Being an empath makes others feel safe and heard when they're with us, it's what makes us wonderful healers, and it's what enables us to experience such amazing levels of joy from nature, animals, children, and more. As I'm writing this, I'm laughing at the realization that I have four kids and six dogs and thrive in nature. My fellow empath friends, while we can experience soul-crushing blows, heartache, intense emotional pain, anguish, and despair, we can also experience unimaginable levels of joy, bliss, hope, and love.

Until we know we're an empath, however, life can be challenging and confusing. I always got so upset with myself that I just couldn't handle things like other people. I couldn't understand why it was so hard for me to go through one of those mock haunted houses at Halloween, why I'd get so upset when I saw people arguing, or even why certain "proven" allopathic medical treatments that seemed to work for everyone else wouldn't work for me while alternative and more holistic treatments would help tremendously. Where there'd be a circle of kids in middle school watching the bully harass the weaker kid, I'd be the one running for the lunchroom attendant to get help in getting the bully to stop. At the same time, I was never able to comprehend how no one else thought to do that. I'd also be the one escorting a bug outside instead of swatting it (after all, how would *we* feel if some gigantic being wanted to hurt us?). I'm also the one crying tears of joy *every single time* I see a beautiful reunion of loved ones racing toward each other at the airport, feeling every emotion they're feeling as they reunite with their family or friends they're so happy to see. It was only when I learned what an empath was, however (and this was after my betrayals), that I finally understood how little I'd been honoring my empath needs and how, instead, I was trying to be like everyone else.

The way I finally understood it best was when I realized that an empath just doesn't have the same filters shielding out an overload of too much stimulation, noise, darkness, and negativity. So, those qualities and situations penetrate right through. That's the downside. The benefit of not having that filter in place is that empaths feel what others may not pick up on; we can be extremely intuitive and interpret messages that others may miss. It's as if some people have a few layers of bubble wrap on them, while the empath has only the sheerest layer of paper-thin protection. Unfortunately, that's not enough to protect ourselves from energy vampires who feast on us like an easy meal. Since you know I like analogies, here's one that'll explain the energy vampire to the empath. An energy vampire is like a tick that burrows itself deeply onto and through the skin of its victim. Feasting on the victim's blood is how it survives. It's only when you realize that the tick is there that can you remove it and heal.

The empath is so attractive to the energy vampire (let's say the narcissist, for example) because they serve as narcissistic supply. What's that?

It's blood to the tick. Otto Fenichel, a psychoanalyst in 1938, described it as "a type of admiration, interpersonal support or sustenance drawn by an individual from his or her environment and essential to their self-esteem.[5] That means that the qualities of an empath serve as the perfect fuel, which helps to recharge, feed, and fuel the narcissist. The narcissist just doesn't have the same wiring or level of empathy as the empath, and when we understand this, we can slowly begin to realize that we're not the ones who are crazy, making things up or being overly sensitive. We just can't fathom that this is how people are, so we're almost blind to it, until we're not.

Empaths can also have what's called "super traits," something I learned about from Dr. Christiane Northrup and Sandra L. Brown. Sandra Brown conducted an interesting study through Purdue University.[6] Six hundred women were studied who'd been in relationships with people who were antisocial, borderline narcissists all the way to being in a relationship with a psychopath. So often, we can assume that a person in a relationship with someone like that would have a low self-esteem and self-worth, but that wasn't found to be the case. The study found that it had to do with personality characteristics, like agreeableness and conscientiousness, which were the biggest factors. What do I mean? When we have a high level of agreeableness, we value relationships, we're loyal, we're trusting, and we basically have a strong faith in humanity and the human spirit. When we're conscientious, we're making decisions based on our values and integrity. It's our personality that has us giving others the benefit of the doubt and has us "hanging in there" when the going gets tough because we believe we can help and it's the right thing to do. Sound familiar? Again, these are beautiful qualities that shouldn't be squelched. They just weren't appreciated or respected by the energy vampire.

GASLIGHTING

So, let's say you're realizing, whether you're an empath or not, that you've been on the receiving end of an energy vampire. Stay with me because we're going to take it one step further. If you've been questioning your sanity or if you feel like you need to record conversations for "proof" that someone said something (only to later deny it), you're about to learn exactly what's really been going on. It's something else an empath is a prime target for as well. It's gaslighting. If you're not familiar with gaslighting and it's been happening to you, you're about to feel so much confirmation coming your way. You're going to realize that you were simply under the spell of someone who used your beautiful qualities to manipulate and control. Again, just as not all people who are betrayed are empaths and not all energy vampires betray, not all gaslighters betray either, although many do.

So, what is gaslighting? "Gaslighting is a form of psychological manipulation in which a person seeks to sow seeds of doubt in a targeted individual or in members of a targeted group, making them question their own memory, perception, and sanity."[7] How do you know you're being gaslighted? *Psychology Today* published a piece sharing 11 signs you're being gaslighted. I'll sum them up here:[8]

1. They tell blatant lies.
2. They deny they said something, even though you have proof.
3. They use what is near and dear to you as ammunition (think kids, friends, etc.).
4. They wear you down over time.
5. Their actions don't match their words.
6. They throw in positive reinforcement to confuse you.
7. They know that confusion weakens people.
8. They project (accuse you of what they're actually doing).
9. They try to align people against you.
10. They tell you or others that you're crazy.
11. They tell you that everyone else is a liar.

If this is the first time you're learning about this, I know how hard this can be. I also want you to know that you weren't a sucker for falling for it or anything else you may be saying to yourself that's negative. It's your love, faith in humanity, compassion, willingness to hang in there, hope, belief in others, trusting nature, and more that made you the perfect host for the tick. I'll never forget one of my clients who was completely blindsided by a narcissistic gaslighter. To protect her privacy, I'll call her Beth.

Beth fell in love with a handsome, charming, and charismatic man who seemed to say and do all of the right things. Early in the relationship, he "love bombed" her, meaning he poured so much affection and attention on her that she felt like she was living a fairy tale. Once she was under his spell, the love bombing slowly stopped. Unfortunately, by this point, he's become almost an addiction for her. She craved more, and not knowing why he slowly went from hot to cold, she took the increasing coldness to mean that it had to be because of something she wasn't saying or doing. So, she did all she could to get his attention and affection. He just didn't seem nearly as interested as he'd been earlier in the relationship, so she kept trying harder and harder, giving all she could, all the time.

Whenever he'd reenter the picture (needing more narcissistic supply), she'd grab on, believing he was back because of how much he valued her and their relationship. After all, didn't he feel the same way she did? He'd have all kinds of reasons (excuses) for why he didn't call back, he'd break plans, and his excuses all seemed valid. He soon started complaining about his finances, even saying that his absence was sometimes because he was embarrassed that he couldn't take her out the way she deserved. He talked about how sad he felt that he couldn't take her to exotic places, buy her extravagant gifts, and shower her with beautiful things. She didn't care about any of that; she just wanted his love. His finances seemed to really take a turn in his business (a business she didn't quite understand), so after he shared "an embarrassing and vulnerable story" about his hardships, she reached for her checkbook and wrote him an enormous check with the intention of helping him get back on his feet. After all, he just wanted to be able to feel secure and buy her a few things, right?

A few weeks went by, and he just wasn't returning her calls or texts. Could he really be that busy? She'd get the briefest of texts telling her "I'll call you tomorrow" or "See you soon" that started to feel empty and hard to believe. She had an uneasy feeling. Something just didn't seem right. One night, and desperately feeling a need for answers, she scrolled his social media profiles. There he was, having the time of his life—with another woman.

The enormous financial gift she gave put her in her own financial difficulty. When she confronted him, he used every cruel tactic in the "gaslighter's handbook." She *still* didn't want to believe what was so obvious (our unyielding faith in humanity) even though the facts were clear. She didn't want to believe that she'd been taken and that the "love" they had wasn't real. Remember, we don't move forward until and unless we accept our betrayal. When she was ready, I remember holding her hand and slowly reading her that list of 11 characteristics of a gaslighter. She cried, knowing that's exactly who he was. By the time her healing was complete, she felt such compassion for him along with any of his future victims he'd surely seek as prey.

I know that wasn't a happy story, but I want you to know that you're not alone and that gaslighting is unfortunately more common than we think. So, what can you do to protect yourself? While knowledge is power, wisdom is the experiential version of that knowledge. That means that you learn things on one level. Let's say you're reading a book on how to play tennis. You learn it on an entirely different level when you get on the tennis court and play. Learning who you are, what you need, and whom to steer clear of is a powerful first step. Being blindsided by someone who does these things allows you to know firsthand what it feels like. Hopefully, it's that feeling that serves as a strong reminder of what you *don't* want in a friend, partner, or anyone else you're spending your precious time with going forward.

❧

HONORING YOUR EMPATH SELF

In wrapping up this chapter, I can feel my fellow empaths feeling a big exhausted. On the one hand, you're discovering who you are, and on the other, you're upset that your beautiful qualities were used and abused. On the one hand, you love how easily you're called to give, and on the other, you wish others wouldn't take so easily. On the one hand, you love the deep connection you're able to experience with certain people, and on the other, you wish you could just talk about trivial things like everyone else. Yes, being an empath can be exhausting, especially if you don't know how to protect yourself. Remember, you don't have those extra layers that shield you against the harsh elements life can sometimes throw at you. You also don't have the heart to firmly set boundaries unless you're pushed to the brink, and you're probably realizing that people push as far as we let them. All of this can make your head spin. I know that's what it did for me—until I finally realized the gift in it.

When it's obvious that people need a shift in consciousness—that they need to wake up and be more loving and kinder and show more compassion—it's the empaths who light the way. When everyone is using fear and anger to get their point across, the empath is using love. As others can miss the beauty in music or art, it's the empath who's brought to tears. Yes, being an empath has its lows and, thankfully, a tremendous amount of highs as well, so here's what I suggest so that you can protect your empath self. Here's my empath to-do list:

1. Do an energy check—do you need rest and time to replenish? Give that to yourself. You charge your phone each night; you need recharging too.
2. Trust your gut—is someone saying one thing but you're sensing something else? Trust your gut. Your narcissistic friend/family member/partner may lie, but your gut never does.
3. Give yourself more of what you need—empaths have a gift of sensing what others may need, but that doesn't mean others are doing that for you. So, give that to yourself. Do you need more time in nature, a more peaceful environment, music, art, plants, or animals? How can you give yourself more of what you need?
4. Create new boundaries for yourself and others—were you giving in to something (watching disturbing TV shows, for example) that make you feel nervous, anxious, or afraid? Just because it doesn't upset other people doesn't mean it's right for you. Say no to things that don't make you feel good and say yes to things that do. Make your yeses and nos nonnegotiable as you learn to respect your new rules and boundaries that are more aligned with who you are and what works best for you.

I want to close this chapter by celebrating how far you've come—especially if none of this was clear until now. Think about it. Here you were, doing your best and wondering why things were always different and more challenging for you. You couldn't understand why you felt the way you did and why you just seemed to always attract people who mistreated or disrespected you. It never made sense why you reacted or responded the way you did, and if that weren't bad enough, you were made to feel like you were somehow wrong or flawed for being who you were—even if you didn't even know who you were at the time.

Because of that, it sometimes just felt safer and better to hide, to keep who you were to yourself instead of taking the risk of being misunderstood or shamed.

YOU ARE AN EMPATH

You are an empath, a beautiful, heart-centered soul that lights the way for others. It's your vulnerability that's your strength and your unwavering faith in others that shows others what's possible when they wake up with the help of your light. You're the one who takes the hit, but you're also the one who rises up, even more powerful than before. You, my empath soul friend, are just like bamboo. While other flowers and plants have their day to shine, bamboo stays underground for what seems like forever. Only when it's good and ready does it powerfully emerge through the ground with a force and strength that's unmistakable. It doesn't apologize for its strength or beauty; it just knows it's bamboo, and that's just what it does. So, while you may be licking your wounds and hiding underground for a while, when you're ready, you'll burst forth with a confidence that's earned through your hard work, your character, and your quiet strength.

Here are a few quotes that perfectly capture the essence of an empath:

> Highly sensitive people are too often perceived as weaklings or damaged goods. To feel intensely is not a symptom of weakness, it is the trademark of the truly alive and compassionate. It is not the empath who is broken, it is society that has become dysfunctional and emotionally disabled. There is no shame in expressing your authentic feelings. Those who are at times described as being a "hot mess" or having "too many issues" are the very fabric of what keeps the dream alive for a more caring, humane world. Never be ashamed to let your tears shine a light in this world.
>
> —Anthon St. Maarten

As empaths, our high level of sensitivity means that we are prone to feeling like eternal outsiders who are in the world but not quite of the world.

—Aletheia Luna

Dear empath:

You are a being of immense depth, wisdom, and compassion. You are a pioneer and trailblazer of humanity, a model for others on how to be sensitive and powerful. All the strength and love you need is already within you, waiting to be discovered.

—Mateo Sol

Take a moment now to realize how far you've come. We have one last chapter to go, and I'll be talking about how to trust in the new you and where to go from here. That's where we're going to take everything you've done and wrap it up in a pretty bow. I'll be giving you some strategies to make sure you stay on track and what to do when you fall. You'll see the road you traveled, and if my predictions are correct, you may feel inspired to share your growth with others. You've done such a great job—now just one more stop before you "graduate." Let's keep going, and I'll meet you in the next and final chapter.

• *14* •

Trusting in the New You
and Where You Go from Here

*W*hile we're never truly broken, betrayal certainly causes us to feel like we are. We've been blindsided, shocked, overwhelmed, confused, and deeply hurt. We've experienced physical symptoms that we're healing from. We're learning how to rebuild our bodies, our minds, our hearts, and our lives. We're learning how to trust again, love again, and feel safe again. We're learning how to make our betrayal a pivotal chapter of our story and not our entire story. We're transforming, re-creating ourselves as a result of an experience we never thought we'd have to deal with. We're members of a club we never wanted to be a part of, and we're doing the best we can from where we are now. If we've done the work, we're also experiencing Post Betrayal Transformation (PBT), where we're actually stronger, wiser, and more empowered *because* of our experience.

There's a beautiful quote by Rumi: "The wound is the place where the Light enters you." That light allows the brightest, boldest, and most vibrant light to shine from within and through you to all those on your path. You've been there and back and have not only re-created yourself but also created a sense of self-worth, confidence, and unshakable strength that's palpable.

WHERE DO YOU GO FROM HERE?

So how do you trust in this new bad*ss version of yourself, and where do you go from here? That's what this chapter is all about. You'll also hear from some of my study participants who've achieved PBT and what they want everyone to know. Take Jo, who said, "If they don't allow themselves to go through the pain and fear, and they stay in what seems to be their normal, they will never allow themselves to have the chance to be at peace and feel extraordinary. There is an absolute beautiful picture at the end of that feeling. They can see the rainbow, they can see the beautiful clear blue sky, they will not have the cloud of sadness in their innermost being, and they'll be smiling and feeling pure emotion. That's real, and they're going to be able to really live life to the fullest. I certainly am!"

In this chapter, we'll revisit all you've done to get here. You'll see how your experience has made you stronger, better, and wiser, and you'll realize that you're so much stronger than you thought. You'll know how to protect yourself, and you'll have the confidence to maintain your new boundaries formed because of all you've learned. You'll have a sharpened BS meter in place that instinctively knows when something isn't right, and you'll be encouraged to trust it—because you've learned the hard way what happens when you quiet that wise inner voice. Your intuition will be sharpened, your resolve strengthened, and your belief in humanity restored. Finally, you'll feel an enormous sense of pride in how strong, resilient, brave, and courageous you are. As my study participant Marie put it, "You're stronger than you think, and you have everything you need." I'll end by inviting you to write a loving and compassionate letter to yourself. This heartwarming love letter sets in stone all you've overcome and solidifies the beautifully healed new you while signaling to the Universe that you're ready for an exciting next chapter. Are you ready? We have a lot to do, so let's get started.

HABITS TO HELP YOU STAY ON TRACK

Since it's unrealistic to say that you'll never be disappointed or hurt by others again, here's what a few of the Fab 14 recognized in themselves when it happens to them. Monica mentioned how she still falls off track sometimes but that, when she does, she uses spirituality and the tools she's found useful to help her climb back up again. Marie mentioned how "attitude adjustments" help her when she needs to update her perspective. Arielle mentioned that as she grows, new challenges arise that bring up new fears, although they encourage her to grow further. What do I do? I journal, meditate, learn, surround myself with like-minded soulful friends, work on my mind-set, and remind myself how far I've come on my PBT journey. I love that saying: "We're either growing or we're dying." So, what's *your* growth based on when it comes to healing from betrayal?

Your growth and healing are determined by the decisions you make. Remember, the three reasons that we don't fully heal from betrayal: we're refusing to accept our betrayal, we're numbing/distracting/ avoiding, or the betrayer has no consequences within your relationship. It really has very little to do with the depth or complexity of the betrayal and has more to do with your willingness and approach to move forward. There's no judgment if you're doing any of those things that hold you back; just know that you're keeping your healing at bay. It's when you do the work in going through each of the Five Stages from Betrayal to Breakthrough that you move toward healing and that healing is available to you whenever you're ready. I remember one participant who said that her betrayal impacted her so deeply that she immediately went to her doctor, who put her on what she called "happy pills" for anxiety and depression. While it may have helped her get through her day, she didn't heal nearly as quickly as another participant who faced it head-on, relentlessly determined to use her betrayal as an opportunity to bounce back better than before. Again, these are personal decisions; always make the choice that feels intuitively right for you.

WHAT YOU REBUILD WHEN YOU HEAL

Why can betrayal be so challenging to heal from? Because aspects of the self are hard hit when we're blindsided by a betrayal. We need to rebuild ourselves after we feel so blatantly rejected and abandoned. We need to re-create a new sense of belonging, confidence, worthiness, and, if it's a romantic betrayal, a new sense of desirability too. We need to strengthen and rebuild our ability to trust while we rebuild our self-esteem, self-love, and self-identity. We need to relearn how to move through relationships while redefining new priorities that may not have been important to us before. We need to completely shift what it is that'll allow us to feel safe while we create new beliefs, a new worldview, and a new way to trust. We need to honor ourselves while being careful to prevent self-sabotage, which we may do if we're not careful because it can seem easier to go back to what we knew versus staying committed to where we're headed. This takes discipline and focus. If we're not careful, we can self-sabotage and, as a result, betray ourselves—not because the old way was good but because it was familiar. You've come way too far to betray yourself by neglecting to own your truth or neglecting to honor your needs and what's in your best interest. This takes work and a commitment to keep healing.

Betrayal impacts us physically, mentally, emotionally, psychologically, and spiritually. It also sets the stage for transformation in these areas. When the way we look at the world, ourselves, and others is all destroyed by betrayal, we're also being set up to create an entirely new worldview and self as a result. When we do, we experience PBT, and that's a state you deserve to experience. Other types of traumas don't necessarily require you to rebuild your self-esteem or have you question your worthiness or sanity, but betrayal does. It also has you confronting feelings of judgment, shame, humiliation, and vulnerability, all of which need to be uncovered and addressed.

Building and re-creating all of those aspects of the self takes patience, persistence, and self-love. While all traumas take time to heal and recover from, it's the personal and intentional nature of betrayal that creates a need for a specific healing path. The good news? You can heal from all of it, and it's my hope that you've been healing as you've been moving through these chapters. When you do, you create a newer and better version than before. Marie said it perfectly when she compared her healing journey to mosaics: "What are mosaics?" she asks. "Broken tile. It's the way we put those tile pieces back together that creates beauty."

Healing and recovery is a process. Maybe you're eating healthier because you're showing yourself more self-love and self-care. If so, you're rewarding yourself with a healthier and leaner body, which also helps you feel more confident and attractive, as your betrayal may have had you question how beautiful you really are. Rebuilding that lean, fit, healthy body is foundational to helping you feel better from your experience and is a great place to start.

Maybe you've rewired your mind-set and simply refuse to indulge in those painful triggers that derailed your mood whenever they'd emerge. Maybe you truly see the gift left in the wake of your betrayal, and it's serving as a springboard to a new path you're now finding yourself on. Maybe your betrayal has you meeting new like-minded friends who value honesty and integrity, and it's these new friends you're now traveling on your path with. Maybe your betrayal created such a profound perspective that you don't "sweat the small stuff" as you're realizing how insignificant those things really are. At the same time, maybe you've realized how precious life is, and it's those small but precious moments you missed in the past that are important to you now. It's possible that you're unwilling to settle for mediocre in *any* category that is important to you. Or maybe you learned that you're an empath and you now treat yourself in a way that feels loving and kind based on what you need.

You may realize that you have access to a completely new type of relationship with others that you didn't have access to before. You may see that you crave deeper and more meaningful connections, and that's exactly what you choose. You may have done some deep forgiveness work, and your body, mind, and heart have healed as a result. You may realize that you want to spend your time and money on new areas as you sense a growing new interest bubble up. You may now have the confidence to speak up, do something different, or try something new. You may realize that there's no better time than *right now* to make those changes that your practical self has been putting off. You may start laughing more, loving more, and living more fully as you see and understand things from a deeper soul level. Finally, you may care less about what people think, how you're perceived, or what people may say about you. Isn't that a relief?

If you're like me, you also feel confident and proud as you look back at all of the hard work you've done. Let's face it: as horrible as your betrayal was, the strength you're feeling now is earned—it certainly wasn't handed to you. You never would have become this 2.0 version of yourself had your experience not happened. Does that mean you want to thank your betrayer for what they did? Well, that's entirely up to you, and, if so, you have my deepest respect. You're more evolved than me.

What else can it lead to? In my case, it also led to another wedding—with Adam. We didn't renew our vows: we married each other again—this time with new rings, new vows, a new dress, and our four children as our bridal party. Can people really change? I questioned that myself, but when I thought about it, the "old me" doesn't exist anymore, and the "old him" just can't be found (if so, I never would have considered it). This new marriage is based on a new level of understanding, commitment, integrity, and trust. The new me doesn't allow for any type of mistreatment, and the new him wouldn't dare do anything to show any level of disrespect. He values and appreciates life from an entirely new perspective. He understands the profound hurt he caused to me, my family, and even my friends and is taking his second chance seriously. It's been the biggest shake-up and wake-up call for my entire family, and we've all grown tremendously as a result.

Of course, this isn't the case with certain betrayals (I shared that in my family betrayal, I just healed and moved on). Each relationship gives you opportunities to learn and grow. Maybe the relationship ran its course and you've learned what you needed to learn from the experience. Or maybe the death of that relationship allows for the birth of something new. It's something you can't predict, and the only way a new possibility has an opportunity to emerge is truly when you let go of the relationship that you had without any idea or expectation of what will show up when you do. It involves letting go, surrendering to the unknown, and trusting that you'll be led to what's in your best interest. It's believing that the Universe really does have your back and that, although the path isn't clear, through your healing, you're paving a new path that serves you best.

That's the gift of betrayal. Remember the analogy of the house and the difference between patching it up and rebuilding it? Betrayal levels that house and allows for something completely new to be built. There are two other things betrayal shows us too. It can reveal someone's true colors, showing us who they truly are once we learn the painful truth. It can also show us who someone had temporarily become as they see firsthand the depth of hurt their actions have created. From that space, they can then use the painful experience they now see so clearly as an opportunity to become the best versions of themselves they're meant to be.

FINAL THOUGHTS FROM THE FAB 14

The Fab 14 had some specific messages they wanted to share with you, so as we begin to wrap up, here's what they want you to know:

Cleo: "Life's tough. Relationships are tough. Don't let people set your time line. It's a process that's different for everyone."

Anne: "Join groups. I think they're very beneficial. Even if you're not the type to speak up at these meetings, you always hear something that's going to resonate in your heart and soul that gives you a little hope as you sit there and encourage somebody. These group meetings are very important, therapy is important, being able to be honest and express yourself with close trusted friends is very important. You really have to focus on taking care of yourself and choose your priorities in life. Family, that's my priority."

Juliana: "Trust that you are in the right place at the right time because you're always where you're supposed to be. You're given something for a reason. Learn the lesson and learn it on the first go around because it doesn't get any prettier. It gets harsher, really."

Patti: "Healing is a process, and while therapy helped, the growth through spirituality continues to drive my healing journey."

Denny: "It's not your fault, and there's light at the end of the tunnel. Whether that light is that you're going to heal your marriage or you're going to move on. Just have faith. Have faith that what needs to happen will happen. You have to be strong, as strong as you can, and get yourself a support group."

Suzanne: "You cannot sit in your despair. You have to get up, and you have to figure out how will I navigate through this betrayal? It happened, you can't change it. It sucks, it's awful. You can blame everybody else, but somehow, you're a part of it, and you've just got to get up every single day and do a little bit to move forward."

Djena: "Women are so hard on themselves. We need to be kinder to ourselves, loving ourselves as easily as we love others."

Dana: "You want to know what's going on because you don't want that to stay like a virus in the marriage. You want to stop it, and then you want to be able to heal it and then move forward. That's so painful, but it's worth it. I never knew how insidious it was in every part of my being."

Marie: "I find that what helps people in my experience move through things is to feel they're not alone in it. It's not like misery loves company; it's to understand this isn't exclusive to you."

Arielle: "You can get through it, and there are amazing people out there that will love you, that you would love—if you're open to it. Get through it; there's light at the end of the tunnel."

Nanette: "You can't put your happiness in someone else's hands. It has to come from within yourself. You've got to figure it out. You have to be independent. Who are you and what do you want in your life? You need to know that, and if you don't know, that's what you need to work on. I am not Mrs. so and so. I'm me, and I need to figure out who is this "me" and what do I want."

Monica: "There is something good to learn. If you can go deep enough. If you can go and feel the pain, go through the pain. Go through those emotions because if you push them away, they're just going to come back. What we resist will persist. And it just keeps on coming back. We're not always going to have good times. And we're not always going to have bad times. But sometimes, it's how we deal with it as we go through it and how we have that fortitude. But really, that betrayal, just look at it. Journal about it. Talk about it. Express it. In the best way you know how, right now. Even if it's just a few little things. Do some movement, walk, get the energy out. But get the energy moving. Change the energy. It's all good, it's all good. It's a journey."

NEXT STEPS

What else does your healing bring? A new wisdom, depth, and perspective in how to view your betrayal from a more healed place. We see our event more clearly and experience more positive emotions from this stronger vantage point. We see this as the wisdom earned as a result of what we've been through. I love this quote by Jim Rohn because it seems to meet us at whatever state of healing and growth we may be in: "Don't wish it was easier wish you were better. Don't wish for less problems, wish for more skills. Don't wish for less challenge, wish for more wisdom." Here's one of my favorite quotes because it truly takes into account the power relationships have on us:

> I suppose that since most of our hurts come through relationships, so will our healing, and I know that grace rarely makes sense for those looking in from the outside.
>
> —Wm Paul Young, *The Shack*

WRITING YOUR LOVE LETTER TO THE OLD YOU

So, where does this leave you and your wise new self? It's a great time to write a beautiful letter to yourself. In the letter, you're going to want to write in a loving and compassionate tone. Tell your "old self" how proud you are of the work you did. Acknowledge *every* change you made, *every* hurdle crossed, *every* trigger overcome, and what you see so clearly now. It's important because it's when you're writing that letter that you'll see the road you traveled, and it's that road you took that got you to where you are right now. Also, it then becomes something you may want to share with others, who may unfortunately be experiencing what you've now healed from.

NEXT STEPS

You also may want to take your healing to the next level by joining us in the PBT Institute Membership Community or joining us there to become a Certified PBT Coach or Practitioner or any other program or certification that meets your needs at this time. You can find out more here: https://ThePBTInstitute.com. Of course, we aren't the only institute offering such services, and you may be able to find something local through your doctor, your therapist, your library, or other local resource.

When I was wrapping up the study and all we found, I experienced a moment I'll never forget. I thought about how incredible it would be if people could get the help they need to heal from their betrayals when they need it most. I imagined that at a time when we're the least likely to seek support, we can at least gain access to information in the comfort of our own space through books or online resources. I imagined that if we're willing to seek support from others, we'd have access to those who truly understand what's needed to help us move forward. I imagined people healing from what they never saw coming and what they never thought they could recover from.

Taking that vision to the next level, our programs, products, and services were quickly under way. It also seemed as if every time I said the word "betrayal," eyes would widen as people suddenly realized that an unhealed betrayal had been following them around for decades, dimming every experience that was meant to be filled with joy. They realized habits firmly in place to protect them so that no one would ever get close to their heart again. They realized how they were too afraid to ask for that raise or promotion they deserved because their confidence was shattered due to an unhealed betrayal. They realized how they were going to the most well-meaning doctors, therapists, healers, and coaches to manage stress-related symptoms, illnesses, and disease. At the root of all that stress? An unhealed betrayal. They realized how much of their lives weren't lived fully because their unhealed betrayal kept them sick, sad, and stuck.

It's my greatest hope and intention that, together, we pay it forward—whether that means sharing what helped you with those around you or becoming a part of the PBT team or any other group you feel called to work with as you formally help others based on the road you traveled that took you to where you are now. Imagine a world where we heal and through our healing there's a ripple effect: the healed mom or dad who impacts their children so that they have stronger and healthier relationships and make better choices because these children feel better about themselves, the healed coworker who has compassion for the other coworker who felt that desperate need to outshine others as they took credit for their idea (because we know that that type of behavior is coming from a place of scarcity and lack), or the healed sibling who resets boundaries with the other sibling so that they can harmoniously maneuver their relationship as best they can, respecting each other for their differences versus tearing each other down through their words.

That ripple effect will impact the betrayers too. It'll help the person who took advantage of their position of authority as they take full responsibility for the harm they caused. Who knows? Maybe they commit to doing all they can to right the wrong and never abuse their power again. It can help the friend who told your secret and apologizes, promising to never do it again if you're willing to give them another chance. It can help the partner who broke your heart understand the damage done by their actions as they vow to never break another heart again— whether yours or another's. Where does that leave you? It leaves you knowing you made a difference. You healed, leaving a beautiful legacy of healing and love behind you.

MY WISH FOR YOU

I'd been asked to give the commencement speech for my PhD graduating class. By the time the study was through, I had an entirely new
definition of success and life. I believe that healing from betrayal *is* success, and here's part of what I shared with the graduating class. I hope
it helps you:

What is success? The newest car, the biggest house, the prettiest
face, or the most perfectly behaved children as determined by societal
standards? If so, who are we when those external measures fade over
time?

If your measure of success is achieved through the accolades others bestow upon you, who are you when you no longer receive those
accolades?

If your measure of success is judged by what you collect, what happens when you stop collecting?

If success is achieved at the expense of family, integrity, connection,
meaning, or contribution, can it really be considered a success?

Who are you if you come in last place, if you don't raise your hand,
if you take a longer route or travel a different path?

What became so apparent during this journey was how fleeting and
empty external measures of success can be, especially when we understand that we're feeding the unrelenting needs of the ego versus nourish-
ing ourselves fully with our soul's calling for deep, rich, and meaningful
experiences. How has this created a new definition of success? Here's
what I now see so clearly:

When you can enjoy the quiet of your own company, that's success.

When you can easily open your heart for someone in need, that's
success.

When you can think about those you love as a smile curls your lips
and a warmth envelops your heart, that's success.

When you can surrender and grow comfortable with the discom-
fort of the unknown, that's success.

When you think of giving up, giving in, and going back to what
was old and familiar, then refuse and remain on your journey forward,
that's success.

Success is facing your fears, slaying your dragons, healing your
wounds, and loving yourself.

Success is thanking your ego for trying to protect you as you choose to trust the voice of your highest self instead.

Success is knowing that even if you have nothing, you have everything you need to create a life that's rich, fulfilling, and beautiful.

Success is the outpouring of love from within *regardless* of what external signs of validation you receive.

Success is using your biggest obstacles as the catalysts to reveal your greatest gifts.

Success is knowing that you are worthy, deserving, and lovable—simply because you exist.

Hellen Keller said, "Character cannot be developed in ease and quiet. Only through experience of trial and suffering can the soul be strengthened, ambition inspired, and success achieved."

With that, here's my wish for you:

May you seek the support and resources you need to achieve transformation and healing so that you become stronger, wiser, happier, and healthier than you ever imagined.

May you find the gift left in the wake and rubble of your biggest challenge.

May you realize how lovable, worthy, and deserving you are as you heal from what you thought would kill you.

May you use your healing to drive humanity forward.

May your new insights light a path to the trail you're now ready to blaze.

May you reflect with pride on how far you've come, then lovingly allow for your next and most exciting chapter to unfold.

May you serve as a role model and mentor, enthusiastically yet humbly sharing your light so that others are inspired to do the same.

You got this.

With love and my deepest admiration,
Dr. Debi

Notes

CHAPTER 1

1. Thibaut, J. W., & Kelley, H. H. (1959). *The social psychology of groups.* New York: Wiley.

2. French, R., Case, P., & Gosling, J. (2009). Betrayal and friendship. *Society and Business Review, 4*(2), 146–158.

3. Silver, A. (1989). Friendship and trust as moral ideals: An historical approach. *European Journal of Sociology/Archives Européennes de Sociologie, 30*(2), 274–297.

4. Couch, L., Jones, W., & Moore, D. (1999). Buffering the effects of betrayal: The role of apology, forgiveness, and commitment. In J. Adams & W. Jones (Eds.), *Handbook of interpersonal commitment and relationship stability* (pp. 451–469). New York: Kluwer Academic/Plenum.

5. Hansson, R. O., Jones, W. H., & Fletcher, W. L. (1990). Troubled relationships in later life: Implications for support. *Journal of Social and Personal Relationships, 7*(4), 451–463.

6. Delbridge, A. (2001). *The Macquarie Dictionary.* Sydney: Macquarie Library.

7. Steinmetz, S. (Ed.). (1993). *The Random House Webster's Dictionary.* New York: Ballantine Books.

8. Leary, M. R. (Ed.). (2001). *Interpersonal rejection.* New York: Oxford University Press.

9. Gaylin, W. (1984). In defense of the dignity of being human. *Hastings Center Report, 14*(4), 18–22.

10. Morrison, E. W., & Robinson, S. L. (1997). When employees feel betrayed: A model of how psychological contract violation develops. *Academy of Management Review, 22*(1), 226–256.

11. Leary, M. R., Springer, C., Negel, L., Ansell, E., & Evans, K. (1998). The causes, phenomenology, and consequences of hurt feelings. *Journal of Personality and Social Psychology, 74*(5), 1225.

12. Herman, J. L. (1997). *Trauma and recovery* (Rev. ed.). New York: Basic Books.

13. Edwards, V. J., Freyd, J. J., Dube, S. R., Anda, R. F., & Felitti, V. J. (2012). Health outcomes by closeness of sexual abuse perpetrator: A test of betrayal trauma theory. *Journal of Aggression, Maltreatment & Trauma, 21*, 133–148.

14. Van Hook, M. P. (2016). Spirituality as a potential resource for coping with trauma. *Social Work and Christianity, 43*(1), 7–25.

15. Anda, R. F., Felitti, V. J., Bremner, J. D., Walker, J. D., Whitfield, C. H., Perry, B. D., & Giles, W. H. (2006). The enduring effects of abuse and related adverse experiences in childhood. *European Archives of Psychiatry and Clinical Neuroscience, 256*(3), 174–186.

16. DePrince, A. P., & Freyd, J. J. (2002). The intersection of gender and betrayal in trauma. In R. Kimerling, P. C. Oumette, & J. Wolfe (Eds.), *Gender and PTSD* (pp. 98–113). New York: Guilford Press.

17. Cutler, S. E., & Nolen-Hoeksema, S. (1991). Accounting for sex differences in depression through female victimization: Childhood sexual abuse. *Sex Roles, 24*(7), 425–438.

18. Hayes, S. C., Wilson, K. G., Gifford, E. V., Follette, V. M., & Strosahl, K. (1996). Experiential avoidance and behavioral disorders: A functional dimensional approach to diagnosis and treatment. *Journal of Consulting and Clinical Psychology, 64*(6), 1152.

19. Hayes, S. C., Wilson, K. G., Gifford, E. V., Follette, V. M., & Strosahl, K. (1996). Experiential avoidance and behavioral disorders: A functional dimensional approach to diagnosis and treatment. *Journal of Consulting and Clinical Psychology, 64*(6), 1152.

20. Charny, I. W., & Parnass, S. (1995). The impact of extramarital relationships on the continuation of marriages. *Journal of Sex & Marital Therapy, 21*(2), 100–115.

21. Levine, T. R., McCornack, S. A., & Avery, P. B. (1992). Sex differences in emotional reactions to discovered deception. *Communication Quarterly, 40*(3), 289–296.

22. DePaulo, B. M., & Kashy, D. A. (1998). Everyday lies in close and casual relationships. *Journal of Personality and Social Psychology, 74*(1), 63.

23. Levine, T. R., McCornack, S. A., & Avery, P. B. (1992). Sex differences in emotional reactions to discovered deception. *Communication Quarterly, 40*(3), 289–296.

24. Asmus, M. J., Barros, M. D., Liang, J., Chesrown, S. E., & Hendeles, L. (2001). Pulmonary function response to EDTA, an additive in nebulized bronchodilators. *Journal of Allergy and Clinical Immunology, 107*(1), 68–72.

25. Barnum, R. P. (1998). Home-filtered water fails lead test: System brands named in S.F. study cover half the market. *San Francisco Chronicle*, p. A1.

26. Sunscreen takes the heat. (1998, February 24). *Chicago Tribune*, p. C3.

27. Koehler, J. J., & Gershoff, A. D. (2003). Betrayal aversion: When agents of protection become agents of harm. *Organizational Behavior and Human Decision Processes*, 2(90), 244–261.

28. Grégoire, Y., & Fisher, R. J. (2008). Customer betrayal and retaliation: When your best customers become your worst enemies. *Journal of the Academy of Marketing Science, 36*(2), 247–261.

29. Elangovan, A. R., & Shapiro, D. L. (1998). Betrayal of trust in organizations. *Academy of Management Review, 23*(3), 547–566.

30. Grégoire, Y., Tripp, T. M., & Legoux, R. (2009). When customer love turns into lasting hate: The effects of relationship strength and time on customer revenge and avoidance. *Journal of Marketing, 73*(6), 18–32.

CHAPTER 2

1. Fitness, J., & Mathews, S. (1998). *Emotions, emotional intelligence, and forgiveness in marriage.* Paper presented at the *9th International Conference on Personal Relationships*, Saratoga Springs, NY.

2. Charny, I. W., & Parnass, S. (1995). The impact of extramarital relationships on the continuation of marriages. *Journal of Sex & Marital Therapy, 21*(2), 100–115.

3. Charny, I. W., & Parnass, S. (1995). The impact of extramarital relationships on the continuation of marriages. *Journal of Sex & Marital Therapy, 21*(2), 100–115.

4. Miller, W. I. (1993). *Humiliation.* Ithaca, NY: Cornell University Press.

5. Jones, W. H., & Burdette, M. P. (1994). Betrayal in relationships. In A. L. Weber & J. H. Harvey (Eds.), *Perspectives on close relationships* (pp. 243–262). Needham Heights, MA: Allyn & Bacon.

6. Fitness, J., & Fletcher, G. J. O. (1993). Love, hate, anger, and jealousy in close relationships: A prototype and cognitive appraisal analysis. *Journal of Personality and Social Psychology, 65*, 942–958.

7. Fehr, B., & Baldwin, M. (1996). Prototype and script analyses of laypeople's knowledge of anger. In *Knowledge structures in close relationships: A social psychological approach* (pp. 219–245). Mahwah, NJ: Lawrence Erlbaum Associates.

8. Romans, S., Belaise, C., Martin, J., Morris, E., & Raffi, A. (2002). Childhood abuse and later medical disorders in women. *Psychotherapy and Psychosomatics, 71*, 141–150.

9. Edmonds, G. W., Hampson, S. E., Cote, H., Hill, P. L., & Klest, B. (2016). Childhood personality, betrayal trauma, and leukocyte telomere length in adulthood: A lifespan perspective on conscientiousness and betrayal traumas as predictors of a biomarker of cellular ageing. *European Journal of Personality*, *30*(5), 426–437.

10. Kendall-Tackett, K., & Marshall, R. (1999). Victimization and diabetes: An exploratory study. *Child Abuse & Neglect*, *23*, 593–596.

11. Anda, R. F., Felitti, V. J., Bremner, J. D., Walker, J. D., Whitfield, C. H., Perry, B. D., & Giles, W. H. (2006). The enduring effects of abuse and related adverse experiences in childhood. *European Archives of Psychiatry and Clinical Neuroscience*, *256*(3), 174–186.

12. Gobin, R. L., & Freyd, J. J. (2014). The impact of betrayal trauma on the tendency to trust. *Psychological Trauma: Theory, Research, Practice, and Policy*, *6*(5), 505–511.

13. Baumeister, R. F., Stillwell, A. M., & Heatherton, T. F. (1995). Personal narratives about guilt: Role in action control and interpersonal relationships. *Basic and Applied Social Psychology*, *17*(1-2), 173–198.

14. Vangelisti, A. L., & Sprague, R. J. (1998). Guilt and hurt: Similarities, distinctions, and conversational strategies. In P. A. Andersen & L. K. Guerrero (Eds.), *Handbook of communication and emotion: Research, theory, applications, and contexts* (pp. 123–154). San Diego, CA: Academic Press.

15. Baumeister, R. F., Stillwell, A. M., & Heatherton, T. F. (1995). Personal narratives about guilt: Role in action control and interpersonal relationships. *Basic and Applied Social Psychology*, *17*(1–2), 173–198.

16. O'Malley, M. N., & Greenberg, J. (1983). Sex differences in restoring justice: The down payment effect. *Journal of Research in Personality*, *17*(2), 174–185.

17. Baumeister, R. F., Stillwell, A. M., & Heatherton, T. F. (1995). Personal narratives about guilt: Role in action control and interpersonal relationships. *Basic and Applied Social Psychology*, *17*(1–2), 173–198.

18. McCullough, M. E., Worthington, E. L., Jr., & Rachal, K. C. (1997). Interpersonal forgiving in close relationships. *Journal of Personality and Social Psychology*, *73*, 321–336.

CHAPTER 4

1. Calhoun, L. G., & Tedeschi, R. G. (2014). *Handbook of posttraumatic growth: Research and practice*. New York: Psychology Press.

2. Bonanno, G. A. (2004). Loss, trauma, and human resilience: Have we underestimated the human capacity to thrive after extremely aversive events? *American Psychologist, 59*(1), 20.

3. Bonanno, G. A. (2004). Loss, trauma, and human resilience: Have we underestimated the human capacity to thrive after extremely aversive events? *American Psychologist, 59*(1), 20.

4. Levine, S. Z., Laufer, A., Stein, E., Hamama-Raz, Y., & Solomon, Z. (2009). Examining the relationship between resilience and posttraumatic growth. *Journal of Traumatic Stress, 22*(4), 282–286.

5. Calhoun, L. G., & Tedeschi, R. G. (2014). *Handbook of posttraumatic growth: Research and practice.* New York: Psychology Press.

6. Walsh, F. (1999). Opening family therapy to spirituality. In F. Walsh (Ed.), *Spiritual resources in family therapy* (pp. 28–58). New York: Guilford Press.

7. Cadell, S., Regehr, C., & Hemsworth, D. (2003). Factors contributing to posttraumatic growth: A proposed structural equation model. *American Journal of Orthopsychiatry, 73*(3), 279–287.

8. Martin, L. M., & Tesser, A. (1996). Clarifying our thoughts. In R. S. Dyer (Ed.), *Ruminative thoughts: Advances in social cognition* (pp. 189–209). Mahwah, NJ: Lawrence Erlbaum Associates.

9. Calhoun, L. G., Cann, A., Tedeschi, R. G., & McMillan, J. (2000). A correlational test of the relationship between posttraumatic growth, religion, and cognitive processing. *Journal of Traumatic Stress, 13*(3), 521–527.

10. McMillen, J. C., & Fisher, R. H. (1998). The Perceived Benefit Scales: Measuring perceived positive life changes after negative events. *Social Work Research, 22*(3), 173–187.

11. Tedeschi, R. G., & Calhoun, L. G. (1996). The Posttraumatic Growth Inventory: Measuring the positive legacy of trauma. *Journal of Traumatic Stress, 9*(3), 455–471.

12. Calhoun, L. G., & Tedeschi, R. G. (2014). *Handbook of posttraumatic growth: Research and practice.* New York: Psychology Press.

CHAPTER 6

1. Peter Levine, https://www.frontiersin.org/articles/10.3389/fpsyg.2015.00093/full.

2. Pat Ogden, PhD, Clare Pain, MD, Kekuni Minton, PhD, and Janina Fisher, PhD, https://www.sensorimotorpsychotherapy.org/article%20APA.html.

CHAPTER 8

1. Pennebaker, J. W., & Seagal, J. D. (1999). Forming a story: The health benefits of narrative. *Journal of Clinical Psychology, 55*(10), 1243–1254.
2. Calhoun, L. G., & Tedeschi, R. G. (2014). *Handbook of posttraumatic growth: Research and practice.* New York: Psychology Press.

CHAPTER 12

1. Exline, J. J., & Baumeister, R. F. (2000). Expressing forgiveness and repentance: Benefits and barriers. In M. E. McCullough, K. I. Pargament, & C. E. Thoresen (Eds.), *Forgiveness: Theory, research, and practice* (pp. 133–155). New York: Guilford Press.
2. Wade, N. G., Bailey, D. C., & Shaffer, P. (2005). Helping clients heal: Does forgiveness make a difference? *Professional Psychology: Research and Practice, 36*(6), 634.
3. Paleari, F. G., Regalia, C., & Fincham, F. D. (2009). Measuring offence-specific forgiveness in marriage: The Marital Offence-Specific Forgiveness Scale (MOFS). *Psychological Assessment, 21*(2), 194.
4. Gordon, K. C., Baucom, D. H., & Snyder, D. K. (2004). An integrative intervention for promoting recovery from extramarital affairs. *Journal of Marital and Family Therapy, 30*(2), 213–231.
5. DiBlasio, F. A., & Proctor, J. H. (1993). Therapists and the clinical use of forgiveness. *American Journal of Family Therapy, 21*(2), 175–184.
6. Fitness, J. (2001). Betrayal, rejection, revenge, and forgiveness: An interpersonal script approach. In M. Leary (Ed.), *Interpersonal rejection* (pp. 73–103). New York: Oxford University Press.
7. Friesen, M. D., & Fletcher, G. J. O. (2007). Exploring the lay representation of forgiveness: Convergent and discriminant validity. *Personal Relationships, 14*, 209–223.
8. Younger, J. W., Piferi, R. L., Jobe, R. L., & Lawler, K. A. (2004). Dimensions of forgiveness: The views of laypersons. *Journal of Social and Personal Relationships, 21*, 837–855.
9. McCullough, M. E., Rachal, K. C., Sandage, S. J., Worthington, E. L., Brown, S. W., & Hight, T. L. (1998). Interpersonal forgiving in close relationships: II. Theoretical elaboration and measurement. *Journal of Personality and Social Psychology, 75*, 1586–1603.
10. McCullough, M. E., Worthington, E. L., Jr., & Rachal, K. C. (1997). Interpersonal forgiving in close relationships. *Journal of Personality and Social Psychology, 73*, 321–336.

11. McCullough, M. E., Pargament, K. I., & Thoresen, C. E. (2000). The psychology of forgiveness: History, conceptual issues, and overview. In M. E. McCullough, K. I. Pargament, & C. E. Thoresen (Eds.), *Forgiveness: Theory, research, and practice* (pp. 1–14). New York: Guilford Press.

12. Cody, M. J., Kersten, L., Braaten, D. O., & Dickson, R. (1992). Coping with relational dissolutions: Attributions, account credibility, and plans for resolving conflicts. In J. H. Harvey, T. L. Orbuch, & A. L. Weber (Eds.), *Attributions, accounts, and close relationships* (pp. 93–115). New York: Springer.

13. Jones, W. H., & Burdette, M. P. (1994). Betrayal in relationships. In A. L. Weber & J. H. Harvey (Eds.), *Perspectives on close relationships* (pp. 243–262). Needham Heights, MA: Allyn & Bacon.

14. Coyle, C. T., & Enright, R. D. (1997). Forgiveness intervention with post abortion men. *Journal of Consulting and Clinical Psychology, 65*(6), 1042.

15. Fitness, J. (2001). Betrayal, rejection, revenge, and forgiveness: An interpersonal script approach. In M. Leary (Ed.), *Interpersonal rejection* (pp. 73–103). New York: Oxford University Press.

16. Worthington, E. L. (2001). *Five steps to forgiveness: The art and science of forgiving.* New York: Crown.

17. Hayes, S. C., Wilson, K. G., Gifford, E. V., Follette, V. M., & Strosahl, K. (1996). Experiential avoidance and behavioral disorders: A functional dimensional approach to diagnosis and treatment. *Journal of Consulting and Clinical Psychology, 64*(6), 1152.

18. Worthington, E. L. (2001). *Five steps to forgiveness: The art and science of forgiving.* New York: Crown.

CHAPTER 13

1. yourdictionary.com/empathy.

2. Orloff, J. (2017). *The empath's survival guide: Life strategies for sensitive people.* Louisville, CO: Sounds True.

3. Northrup, C. (2018). *Dodging energy vampires: An empath's guide to evading relationships that drain you and restoring your health and power.* Carlsbad, CA: Hay House.

4. Empath Self-Assessment: https://drjudithorloff.com/quizzes/empath-self-assessment-test.

5. https://en.wikipedia.org/wiki/Narcissistic_supply.

6. https://saferelationshipsmagazine.com.

7. https://en.wikipedia.org/wiki/Gaslighting.

8. https://www.psychologytoday.com/us/blog/here-there-and-everywhere/201701/11-warning-signs-gaslighting.

Bibliography

Anda, R. F., Felitti, V. J., Bremner, J. D., Walker, J. D., Whitfield, C. H., Perry, B. D., & Giles, W. H. (2006). The enduring effects of abuse and related adverse experiences in childhood. *European Archives of Psychiatry and Clinical Neuroscience, 256*(3), 174–186.

Asmus, M. J., Barros, M. D., Liang, J., Chesrown, S. E., & Hendeles, L. (2001). Pulmonary function response to EDTA, an additive in nebulized bronchodilators. *Journal of Allergy and Clinical Immunology, 107*(1), 68–72.

Barnum, R. P. (1998, June 18). Home-filtered water fails lead test: System brands named in S.F. study cover half the market. *San Francisco Chronicle*, p. A1.

Baumeister, R. F., Stillwell, A. M., & Heatherton, T. F. (1995). Personal narratives about guilt: Role in action control and interpersonal relationships. *Basic and Applied Social Psychology, 17*(1–2), 173–198.

Bonanno, G. A. (2004). Loss, trauma, and human resilience: Have we underestimated the human capacity to thrive after extremely aversive events? *American Psychologist, 59*(1), 20.

Brown, S. L., & Young, J. R. (2018). *Women who love psychopaths: Inside the relationships of inevitable harm with psychopaths, sociopaths and narcissists*. n.p.: Mask Publishing.

Cadell, S., Regehr, C., & Hemsworth, D. (2003). Factors contributing to posttraumatic growth: A proposed structural equation model. *American Journal of Orthopsychiatry, 73*(3), 279–287.

Calhoun, L. G., Cann, A., Tedeschi, R. G., & McMillan, J. (2000). A correlational test of the relationship between posttraumatic growth, religion, and cognitive processing. *Journal of Traumatic Stress, 13*(3), 521–527.

Calhoun, L. G., & Tedeschi, R. G. (2014). *Handbook of posttraumatic growth: Research and practice*. New York: Psychology Press.

Charny, I. W., & Parnass, S. (1995). The impact of extramarital relationships on the continuation of marriages. *Journal of Sex & Marital Therapy, 21*(2), 100–115.

211

Cody, M. J., Kersten, L., Braaten, D. O., & Dickson, R. (1992). Coping with relational dissolutions: Attributions, account credibility, and plans for resolving conflicts. In J. H. Harvey, T. L. Orbuch, & A. L. Weber (Eds.), *Attributions, accounts, and close relationships* (pp. 93–115). New York: Springer.

Couch, L., Jones, W., & Moore, D. (1999). Buffering the effects of betrayal: The role of apology, forgiveness, and commitment. In J. Adams & W. Jones (Eds.), *Handbook of interpersonal commitment and relationship stability* (pp. 451–469). New York: Kluwer Academic/Plenum.

Coyle, C. T., & Enright, R. D. (1997). Forgiveness intervention with post abortion men. *Journal of Consulting and Clinical Psychology, 65*(6), 1042.

Cutler, S. E., & Nolen-Hoeksema, S. (1991). Accounting for sex differences in depression through female victimization: Childhood sexual abuse. *Sex Roles, 24*(7), 425–438.

Delbridge, A. (2001). *The Macquarie Dictionary.* Sydney: Macquarie Library.

DePaulo, B. M., & Kashy, D. A. (1998). Everyday lies in close and casual relationships. *Journal of Personality and Social Psychology, 74*(1), 63.

DePrince, A. P., & Freyd, J. J. (2002). The intersection of gender and betrayal in trauma. In R. Kimerling, P. C. Oumette, & J. Wolfe (Eds.), *Gender and PTSD* (pp. 98–113). New York: Guilford Press.

DiBlasio, F. A., & Proctor, J. H. (1993). Therapists and the clinical use of forgiveness. *American Journal of Family Therapy, 21*(2), 175–184.

Edmonds, G. W., Hampson, S. E., Cote, H., Hill, P. L., & Klest, B. (2016). Childhood personality, betrayal trauma, and leukocyte telomere length in adulthood: A lifespan perspective on conscientiousness and betrayal traumas as predictors of a biomarker of cellular ageing. *European Journal of Personality, 30*(5), 426–437.

Edwards, V. J., Freyd, J. J., Dube, S. R., Anda, R. F., & Felitti, V. J. (2012). Health outcomes by closeness of sexual abuse perpetrator: A test of betrayal trauma theory. *Journal of Aggression, Maltreatment & Trauma, 21,* 133–148.

Elangovan, A. R., & Shapiro, D. L. (1998). Betrayal of trust in organizations. *Academy of Management Review, 23*(3), 547–566.

Exline, J. J., & Baumeister, R. F. (2000). Expressing forgiveness and repentance: Benefits and barriers. In M. E. McCullough, K. I. Pargament, & C. E. Thoresen (Eds.), *Forgiveness: Theory, research, and practice* (pp. 133–155). New York: Guilford Press.

Fehr, B., & Baldwin, M. (1996). Prototype and script analyses of laypeople's knowledge of anger. In *Knowledge structures in close relationships: A social psychological approach* (pp. 219–245). Mahwah, NJ: Lawrence Erlbaum Associates.

Fitness, J. (2001). Betrayal, rejection, revenge, and forgiveness: An interpersonal script approach. In M. Leary (Ed.), *Interpersonal rejection* (pp. 73–103). New York: Oxford University Press.

Fitness, J., & Fletcher, G. J. O. (1993). Love, hate, anger, and jealousy in close relationships: A prototype and cognitive appraisal analysis. *Journal of Personality and Social Psychology, 65,* 942-958.

Fitness, J., & Mathews, S. (1998). *Emotions, emotional intelligence, and forgiveness in marriage.* Paper presented at the 9th International Conference on Personal Relationships, Saratoga Springs, NY.

French, R., Case, P., & Gosling, J. (2009). Betrayal and friendship. *Society and Business Review, 4*(2), 146–158.

Friesen, M. D., & Fletcher, G. J. O. (2007). Exploring the lay representation of forgiveness: Convergent and discriminant validity. *Personal Relationships,* 14, 209–223.

Gaylin, W. (1984). In defense of the dignity of being human. *Hastings Center Report, 14*(4), 18–22.

Gobin, R. L., & Freyd, J. J. (2014). The impact of betrayal trauma on the tendency to trust. *Psychological Trauma: Theory, Research, Practice, and Policy, 6*(5), 505–511.

Gordon, K. C., Baucom, D. H., & Snyder, D. K. (2004). An integrative intervention for promoting recovery from extramarital affairs. *Journal of Marital and Family Therapy, 30*(2), 213–231.

Grégoire, Y., & Fisher, R. J. (2008). Customer betrayal and retaliation: When your best customers become your worst enemies. *Journal of the Academy of Marketing Science, 36*(2), 247–261.

Grégoire, Y., Tripp, T. M., & Legoux, R. (2009). When customer love turns into lasting hate: The effects of relationship strength and time on customer revenge and avoidance. *Journal of Marketing, 73*(6), 18–32.

Hansson, R. O., Jones, W. H., & Fletcher, W. L. (1990). Troubled relationships in later life: Implications for support. *Journal of Social and Personal Relationships,* 7(4), 451–463.

Hayes, S. C., Wilson, K. G., Gifford, E. V., Follette, V. M., & Strosahl, K. (1996). Experiential avoidance and behavioral disorders: A functional dimensional approach to diagnosis and treatment. *Journal of Consulting and Clinical Psychology, 64*(6), 1152.

Herman, J. L. (1997). *Trauma and recovery* (Rev. ed.). New York: Basic Books.

Jones, W. H., & Burdette, M. P. (1994). Betrayal in relationships. In A. L. Weber & J. H. Harvey (Eds.), *Perspectives on close relationships* (pp. 243–262). Needham Heights, MA: Allyn & Bacon.

Kendall-Tackett, K., & Marshall, R. (1999). Victimization and diabetes: An exploratory study. *Child Abuse & Neglect, 23,* 593–596.

Koehler, J. J., & Gershoff, A. D. (2003). Betrayal aversion: When agents of protection become agents of harm. *Organizational Behavior and Human Decision Processes, 2*(90), 244–261.

Leary, M. R. (Ed.). (2001). *Interpersonal rejection.* New York: Oxford University Press.

Leary, M. R., Springer, C., Negel, L., Ansell, E., & Evans, K. (1998). The causes, phenomenology, and consequences of hurt feelings. *Journal of Personality and Social Psychology, 74*(5), 1225.

Levine, S. Z., Laufer, A., Stein, E., Hamama-Raz, Y., & Solomon, Z. (2009). Examining the relationship between resilience and posttraumatic growth. *Journal of Traumatic Stress, 22*(4), 282–286.

Levine, T. R., McCornack, S. A., & Avery, P. B. (1992). Sex differences in emotional reactions to discovered deception. *Communication Quarterly, 40*(3), 289–296.

Martin, L. M., & Tesser, A. (1996). Clarifying our thoughts. In R. S. Dyer (Ed.), *Ruminative thoughts: Advances in social cognition* (pp. 189–209). Mahwah, NJ: Lawrence Erlbaum Associates.

McCullough, M. E., Pargament, K. I., & Thoresen, C. E. (2000). The psychology of forgiveness: History, conceptual issues, and overview. In M. E. McCullough, K. I. Pargament, & C. E. Thoresen (Eds.), *Forgiveness: Theory, research, and practice* (pp. 1–14). New York: Guilford Press.

McCullough, M. E., Rachal, K. C., Sandage, S. J., Worthington, E. L., Brown, S. W., & Hight, T. L. (1998). Interpersonal forgiving in close relationships: II. Theoretical elaboration and measurement. *Journal of Personality and Social Psychology, 75*, 1586–1603.

McCullough, M. E., Worthington, E. L., Jr., & Rachal, K. C. (1997). Interpersonal forgiving in close relationships. *Journal of Personality and Social Psychology, 73*, 321–336.

McMillen, J. C., & Fisher, R. H. (1998). The Perceived Benefit Scales: Measuring perceived positive life changes after negative events. *Social Work Research, 22*(3), 173–187.

Miller, W. I. (1993). *Humiliation.* Ithaca, NY: Cornell University Press.

Morrison, E. W., & Robinson, S. L. (1997). When employees feel betrayed: A model of how psychological contract violation develops. *Academy of Management Review, 22*(1), 226–256.

Northrup, C. (2018). *Dodging energy vampires.* London: Hay House.

Ogden, P., Pain, C., Minton, K., & Fisher, J. (2000). Sensorimotor psychotherapy: One method for processing traumatic memory. *Traumatology, 6*(3), Article 3. https://www.sensorimotorpsychotherapy.org/article%20APA.html.

O'Malley, M. N., & Greenberg, J. (1983). Sex differences in restoring justice: The down payment effect. *Journal of Research in Personality, 17*(2), 174–185.

Orloff, J. (2018). *The empath's survival guide: Life strategies for sensitive people.* Boulder, CO: Sounds True, Inc.

Orloff, J. (2018). Empath self-assessment. https://drjudithorloff.com/quizzes/empath-self-assessment-test.

Paleari, F. G., Regalia, C., & Fincham, F. D. (2009). Measuring offence-specific forgiveness in marriage: The Marital Offence-Specific Forgiveness Scale (MOFS). *Psychological Assessment, 21*(2), 194.

Payne, P., Levine, P. A., Payne, & Crane-Godreau, M. A. (2015). Somatic experiencing: Using interoception and proprioception as core elements of trauma therapy. *Frontiers in Psychology.* https://doi.org/10.3389/fpsyg.2015.00093.

Pennebaker, J. W., & Seagal, J. D. (1999). Forming a story: The health benefits of narrative. *Journal of Clinical Psychology, 55*(10), 1243–1254.

Romans, S., Belaise, C., Martin, J., Morris, E., & Raffi, A. (2002). Childhood abuse and later medical disorders in women. *Psychotherapy and Psychosomatics, 71,* 141–150.

Silver, A. (1989). Friendship and trust as moral ideals: An historical approach. *European Journal of Sociology/Archives Européennes de Sociologie, 30*(2), 274–297.

Steinmetz, S. (Ed.). (1993). *The Random House Webster's Dictionary.* New York: Ballantine Books.

Sunscreen takes the heat. (1998, February 24). *Chicago Tribune,* p. C3.

Tedeschi, R. G., & Calhoun, L. G. (1996). The Posttraumatic Growth Inventory: Measuring the positive legacy of trauma. *Journal of Traumatic Stress, 9*(3), 455–471.

Thibaut, J. W., & Kelley, H. H. (1959). *The social psychology of groups.* New York: Wiley.

Van Hook, M. P. (2016). Spirituality as a potential resource for coping with trauma. *Social Work and Christianity, 43*(1), 7–25.

Vangelisti, A. L., & Sprague, R. J. (1998). Guilt and hurt: Similarities, distinctions, and conversational strategies. In P. A. Andersen & L. K. Guerrero (Eds.), *Handbook of communication and emotion: Research, theory, applications, and contexts* (pp. 123–154). San Diego, CA: Academic Press.

Wade, N. G., Bailey, D. C., & Shaffer, P. (2005). Helping clients heal: Does forgiveness make a difference? *Professional Psychology: Research and Practice, 36*(6), 634.

Walsh, F. (1999). Opening family therapy to spirituality. In *Spiritual resources in family therapy* (pp. 28–58). New York: Guilford Press.

Worthington, E. L. (2001). *Five steps to forgiveness: The art and science of forgiving.* New York: Crown.

Younger, J. W., Piferi, R. L., Jobe, R. L., & Lawler, K. A. (2004). Dimensions of forgiveness: The views of laypersons. *Journal of Social and Personal Relationships, 21,* 837–855.

Young, W. P. (2008). *The shack.* London: Hachette.

www.yourdictionary.com/empathy

https://en.wikipedia.org/wiki/Narcissistic_supply

https://en.wikipedia.org/wiki/Gaslighting

www.psychologytoday.com/us/blog/here-there-and-everywhere/201701/11-warning-signs-gaslighting

Index

About the Author

Debi Silber, PhD, president of the PBT (Post Betrayal Transformation) Institute (https://ThePBTInstitute.com), is a holistic psychologist and a health, mind-set, and personal development expert. She is an award-winning speaker, keynoting events such as the Women's Summit at Bryant University, the American Heart Association's Go Red event, the Women's Leadership Conference, MGM Grand, and many more.

Dr. Silber is a two-time TEDx speaker, has contributed articles and insights to *The Dr. Oz Show*, *Fox*, *CBS*, *News 12*, multiple times to the *Huffington Post*, *Forbes*, *Shape*, *Self*, *WebMD*, *Working Mother*, *Glamour*, *Ladies Home Journal*, *Women's World*, *MSN*, and *YahooShine*, to name a few. She was a featured expert on the local CBS affiliate show *Live It Up* and on websites such as Working Mother, Medium, and Thrive Global; has been featured as a self-improvement expert in four books, including *Power Moms: The New Rules for Engaging Mom Influencers Who Drive Brand Choice*; and was even profiled in the textbook *Exploring Global Issues: Social, Economic, and Environmental Interconnections*, which aims to inspire students to pursue similar careers. She is also host of her recently launched podcast, *From Betrayal to Breakthrough*, and is a popular podcast, virtual summit, and media guest.

A holistic registered dietitian with a master's degree in nutrition, a certified personal trainer, and a Whole Health Coach™, she has two certifications in pre- and postnatal fitness with specialty recognition in weight loss and weight maintenance, is a functional diagnostic nutritionist, and has just completed her PhD in transpersonal psychology (the psychology of transformation and human potential), for which she conducted a groundbreaking study on how women experience betrayal— what holds them back and what helps them heal. She has achieved various honors, such as winning the 2018 Future of Health award, where her discoveries on betrayal were voted on and recognized by more than 500 health and wellness professionals; the 2017 Long Island Business News Award-Achievements in Health Care; Health Tap's 2015 Nutrition Industry winner; 2014 Top Ranked U.S. Executive by the National Council of American Executives; and a Notable American Woman.

She's the author of several self-published books, including *The Unshakable Woman: 4 Steps to Rebuilding Your Body, Mind and Life after a Life Crisis* (Createspace, foreword by J. J. Virgin); *The Unshakable Woman—The Workbook* (Createspace); *The Lifestyle Fitness Program: A Six Part Plan So Every Mom Can Look, Feel and Live Her Best* (Morgan James, recommended by Jack Canfield and *Parenting* magazine); and *A Pocket Full of Mojo: 365 Proven Strategies to Create Your Ultimate Body, Mind, Image and Lifestyle* (Createspace, recommended by Brian Tracy and Marshall Goldsmith). *A Pocket Full of Mojo* was purposely written to be sold as a bulk book option to companies serving as a low-investment corporate wellness tool, which she has sold to PayPal, Life Time Fitness clubs, and law and accounting firms.

She's married (twice) to her husband Adam, and they have four children (Dani, Dylan, Camryn, and Cole) and six dogs (Scooby, Roxy, Gigi, Nike, Kylie, and Brody). Debi's greatest passion is helping others heal physically, mentally, and emotionally from the trauma of betrayal.

Please stay in touch! Join our community at https://ThePBTInstitute .com and and share your success! I'd love to hear about your journey, and I know it'll inspire others too. Stay in touch on social media by going to:

www.facebook.com/InspireEmpowerTransform
www.facebook.com/groups/WomenHackingBetrayal
twitter.com/DebiSilber
www.instagram.com/debisilber
www.linkedin.com/in/debisilber
Or e-mail me at: Debi@PBTInstitute.com